I0868085

Performance and Personhood in Caribbean Literature

New World Studies

J. Michael Dash, *Editor*

Frank Moya Pons and
Sandra Pouchet Paquet,
Associate Editors

Performance and Personhood in Caribbean Literature

FROM ALEXIS TO THE DIGITAL AGE

Jeannine Murray-Román

University of Virginia Press
Charlottesville and London

the modern language initiative

THIS BOOK IS MADE POSSIBLE BY A COLLABORATIVE GRANT FROM THE ANDREW W. MELLON FOUNDATION.

University of Virginia Press
© 2016 by the Rector and Visitors of the University of Virginia
All rights reserved
Printed in the United States of America on acid-free paper

9 8 7 6 5 4 3 2 1

Library of Congress Cataloging-in-Publication Data

Murray-Roman, Jeannine, 1977–
Performance and personhood in Caribbean literature : from Alexis to the digital age / Jeannine Murray-Roman.
pages cm. — (New world studies)
Includes bibliographical references and index.
ISBN 978-0-8139-3847-9 (cloth : alk. paper)
ISBN 978-0-8139-3848-6 (pbk. : alk. paper)
ISBN 978-0-8139-3849-3 (e-book)
1. Caribbean literature—20th century—History and criticism. 2. Performance in literature. 3. Self-perception in literature. 4. Literature and society—Caribbean Area—History—20th century. I. Title.
PN849.C3M865 2016
809'.89729—dc23

2015022971

Contents

Acknowledgments

THIS BOOK COULD NOT EXIST WITHOUT a tremendous amount of personal and institutional support. I am grateful to the Graduate Division of the University of California, Los Angeles, and Reed College Office of the Dean for consistently funding the project. I also thank Intellect Books for permission to reprint portions of "Literary Tourism, *littérature monde*, and the ethics of conversation in Ernest Pépin's *L'Envers du décor*," first published in the *International Journal of Francophone Studies* 12.2/3 (2009). The book has benefited immeasurably from having incisive commentary on its early versions at the Caribbean Studies Association and American Comparative Literature Association conferences, particularly the "Theories of Caribbean Comparatism" seminar convened in New Orleans in 2010 by Natalie Melas and Gerard Aching; "Comparative Caribbeans" at Emory University in 2011; "Caribbean Crossroads" at University of California, Santa Barbara, in 2012; as well as talks at Howard University and University of Miami. The questions, concerns, and interest I received at these events have been invaluable in shaping my thinking. In a similar way, the manuscript's anonymous reviewers solicited by the University of Virginia Press have pushed me to strengthen the book in every way. I was awed by the care they took in engaging with my work, and I remain motivated by their investment in seeing through the evolution of the manuscript. Along with my editor, Cathie Brettschneider, at the University of Virginia Press, they were instrumental in helping me bring this book into being. I am grateful to Albert Chong for permission to use his work *Dancing with the Palo* as the cover image, and to Angie Harmon, Anna Kariel, and Ellen Satrom at the University of Virginia Press, as well as Susan Murray and Lauren Nelson, for their assistance in preparing the manuscript.

I am also incredibly lucky to have been mentored by brilliant women and men who modeled for me—and invited me to share—a collaborative and open approach to academic work. First and foremost, my dissertation chair, Françoise Lionnet, who is the most creative, productive, and generous person I know. At Dartmouth: my undergraduate thesis advisors, Kate Conley and Gerd Gemünden; and my master's year advisors, Mary Jean Green and Marianne Hirsch; at UCLA: Robin Derby, Susan Foster, Jorge Marturano, Jenny Sharpe, and the 2009–2011 Fellows in the Mellon Postdoctoral Program, Cultures in Transnational Perspective, led by Shu-mei Shih and Françoise Lionnet. From them, I learned so much, perhaps most importantly that scholarship need not be an isolated struggle. Instead we organized our work around exchanges: talking about writing and research during walks in the Santa Monica mountains and over good food, from epic meals to Trader Joe's triple-cream brie. Throughout the years, I have been fortunate to share my working life with beloved writing partners, colleagues, and friends: Harmony Bench, Zara Bennett, Cindy García, Tanya González, Hannah Kosstrin, Peter Lehman, and Ali Potvin; the UCLA comp lit crew, Talar Chahinian, Myrna Douzjian, Marian Gabra, Lisa Felipe, Neetu Khanna, and Guilan Siassi; at Reed College, Kate Bredeson, Mary Ashburn Miller, Sarah Wagner-McCoy, and Catherine Witt. The long conversations and happy afternoons with you have sustained me. My most profound and expansive gratitude always goes to my friends and to my family. Carmen Román-Murray and Ed Murray, Topo and Michael La Masse: you have my heart.

Finally, I want to acknowledge how much the field of comparative Caribbean literary studies has changed over the past decade. In 2005, my dissertation prospectus featured an impassioned defense for why a comparative and multilingual approach to Caribbean literature was vital and necessary, even if difficult and rare. At that time, Gerard Aching's *Masking and Power* (2002), Brent Hayes Edwards's *The Practice of Diaspora* (2003), J. Michael Dash's *The Other America* (1998), and Silvio Torres-Saillant's *Caribbean Poetics* (1997) were some of the only analyses of Caribbean literature that explicitly used comparative methodologies. At this moment of publication in 2016, however, many monographs exploring the potential of interdisciplinary and multilingual approaches have, happily, obviated the need for such justifications. Sybille Fischer's *Modernity Disavowed* (2004), Natalie Melas's *All the Difference in the World* (2007), Guillermina De Ferrari's *Vulnerable States* (2007), Paul Miller's *Elusive Origins* (2010), Omise'eke Natasha Tinsley's *Thiefing*

Sugar (2010), Raphael Dalleo's *Caribbean Literature and the Public Sphere* (2011), Sara Johnson's *Fear of French Negroes* (2012), Tanya Shields's *Bodies and Bones* (2014), and Rosamond King's *Island Bodies* (2014) are only some of the many analyses of Caribbean literature that have amply demonstrated the value of reading across national language disciplinary boundaries and the colonial legacies that such boundaries reinscribe. My proposal that performance allows us to identify through-lines in regional literary practices adds to the approaches they already take and is inspired by their work.

Introduction

A STARTING POINT FOR ENGAGING the intersection of the performing arts and literature in the Caribbean region is the famous exchange between the storyteller and the writer-figure in Patrick Chamoiseau's *Solibo Magnifique*: "To write is to take the *lambi* out of the sea to shout: here's the conch! The word replies: where's the sea? But that's not the most important thing, I'm going and you're staying. I spoke to you, you're writing, announcing that you come from the word. You give your hand over the distance. It's all very nice, but you just touch the distance" (28; see French in Chamoiseau 53). A spatial analogy evokes the problems of converting orality, performance, or moving bodies into literature. In aiming for permanence, the writer privileges explanation whereas the storyteller orients him- or herself toward action. But instead of dismissing efforts to use local languages and corporeal forms of making meaning in literature, we can read this critique as a challenge that sets forth the scope of work for Caribbean writers who take on the task of representing the spoken word and the moving body. If we follow the storyteller's assessment, the act of writing performance never fully achieves its goal—it only "touches the distance," thereby marking a writer's effort and the extent of her failure. Given the impossibility of the task, in *Performance and Personhood in Caribbean Literature* I ask, Why is the representation of performance so pervasive in Caribbean literature?

Reggae, salsa, the rituals associated with the African-based religions of Vodou or *santería*, Carnival: these are only a few of the cultural traditions that circulate in the Caribbean basin. Globally, the region is best known for its local performance practices, and the representations of performance events are omnipresent in the region's literature. Descriptions of performance are as striking in the text when the text is itself about a performance, like Rosario Ferré's short story "Maquinolandera," which is structurally based on the refrain of a song, as they are when we break away from the plot and read about how protagonists are transported by participating in a performance event, for example while dancing with friends or during long nights of storytelling, as featured in Ernest Pépin's *L'Envers du décor.* Concentrating on the Afro-diasporic dance circle, or the cypher, this book is dedicated to the roles that the representations of social performance play in Caribbean fiction. I propose that writers look to performance to elicit three aspects of opposition politics: the politics of social relations, historical temporality, and corporeality as a site of knowledge production. First, performance highlights the dynamic relationship between audience members and performers and thus allows writers to imagine modes of community formation and social transformations that would otherwise seem impossible. Second, the capacity to suspend a chronological sense of time in a performance makes apparent nonteleological relationships to both history and futurity. In the breaks from chronology, writers rehearse the futures they want to bring into being and engage past histories and experiment with how those stories might be retold in more generative ways. Finally, the attention performance draws to bodies in motion and to the meaning these bodies make leads to the articulation of expansive conceptions of personhood.

The works I examine demonstrate that Caribbean writers use performance events as a proxy for rehearsing a spectrum of differing conceptions of community, an issue that has particular historical vexations in the region. As Celia Britton demonstrates within the Francophone Caribbean, the history of forced migrations is only the first of the reasons that community is an uncertain and anxiety-provoking problem: "Conceived both in terms of collective practices and institutions and on the subjective level of collective identity, [community] generates a deep-seated anxiety in the French Caribbean" (*Community* 1).[1] In addition to serving as a particular formation of a contingent community, the dance circle also provides a place for reworking relationships. To explore the intersection of performance and community in the Caribbean context, I begin with Frantz Fanon's description of "le cercle de la dance" in *Les Damnés de la terre.* The brief but evocative representation of a dance circle of colonized persons, which speaks not only to anticolonial thought but dance studies as well, is noted by Thomas DeFrantz in his definition of social dance: "The dancing bodies and their audiences merge. As Frantz Fanon writes, 'The circle of the dance is a permissive circle: it protects and permits. . . . There are no limits—inside the circle'" (*Dancing Revelations* 197). Precisely because audiences and performers together form social dance, the dance circle emphasizes the interpersonal relationships possible only in such a circle, transient and ephemeral as it may be. In this introduction, I analyze this evocative moment in Fanon's thinking in order to call forth the ways in which the circle can become a space for challenging colonialism and its legacies. I propose that the dance circle, as represented in contemporary Caribbean novels, is one distinct type of performance heralded as a quasi-utopian space where it is possible to practice social transformations and alternative formations of community that would otherwise seem impossible.

Just as it breaks with the status quo by offering alternative spaces, the temporality of performance facilitates the interruption of the plotlines of Caribbean texts: over and again, characters in these texts comment on their temporal disorientation after leaving a performance event. Performance can momentarily step outside of chronological time, and the conventions of theater present the audience with new contexts to serve as reality for the duration of the play. Therefore, performance events provide writers with the opportunity to rewrite history by filling in silences or ignored experiences, to activate the past's knowledge and emotions in the present, or to rehearse the futures they want to bring into being. The Augustinian concept of "*distentio*," as developed by Paul Ricoeur in *Time and Narrative*, maps onto the way that these writers evoke nonchronological conceptions of time: through "*distentio*," the present is distended to include the past and the future. Although these descriptions create a sense of time's expansiveness, they are only possible within the moment of performance, when there is a break from the internal progress of the narrative. The textual representation of performance therefore produces two approaches to temporality: rupture and expansion. The break interrupts the sense of time's inexorable passage and, as a result, in novels like Jacques Stephen Alexis's *Les Arbres musiciens*, where it would seem that Haiti's loss of sovereignty to U.S. imperialism is a foregone conclusion, the excursus from the plot into the dance circle disrupts the perception that the future is indistinguishable from the oppressive present.

I characterize such detailed descriptions of performance events as ekphrases, defined as moments of exceptional vividness of narration. My use of ekphrasis as a way of identifying such textual engagements with performance practices implies that this moment of description breaks from the text's norms while remaining integral to it. This textual dynamic imitates that of the jazz break, "a short suspension of the rhythm or the flow of the music" that makes way for a soloist's improvisation.[2] Within the fixity of the printed word, the break evokes the possibility for improvisation's experimentation. I work from Fred Moten's *In the Break* not only for the idea of the break as a structural relationship between Afro-diasporic performance and writing, but also for his proposal that what happens in the breaks is "a revaluation or reconstruction of value, one disruptive of the oppositions of speech and writing, and spirit and matter" (14). Inspired in great part by Moten's research on ontology and heuristics in performance, my textual analyses elaborate redefinitions of personhood that are justified by the demonstration that performance is a site of knowledge production. I structure several chapters to showcase how the moments of ekphrastic writing draw on the principles of the genre of performance as well as the energy generated in the dance circle that is rarely sustained once outside of it. I nevertheless suggest that these representations of performance do not treat performance solely as an escape from the present, but instead take the occasion to rehearse the social relations and transformations that are desired for the present.[3] It is precisely the use of performance as an exceptional event, the impact of which is not confined to the event itself, which makes the representation of performance such fertile ground for Caribbean writers.

Within the break engendered by the representation of the performance event, the present can be drawn out to instantiate both memories of the past and the imagination of the future. On the basis of these inclusions, the temporality of performance creates an opportunity to reshape the present. The particular spatial and temporal configurations of the circle exist to protect the participants' exploration of their own lived experiences. Guillermo Cabrera Infante and Patrick Chamoiseau, for example, describe the suspension of time as being felt in the body, a corporeal sensibility that contradicts information provided by the clock.[4] The body's experience generates knowledge about the world that stands in opposition to official information imposed from the metropole, the (former) colonial capitals of Paris and London. As the characters voice their wonder at their feeling of temporality that moves at a different pace and in different directions than their watch's indications, they articulate a temporal divergence from what Anne McClintock terms "panoptical time." Starting from Johannes Fabian's chronological time, McClintock aligns chronology with colonial divisions of global space and defines panoptical time as "the image of global history consumed—at a glance—in a single spectacle from a point of privileged invisibility" (36). Shifting away from such a construction of global history, with its attendant racial hierarchies, is part of the work of representing social performance in these texts. I argue that Caribbean writers demonstrate how the cultural production for which the region is so well known is both a repository for historical knowledge and a space for the invention of new knowledge. This is my focal point for how Caribbean writers do what Wilson Harris has identified as the purview of global postcolonial peoples: "The true capacity of marginal and disadvantaged cultures resides in their genius to tilt the field of civilization so that one may visualize boundaries of persuasion in new and unsuspected lights to release a different apprehension of reality, the language of reality, a different *reading* of texts of reality" (183). In their representations of performance, Caribbean writers show their readers how to read and interpret what is articulated within the dance circle as knowledge. They position themselves as explaining the performing body's action through ekphrastic description, the virtuosic performance practices through which Caribbean peoples "tilt the field of civilization" away from the single perspective of panoptical time. Reading Caribbean literature in this light, I ask, What kinds of epistemological tilts does the turn to performance enable?

Performance and Personhood in Caribbean Literature seeks to articulate a regional writing practice within the textual depictions of performance, a practice that is marked by the aesthetic experimentation that occurs in the ekphrastic compensation of writing across the arts, as well as a written explanation of the social praxes and knowledge formations that are produced in a dance circle. Especially by providing the occasion for investigating bodies as sites of knowledge, representations of performance can be used to contest the still commonly held assumption against which Walter Mignolo argues in his passionate argument for epistemic disobedience that "the first world has knowledge, the third world has culture; Native Americans have wisdom, Anglo Americans have science" (160). As I will show, literary representations of performances highlight the ways in which cultural practices house knowledge. Furthermore, corporeal movement is represented *not* as an unthinking and automatic reflex to its environment, but rather as articulating thought in movement. This shift from evaluating corporeal performance as an object of analysis to an episteme (D. Taylor xvi), and from automatic reflexes to kinesthetic intelligence, is a move that is well established in the fields of performance studies and dance studies. In analyzing the representation of social performance in Caribbean writing, I propose that the meaning-making capacities of performing bodies function as a given in these texts and that, furthermore, their movement is described in such a way as to make their epistemic contributions evident. The question of how to redefine knowledge is an undercurrent of writing performance that I aim to surface in order to show how the intersection of writing and performance practices in Caribbean literature is a site for reconsidering the allotment of personhood in (post)colonial worlds.

Personhood and the Fanonian Circle

Foundational to the way that I trace the relationship between performance and personhood is Fanon's ekphrastic description of the dance circle. In the middle of "Concerning Violence" in *Wretched of the Earth*, Fanon reflects on how colonized peoples use performance events to manage the muscular tensions that result from their unfulfilled desire to upend colonial hierarchies.

> Sur un autre versant, nous verrons l'affectivité du colonisé s'épuiser en danses plus ou moins extatiques. C'est pourquoi une étude du monde colonial doit obligatoirement s'attacher à la compréhension du phénomène de la danse et de la possession. La relaxation du colonisé, c'est précisément cette orgie musculaire au cours de laquelle l'agressivité la plus aiguë, la violence la plus immédiate se trouvent canalisées, transformées, escamotées. Le cercle de la (88) danse est un cercle permissif. Il protège et autorise. A heures fixes, à dates fixes, hommes et femmes se retrouvent en un lieu donné et, sous l'œil grave de la tribu, se lancent dans une pantomime d'allure désordonnée mais en réalité très systématisée où, par des voies multiples, dénégations de la tête, courbure de la colonne, rejet en arrière de tout le corps, se déchiffre à livre ouvert l'effort grandiose d'une collectivité pour s'exorciser, s'affranchir, se dire. Tout est permis . . . dans le cercle. Le monticule où l'on s'est hissé comme pour être plus près de la lune, la berge où l'on s'est glissé comme pour manifester l'équivalence de la danse et de l'ablution, du lavage, de la purification sont des lieux sacrés. Tout est permis car, en réalité, l'on ne se réunit que pour laisser la libido accumulée, l'agressivité empêchée, sourdre volcaniquement. (87–88)

> On another level we see the native's emotional sensibility exhausting itself in dances which are more or less ecstatic. This is why any study of the colonial world should take into consideration the phenomena of the dance and of possession. The native's relaxation takes precisely the form of a muscular orgy in which the most acute aggressivity and the most impelling violence are canalized, transformed, and conjured away. The circle of the dance is a permissive circle; it protects and permits. At certain times on certain days, men and women come together at a given place, and there, under the solemn eye of the tribe, fling themselves into a seemingly unorganized pantomime, which is in

> reality extremely systematic, in which by various means, shakes of the head, bending of the spinal column, throwing of the whole body backward—may be deciphered as in an open book the huge effort of a community to exorcise itself, to liberate itself, to explain itself. There are no limits—inside the circle. The hillock up which you have toiled as if to be nearer to the moon; the river bank down which you slip as if to show the connection between the dance and ablutions, cleansing and purification—these are sacred places. There are no limits—for in reality your purpose in coming together is to allow the accumulated libido, the hampered aggressivity, to dissolve as in a volcanic eruption. (Farrington translation 57)

Fanon goes on to reject these modes of performance, along with spiritual rites and mythology, because his aim is for colonized persons to use their energies to fuel systemic revolt and not, as he suggests in this description, to dilute those energies in the relief that the practices of performance afford. Yet here, he also acknowledges the importance of the Afro-diasporic dance circle as a site where knowledge formation takes place. Within the circle, the body's movements are directed by one's own self in kinesthetic conversation with a chosen community—not under the command of another. By virtue of their participation in the circle, colonized persons challenge definitions of personhood that relegate them to a category of being that is less than fully human. As such, while the dance circle may not contribute to the revolutionary trajectory that Fanon outlines, by serving as a safe space for artistic experimentation and self-articulation, it challenges colonial frameworks. It is therefore an important site for rehearsing social transformations.

Fanon insists on the intelligibility of the corporeal movement within the dance circle: when the body performs, the community created in the circle works to "s'affranchir, se dire." "Se dire," technically to say to oneself or claim about oneself, can be broadly interpreted in this context as articulating oneself. Self-definition and self-emancipation ("s'affranchir") are equated through juxtaposition such that the circle where these acts occur becomes the place where dreams of self-possession can take material form. Moments before this passage, Fanon writes about the strict limitations of movement placed on a colonized person, limitations that lead to dreams of "muscular prowess, his dreams are of action and aggression. I dream I am jumping, swimming, running, climbing. . . . During the period of colonization, the colonized person never stops achieving his freedom from nine in the evening until six in the morning" (Farrington 52).[5] The dance circle, where there are no such limitations of movement, offers a waking version of the dreams of surpassing colonialism's constraints. The medium of performance can be used to enact dreams because, as the theater practitioner Aleksandra Wolska maintains about performance practices, the art of the performative is to make something happen out of almost nothing (95). Despite his overt reservations, it is entirely fitting that Fanon identifies performance practices as the modes through which the community's work of transforming subjugation into its opposite takes physical form. In the circle, Fanon identifies the coexistence of the dreams of an energetic and unconstrained body with the legibility of an Afro-diasporic movement tradition.

Performance and Personhood in Caribbean Literature shows that Caribbean writers describe the dynamics of the dance circle in order to reflect on the intellectual/corporeal labor of defining personhood that takes place within it. Gerard Aching's work on Frederick Douglass's *Narrative* and subjectivity in the context of Hegel's metaphors of slavery is instructive in this regard. Drawing on historians and philosophers such as Paul Escott and Howard McGary, Aching suggests we "deepen our understanding of the slave's work not only as forced labor but also as the psychic work of grappling with internalized forms of oppression" ("Slave's Work" 916). Fanon's description of the dance circle indicates that the circle functions as a site where the psychic work of grappling with the oppression that is the continuing legacy of slavery and colonialism can be reworked through inventive corporeal articulations. Fanon's evocation of performance is therefore at the heart of this study because it outlines the relationship between the scene of the dance circle, the techniques of ekphrastic writing about performance, and an epistemology that places corporeality at the center of definitions of thought, intelligence, and knowledge. The work that the text does is to render corporeal movement intelligible for global readerships, even as it maintains that the intelligibility is housed in the movement itself. Inspired by, but not limited to, the exact form of the dance circle, I term the "Fanonian circle" the textual moments when the author represents the Afro-diasporic circle such that the narrative explicates how corporeal movement expresses ideas or articulates knowledge, and positions ekphrastic writing as a form of translation from kinesthetic semiotics (Desmond 33) to literary text.[6] Here, Fanon conjoins psychic with physical labor as he comments that for the colonized, relaxation is not an experience of leisure, but is a form of self-protection against colonial repression that is achieved through "a muscular orgy." This energy dedicated to creating circles that protect and permit is precisely what I will argue that Caribbean writers attempt to activate when they include ekphrases of performances in their textual works.

The capability of performance to create a sacrosanct space, a space where social formations and conceptions of personhood can be energetically redefined, requires a particular approach. Social performance assumes that engaged participants are not separate from the dancers, musicians, or storytellers, and that everyone present contributes to a shared experience. As Marlene NourbeSe Philip explains in her description of two characters, Totoben and Maisie, and their audience participation in Carnival: "Carnival and marse meaning that you crossing from looking to dancing and back again to looking, from not moving to moving and back again to not moving" (152). In Philip's description, what is particular to Carnival—and social performance more generally—is that the audience members and performers do not have distinct roles; rather, their roles are inseparable from one another. By including the standing/watching audience members *in* the dancing band, Philip equates witnessing with participating. Here "looking" is not passive spectatorship but a dynamic form of support that is absolutely necessary for those who are, in that particular instant, dancing and moving. Not only do audience members at social performances have the potential to act as performers, but in both ritual and secular forms of the circle, the audience takes on the task of holding the circle's energy. In this sense, audience and performer together create the circle's meaning. This aspect of the Fanonian circle, especially resonant in Afro-diasporic traditions, is the point of departure for identifying the corporeal epistemologies of these texts.

Social performance and the dance circle represent only a very small sliver of the range of performances associated with the Caribbean that are described in literature. For example, the ekphrastic description of the dance circle in *Damnés* for both DeFrantz and Paul Gilroy stands in contrast to how the circle's dynamics of Fanon's writing are subsequently transformed when Afro-diasporic dance migrates onto proscenium stages, changing the audience from participant to consumer and attempting to limit the performer's significance to an entertainment commodity. As Gilroy comments, "Creolised creativity entered the arterial system of the modern body politic via the capillaries of popular culture. It made resistance and accommodation into inseparable twins" ("To Be Real" 16). Performances that take place outside of the dance circle, destined for commercial recordings and stages, account for a substantial number of Caribbean and Afro-diasporic performance practices. Such performance events are likewise the subjects of literary representation:

Earl Lovelace's demonstration of how performance can be a social and political dead end in *The Dragon Can't Dance* and performers' commodification in Mayra Santos-Febres's *Sirena Selena* are only two such texts that multiply the textual uses of performance beyond the purview of this study.

Out of the vast repertoire of Caribbean texts that feature performance, I focus exclusively on representations of social performances that could be said to take place within a dance circle. Rather than concentrate on the literary representation of one genre of performance—music, dance, or storytelling—I follow the example of Afro-diasporic performance traditions where dance, drumming, music, or storytelling take place together and are not divided into a western European autonomy of the arts. The texts I compare here all feature performances where audience and performers are indistinguishable from one another in terms of their importance in creating the performance and where performance spaces conjure a temporary sense of possibility that sanctifies the space and the relations experienced therein. As Fanon invokes in describing the circle's spaces: "The hillock up which you have toiled as if to be nearer to the moon; the river bank down which you slip as if to show the connection between the dance and ablutions, cleansing and purification—these are sacred places." In creating a permanent if imperfect trace of that ephemeral communal catharsis in literary representations, writers from Jacques Stephen Alexis to Zoé Valdés seek to recuperate the social, political, and aesthetic possibilities rehearsed in performance events as a starting point for rethinking social and political formations in the Caribbean.

In this regard, this study joins twentieth-century scholarship about the Caribbean in which analysis of cultural production signals a tradition of opposition politics. As Natasha Barnes states, in Anglophone Caribbean scholarship "culture became the foundation for a vanguard Caribbean intellectual tradition in which resistance and opposition emerge as prominent themes from the complex caldron of Afro-creole popular expressivity" (16). Even as I highlight the importance of this lineage in my approach to Caribbean literature, I keep in mind Silvio Torres-Saillant's caution that an engagement with expressive forms cannot be equated with social transformation.[7] Performance as a space for politics is peculiar in that it both bears on everyday life and is limited—for when the audience and performers go their separate ways at the end of the night, challenges arise in how to translate the rehearsals that take place in a utopian space into everyday life.[8] In part, it is because performances can function as excurses from everyday life in their conceptions of space and time that writers can use ekphrases of performance as a respite from the practical impossibilities that constrain the political imagination.

A central organizational logic of the book is therefore how, in the circle where participants lift the limits on the political imagination, the definition of who can be a person can expand in different directions given different contexts. The first chapter sets up this question by examining how Marissa Chibas's performance in her one-woman show *Daughter of a Cuban Revolutionary* (2007) offers a demonstration of substitutability to shift the concept of personhood from the discrete individual to a community's relations. Then, in chapter 2, in the contexts of cultural loss in Patrick Chamoiseau's *Solibo Magnifique* (1998) and slavery in Marlon James's *The Book of Night Women* (2009), I argue that the representations of performance make the case for what scholars in the fields of women's studies and dance studies have referred to as "embodied knowledge," knowledge that is grounded in bodily experience that accounts for the researcher's body, and that blurs boundaries between mind and body (Ellingston). Full personhood is claimed for the category of humans Fanon calls *les damnés* on the basis of their generation of knowledge, in these cases expressed in corporeal performance. The following chapters consider the contexts of exilic communities, prison, and forced displacement; in chapter 4, how Staceyann Chin and Zoé Valdés take to the blogosphere to create a circle of supported experimentation in which the participants are separated by time and place; in the fifth and final chapter's analyses of Rosario Ferré's "Maquinolandera" (1977) and Jacques Stephen Alexis's *Les Arbres musiciens* (1957), I return to the fluid conceptions of personhood of Vodou cosmology. The last sections of each chapter elaborate what I call the texts' corporeal epistemology, the definition of knowledge and philosophical thought that emerges in the textual description of the body's movement while in the circle. Underscoring the degree of removal between a performance and its textual representation, the term "corporeal epistemology" highlights a particular task of writers: to write performance in order to translate embodied knowledge into literary practice.

It is in the ekphrases of performance events that Caribbean writers elaborate corporeal epistemologies, that is, the meaning-making systems that derive from an Afro-diasporic tradition of rhetoric, rhythm, and corporeal movement. The regional practice of representing performance reorganizes how we categorize the production of knowledge, asking us to think about the implications of recognizing the dance circle and the antiphonal, improvisational movement of bodies within the dance circle as a form of embodied knowledge. My focus on what I call the Fanonian circle is a model for how writers evoke in such descriptions the identification of emotional meaning and the intelligibility of performance practices as a form of political expression, in that locating knowledge within performance is part of a broader case for expanding categories of the person beyond the definition of a person as individualized: "The Western European tradition believes each soul to be individual and unique, the inhabitant of only one body" (Blakemore and Jennett). According to this line of thought, in order to be a person, one must have a singular identity that is "'incommunicable'—that is, unique and irreplaceable selves, not exchangeable specimens of a general human stock" (C. Smith 66). The explorations of personhood in the Caribbean texts I consider are counterposed to this assumption, and I begin to push against this definition of personhood with the first chapter's analysis of Marissa Chibas's play, where a performing person practices substitutability as a mode of relation.

I propose that one element of the Caribbean practice of writing performance is the elaboration of a person whose constitution is not bound to the contours of the Enlightenment's legacies of a hermetic individual whose rational mind entitles him or her with the special moral status and legal rights of personhood (C. Smith 72). It also expands beyond personhood in a neoliberal context, wherein a person is defined by the "possession of individual interests and her ability to rank and decide between them" (Elliott 84). I return here to the well-trod terrain of contesting the mind-body split and the Cartesian cogito as person because one avenue of protest against disenfranchisement in these novels is to demand that the natural rights of characters be recognized on that the basis that their performances are a form of knowledge that is different from—but equal in legitimacy to—rationality. The argument that if performance is knowledge, then the performer must be considered a person is one approach to the work Sylvia Wynter takes in her 2003 tour de force "Unsettling the Coloniality of Being/Power/Truth/Freedom: Towards the Human, After Man, Its Overrepresentation—An Argument," in which she argues for "a redescription of the human outside the terms of our present descriptive statement of the human" (268), an articulation that resonates with the shorthand that I use: to broaden personhood. Wynter dedicates much of the essay to demonstrating how "Man," as the "creed-specific conception of what is was to be human" (291), is based on the master codes of European philosophy that, in turn, justify the imperial expansionism that functions due to the category of what she calls "Man's Human Other," defined as such by a "naturally determined enslavement to irrationality" (305). She traces the master codes' epistemic shifts from the opposition of "Redeemed Spirit" to "Fallen Flesh" of the religious subject, through the post-Renaissance secular political subject whose "rationality" separates him from "irrational" subhumans, to global capital's distinctions between "productive members of society" and Fanon's *damnés,* the unproductive, poor, and jobless. Wynter demonstrates the continuous relevance of the mind-body split throughout the cumulative effects of each of these codes and their exclusionary definitions of personhood.

The very term "personhood," or the quality or condition of being a person, implies that who or what is a person is not self-evident. Who or what has access to the rights and responsibilities of a person is not a given, but rests on terrain that shifts according to different social needs. The term itself enters the English lexicon relatively recently,[9] but the mechanisms of fungibility it encodes can be traced to Hobbes, Locke, and, as Amanda Bailey demonstrates, the practice of debt bondage as civil death in early modern England and the foundation of the American colonies. The "alive in body but dead in law" (9) debtor languished in incarceration or worked off her debts as an indentured servant in the colonies; and in both cases, her personhood is compromised in that she suffers the consequences of personhood's responsibilities to the state without enjoying its attending rights. A human's distinction from a person is therefore reflected in the dynamics of social rights and responsibilities, set forth by Kant: "*Person* is a being who has *rights* and is conscious of them. If he has *rights and no duties*, then he is *God*. To have duties and no rights is the characteristic of the *criminal*" (210).[10] In examining the figure of the debtor, Bailey finds that "even as slaves were referred to as property, no legal code in either England or colonial America had ever denied that the slave was a person" (145). Despite the absence of its legal codification of "non-person," Kant's creation of a separate category for the criminal, which is not included in that of the person, points to the ways in which race would establish exclusions around full personhood. It is therefore not surprising that when Saidiya Hartman theorizes the subject of the freedman in post-Emancipation United States, she finds that "for the free(d) individual . . . to be responsible was to be blameworthy" (125) and further, that "the guilty volition enjoyed by the free agent bore an uncanny resemblance to the only form of agency legally exercised by the enslaved—that is, criminal liability"

(126).[11] While the uses of race in the United States are not equivalent to its function throughout the Caribbean region, race is a central element in separating the criminalized *damnés* from the legal category of the person throughout the Americas.

In the context of early-twenty-first-century U.S. political discourse, "personhood" is most commonly heard in debates surrounding reproductive and corporate rights, and Stephen Best has examined the narrative constructions that make and unmake persons in the juridical context in which "person signifies what the law makes it signify" (13). Certainly the current questions where the term is most likely to appear in 2015—at what point does a fetus become a rights-bearing person whose life is protected by the law, and to what extent can a corporation participate in the political process as a person who financially supports her interests—put the category of the person in contention. The fact that the concept of personhood puts "person" in play for debate is the starting point for the argument that subtends my analyses, for while the word "personhood" never appears in any of the primary sources I analyze, the concept allows me to articulate how Caribbean writers use representations of performance to make the case for extending personhood beyond the exclusionary parameters that have been drawn and retraced along the lines of the Cartesian subject.[12] *Performance and Personhood in Caribbean Literature* investigates how Caribbean writers advocate forcefully for their own selves as persons, connecting themselves to the personhood of the landless, the queer, the exiled, and most fundamentally, the enslaved and their descendants. Their advocacy is based in part on demonstrating how persons assert their personhood through performance practices.

The elaboration of personhood that emerges here in the textual representations of performance thus diverges from Enlightenment values in two main directions: one, the primacy of individualism is undercut in favor of relationality, and two, disembodiment as a path toward a universal person is rejected in favor of specificity.[13] In part, I mean specificity in a very literal sense: the political and historical circumstances against which the dance circle takes shape structures the ways in which the protagonists attempt to possess themselves and claim their personhood. From slavery to the uneven power dynamics of the tourist economy, the complex contexts of domination determine how a storyteller's, a singer's, or an audience member's body will move through that space, what movement traditions they will each inhabit, and the different meanings that will be generated through the interaction of a person and her environment. We might think of this work in concert with what George Yancy calls "doing philosophy in Black," where knowledge is generated by "*raced* embodied subjects [who] undergo shared existential crises of struggle within the context of anti-Black racism" (3). The insights and epistemological work that are available from these various perspectives and contexts are, in the textual representations of performance, conjoined with the structured improvisation of the Afro-diasporic dance circle, a combination that Paget Henry theorizes as an Africana metaphysics that he terms *creative realism*, wherein "different perspectives are temporarily allowed to occupy the position of 'center'" precisely because this decentered metaphysics is based on improvisation (*Africana Political Philosophy* 52). Such approaches to deuniversalizing philosophy ground the engagement that Caribbean writers take to depicting performing bodies: chiasmatically rearranging the mind-body divides such that minds move and bodies think is the basis for, first, the project of recognition that there is such a thing as a thinking body and, second, finding modes of textually representing the knowledge housed in their corporealities.

The question that guides my readings is thus, How do Caribbean writers revise the interpretation of corporeal production such that its thinking is recognizable as such? Fanon insists in *Damnés* that the performance events produced by colonized persons do not function as simply as European interpretive practices might have trained his readers to see them. Describing the dance circle as a "seemingly unorganized pantomime, which is in reality extremely systematic," Fanon responds to the philosophical tradition of refusing intelligibility to either corporeal movement or raced, embodied subjects. Such a refusal of intelligibility is a form of epistemic violence, and in this brief ekphrastic description of performance, he challenges those interpretive systems and ideologies of what constitutes knowledge by intimating that corporeal movement is a site of philosophical production. What theories of knowledge emerge from the Afro-diasporic movement traditions when Caribbean writers inscribe their texts with representations of performance events? For example, when antiphony structures conversation and debate; when the storyteller's transformations suggest we change how to ask questions about his life and death; when logic would seem to dictate that it is impossible to challenge an oppressive political system, bodily instinct that creates a direction for contestation reveals itself as kinesthetic intelligence; when songs, dances, and drummed rhythms that tell the story of past events revive those events for their audience's present experience; when a demonstration that a single body can be the site of expression for multiple persons through a practice of substitutability expands definitions of personhood. Each of these examples wrenches knowledge out of the objectivist tradition of "detaching all rationality and reason from embodied experience," as Margaret Thompson Drewal phrases it.[14] Such examples demonstrating how moving bodies are thinking, knowledge-producing bodies mark the ekphrastic representations of performance practices in Caribbean writing.

The Ethics and Aesthetics of Ekphrasis

The critical tradition of examining the Caribbean literary representation of performance into which I enter has three main approaches: (1) a consideration of how literary works themselves act as performances, as in Lizabeth Parivisini-Gebert's essay "Writers Playin' Mas," where she discusses the carnivalesque practice of parody within Caribbean writing and Benítez-Rojo's proposal in *Repeating Island* that Caribbean texts function according to the rules of different kinds of spectacles, from Carnival to television shows (218); (2) a review of how the explicit textual imitation of performance practices potentially impacts different readers, for example Maximilien Laroche's analysis of the relationship between "oraliture" and "littérature" or Rocio Davis's suggestion that Edwidge Danticat's *Krik? Krak!* is an experience of intensifying reading; and (3), tracing the influence of the performing arts on literary practices. The last generally focuses on one specific performance practice, such as a musical instrument or genre, dance tradition, or rite, as in Frances Aparicio's *Listening to Salsa,* which integrates readings of literature about salsa alongside analyses of song lyrics and performance descriptions; or Martin Munro's *Different Drummers*, which examines how West African rhythms developed into particular forms throughout North America and its subsequent influence on literature, or, in focusing on orality, works such as Mervyn Morris's "Printing the Performance" and Carolyn Cooper's *Noises in the Blood*, which aim to develop a terminology to identify the aesthetic techniques, and political ramifications, of oral performance poetry and reflect on its relationship to print matter. Finally, monographs such as Aching's *Masking and Power* theorize the political and philosophical impact of writing performance, or what representing performance practices *does*, proposing that the literary representation of masking and mimicry in Carnival is a social practice that transforms social orders, thus mapping a kind of "politics on a lower frequency" (9). My book draws from each of these approaches and uses multilingual and interdisciplinary comparative methodologies through which we might trace the qualities of social performance in a regional Caribbean writing practice. Rather than focus on one context or performance practice, the criterion for the selection of literary works is the inclusion of an ekphrasis of social performance.

Broadly defined as "the verbal representation of visual representation" (Heffernan 3), ekphrasis is most commonly associated with the intersection of poetry and the plastic arts after Horace's famous phrase "ut pictura poesis."[15] While modern uses of ekphrasis generally limit the term to refer to the exchange between the visual arts and literature, I use Ruth Webb's adoption of the classical use of the rhetorical practice that broadly characterizes ekphrasis as different from narration in that it "includes the details that tell one *how* it happened, how it looked (one might add also how it sounded and felt). The difference, in Nikolaos' terms, is *enargeia*, vividness, an *ekphrasis* in sum is a vivid form of narration" (13). The subject matter itself could include a broad range of actions, events, or works of art, and Webb argues convincingly against limiting its subjects to "the static, the objectified" visual arts (14). I attend to the descriptions of performance, ekphrastic and otherwise, in Caribbean writing in order to call attention to the ways that the description of performance events connects bodies in motion to new bodies of knowledge. This literary technique, which courses through Caribbean writing, can extend the relationship between performers and audience members to that between a text and its readers. Through the vivid description of how a performance event looks, sounds, and feels for its audience, the ekphrasis of performance aims to impact the reader in an analogous way to how the performance impacts the audience.

In the ekphrasis of performance I analyze in this introduction, Fanon's evocation of the ecstatic dance circle both describes a respite from the experience of colonial oppression and is itself, in the narrative of *Damnés*, a break from reflections on oppression. Fanon frames the description of the movement vocabulary of the dancers in the circle with the indication that these movements are the various means or roads that the dancers take to liberate themselves: "des voies multiples, dénégations de la tête, courbure de la colonne, rejet en arrière de tout le corps." The "shakes of the head, bending of the spinal column, throwing of the whole body backward" illustrate the value of polycentrism in Afro-diasporic dance. Just as the body's lines travel in different directions when the head and spine emit energy in different directions, meaning travels in different directions simultaneously. Fanon crucially includes a directional shift in his description: the sudden backward movement of the body marks the moments of radical change that can take place during the performance. This approach to movement and thought in Afro-diasporic intellectual-artistic production lays the groundwork for Fanon's further suggestion that performance as a communicative system is on par with that of writing as we see in the phrase "se déchiffre à livre ouvert l'effort grandiose d'une collectivité pour s'exorciser, s'affranchir, se dire." Turning to the book, Fanon rejects out of hand any possible interpretation of the movements in the dance circle as random or meaningless and endows corporeal performance with the same degree of legitimacy as literature by demonstrating the legibility and therefore intellectual strength of these expressive forms in terms that his metropolitan reader must acknowledge.

But this metaphor of the book, along with the verbs "se déchiffrer" and "se dire," embed into Fanon's defense of Afro-diasporic performance practices the ethical quandaries of writing about what takes place in the dance circle. For while Fanon's reflexive pronouns insistently return the action to the active subject, Farrington's translation highlights the question of address: "The huge effort of a community to exorcise itself, to liberate itself, to explain itself [may be deciphered as in an open book]." To whom does the community explain itself, by whom may the performance be deciphered, and what is the role of the writer in facilitating this exchange? This is where the purposes of performance diverge between the performance event itself and its literary representation. If we recall Philip's description of Totoben's and Maisie's audience participation in Carnival: "The police not understanding that Totoben and Maisie who standing and watching and Maisie and Totoben who dancing in the band is one and the same; they not understanding" (125). Totoben and Maisie understand their doubled role of dancing/looking perfectly well, and it is not for their benefit that Philip must explain that the ease of crossing between the two activities of audience and participant actually eradicates that line and combines the two roles in the activity of participating-by-witnessing. Rather, Philip introduces this explanation of the social performance with a mention of those who do not participate in the circle. In reading Fanon and Philip together to locate the description's addressee, we see that metropolitan readers occupy the same role as the police. Because both writers assume that without explication the reader will come to incorrect interpretations of the dance circle, ekphrasis has a pedagogical function: it offers a corrective to interpretations that might limit the scope of what takes place within the dance circle.

In the literary representation of performance events and rituals, Caribbean writers make legible the intellectual work of performance. Because these rituals are defined by their private intimacy, when estimating the impact of making them public, we are never far from the ethical dilemmas that arise with translation. The pithy Italian saying, "traduttore traditori," where translation is separated from betrayal by the slip of a vowel, evokes the sense that by displacing local concepts into colonial language, the translator betrays both the concepts themselves as well as the people who conceived them.[16] A paratextual question that therefore haunts this project is whether there is any return value to the dance circle's participants when accounts of their performances are published. The majority of the texts I read here are published by editorial houses in Paris, Barcelona, and New York. In order to appeal to the widest possible audience, writers must accommodate metropolitan readers even while challenging Eurocentric assumptions about what constitutes knowledge. Caribbean writers who use ekphrasis to describe and explain the workings of the dance circle translate the circle's activities from corporeal movement to text and explicate creole vocabulary along with Afro-diasporic spiritual rites and movement traditions through metaphors that correspond with the metropolitan reader's cultural codes, such as Fanon's "open book." And their translations are marked by the self-conscious concern, often in the narrator's own voice, that by opening the closed dance circle beyond its participants, they fundamentally transform the circle.

What are the aesthetic and ethical ramifications of writing performance? Whether writers should write about the rituals through which colonized peoples sustain themselves is a fraught question that we can approach from two directions: first, that the ekphrasis betrays the participants of the dance circle who choose to enter the dance circle in part because its privacy provided safety; second, that the ekphrasis betrays the performance on aesthetic grounds, a question that is at the heart of ekphrastic writing well beyond the context of writing Caribbean performance. Asbjørn Grønstad raises this question when he quotes the admission of the art historian T. J. Clark that "I shall call on pictures to do too much work, to stand for an ethics and politics I find I can state only by means of them" (Grønstad 43), and further proposes that using the artistic object as a vehicle for articulation risks "erasing" the artistic object itself. I therefore include in the "Fanonian circle" the metalevel considerations framing the description itself in which writers ruminate about how best to describe a performance event—and voice the concern that ekphrasis erases the performance by using its vivid description as a starting point for literary experimentation. Ekphrastic language is self-reflexive, as Timothy Morton explains: "to try to create an effect of painting in words often throws the readers' attention back on the nature of the words themselves" (*Spice* 34). For even while writers like Chamoiseau embed into the text overt reservations that the project of ekphrasis is necessarily a failure in crucial ways, as in the citation with which I began, they continuously try new approaches to describing performance. That is, betrayal and failure are aesthetically generative. When writers evoke the sounds and movements of a live performance, they experiment with metropolitan languages and invent new forms of orthography, punctuation, vocabulary, and syntax. Throughout this study, I identify the linguistic and aesthetic modes of experimentation that writers invent when under the pressure to render a corporeal experience into a readerly one.

Because this book is dedicated to how writers take on the challenges of writing performance in Caribbean fiction, I want to introduce these practices with two critical essays in which Caribbean writers reflect on their experiences translating Caribbean popular cultures into writing: Antonio Benítez-Rojo's famous example of two women walking during the Cuban Missile Crisis in the introduction to *The Repeating Island*, which links corporeal ritual and regional philosophy, and Mayra Santos-Febres's essays from *Sobre piel y papel* (2004), the very title of which indicates the congress between writing and bodies. In trying to identify what is distinct about Caribbeanness, Benítez-Rojo sets up the "Peoples of the Sea" as having an ideological approach that is not oriented toward apocalyptic destruction: it is aquatic, not terrestrial, and it is organized around "a detour without a purpose" (11) as opposed to the verticality of teleology. In proposing that the Cuban Missile Crisis was anything but Cuban, he turns to the description of walking as performance: "two old black women passed 'in a certain kind of way' beneath my balcony. I cannot describe this 'certain kind of way'" (10).[17] This moment has been rightly excoriated for its essentialism by Frances Aparicio among others, and it has become an iconic moment in Caribbean theory in part because of the controversy that it has generated. Equally important to my purposes here is how this performance becomes a touchstone for thinking about the difficulties of writing performance in the Caribbean context throughout *Repeating Island*.

Benítez-Rojo's initial response to writing performance is an overt statement of his refusal to describe it. Part of how he emphasizes the distinctiveness of performance, as we have already seen with Chamoiseau, is by pointing out where writing fails. However, the distinctiveness of Caribbean social performance is at the core of his argument about what is distinct about the Caribbean region more generally, which lies in what I refer to as the dynamics of the Afro-diasporic dance circle: the "certain kind of way" that he cannot describe is that which "takes away the space that separates the onlooker from the participant" (16). Similarly to Philip's insistence that watching and dancing are not separate activities in Carnival, Benítez-Rojo participates in carving out an important space for social performance within theories of the Caribbean. He grounds this theorization of performance as Caribbeanness in the context of the Cuban Missile Crisis, in which apocalyptic violence engineered by global powers plays itself out on Caribbean land. In linking performance traditions—notably the absence of space between onlooker and participant—to a regional history of surviving limit events instead of hurtling itself toward absolute destruction, Benítez-Rojo suggests that a sense of personal engagement in the specificity of local environments and local practices is a vital distinction between Eurocentric and Caribbean approaches. As he works through how the formation of Caribbean culture is defined by performance, he further indicates that "performance [is defined] not only in terms of scenic interpretation but also in terms of the execution of a ritual, that is, that 'certain way' in which the two Negro women who conjured away the apocalypse were walking" (11). In this light, the "certain kind of way" is an essentialist reference to race and it is also a practice that draws on Afro-diasporic movement traditions as part of a history of Caribbean creolization: a discipline informed by a history of surviving violent trauma.

In contrast to Benítez-Rojo, who places the impossibility of depicting performance at the center of his multiple attempts to depict it, Santos-Febres quickly moves past impossibility and instead takes its necessity as her starting point. In "Español, Clave Caribe," she reflects on the challenges faced by Puerto Rican writers—challenges that she indicates are applicable to anyone writing from a small market or in a minor language. The essay is marked by vocabulary specific to Puerto Rico and includes some of the contractions that are characteristic of Spanish as it is spoken throughout the Caribbean. These writing choices contrast with the author's explanation that Caribbean writers are pushed to standardize their texts, and how, in a bid to make a text fully accessible to every possible audience, publishers will turn any piece of writing into "un libreto de Univisión." This reference to one of the main Spanish-language television channels in the United States points to bland and regionally unspecific writing; the channel's name echoes "universalismo," a concept that earns Santos-Febres's ire elsewhere in the essay collection.[18] As we will see highlighted in chapter 2 on writing and creole languages, publishers' pressure becomes internalized until writers place parameters on their own imaginations. Moreover, this criticism of universalism matches why Afro-diasporic philosophers suggest "doing philosophy" from the historicized perspective of raced, gendered bodies, to use Yancy's phrasing. In the approach I take to reading Caribbean literature regionally, I adopt the ideas that Santos-Febres develops in her pragmatic practice that relies on evoking corporeality. For Santos-Febres, turning to the creativity of speaking, performing, and moving bodies provides a workaround to the problem of writing about local specificities for global audiences.

Santos-Febres acknowledges the challenges posed by writing with regional specificity and proposes that meeting that challenge is a two-pronged task: yes, it is necessary to battle with publishing houses who demand that authors strip their texts of all local expressions, but simultaneously, writers need to create ways of bringing that specificity into the text when staying close to local speech is not an option. She provides no precise methodology, but in an extended metaphor of a chicken dinner as writing, she demonstrates how translation need not result in the permanent loss of specificity, but rather that a sequence of trade-offs can provide roundabout opportunities to inject the feeling of specificity, if not its exact terminology:

> Una tiene que dar del ala pa' comer de la pechuga, eso es conocimiento general. Para darse a conocer hay que hablar claro y preciso. A veces, aunque nos cueste, debemos sacrificar al saoco y la cosa mala en atrás de la claridad. Sin embargo, insisto, repito, y recalco, lo último que se pierde es el sabor. ("Clave" 192)

> She needs to give up some of the chicken wing to get a bite of the breast meat, that is common knowledge. To make oneself known, one must speak clearly and precisely. Sometimes, even if it hurts, we have to sacrifice the stew and "the bad thing" for the sake of clarity. Nevertheless, I insist, I repeat, and I insist again that the last thing you lose is the flavor.

The metaphor begins with Santos-Febres's citation of a proverb that means to trade something good for something better. Drawing on a model for how to negotiate from a position of lesser power, she sidesteps the ethical question surrounding translation and instead offers a workaround, a term I borrow from computer programming to describe an operation that temporarily circumvents a problem rather than permanently eliminate it. Part of Santos-Febres's workaround is to argue for universal access, even while continuing to use the sound of spoken Spanish "pa'" and local vocabulary: she literally says one thing to ensure clarity while doing another to retain specificity. Her shifting subject pronouns reinforce the sense that she is playing with linguistic expectations. For while the rule about how to speak to broad audiences to make oneself known uses the conjugation for the impersonal one in "hay que," Santos-Febres uses the first-person singular voice to insist on flavor, and the protagonist who bargains her chicken leg is identified as "una"—a female-gendered writer figure whose presence tweaks the generalized nature of this proverb. Santos-Febres is rightly imprecise about what lends the text this Caribbean flavor: each writer creates her own workaround.[19] It is the very mention of concessions and exchanges that allows her to make a place in the text for local idioms and specific authorial figures.

My thinking on ekphrasis of Caribbean performance dovetails with Santos-Febres's reflections in her conclusion to "Español, Clave Caribe," where she takes a longer view of these concerns, suggesting that changes in language do not begin with the arbitrators of high culture, such as grammarians or literary critics, but with daily use. These transformations come about because of the corporeal and musical inflections to quotidian language. "Español, Clave Caribe" therefore uses performance as a vehicle for retaining specificity even within an exercise of linguistic and cultural translation:

> La lengua cambia. Y por eso en esta y en otras claves reinventamos el español, lo hacemos nuestro fuera y dentro de los márgenes editoriales, por que es que la cosa no va de otra. Ahora mismo, ahora mismito, en este segundo alguien está pariendo una palabra, un juego con el idioma en frecuencia vacilón, una frase que recombina en la punta de lengua siglos de mestizaje, bachata, ira, opresión, combate, deleite, historia y alianzas. (193)

> Language changes. And for that reason, we reinvent Spanish in this key and others as well; we make it ours inside and outside of the editorial margins, because there's no other way around it. Right now, right right now, this very second, someone is laboring to give birth to a word, a language game in a joking, party frequency, a sentence that recombines centuries of *mestizaje*, *bachata*, anger, oppression, struggle, lust, history, and alliances on the tip of the tongue.

Linguistic transformations take on a sense of urgency in the phrase "ahora mismo, ahora mismito, en este segundo," as if they are passing by both her and us, taking place while she writes and we read. Indeed, the transformations are more than linguistic. Santos-Febres reminds us that the language to which she refers is necessarily embodied when she describes its changes viscerally: rather than the more discreet phrase for giving birth, "dar a luz," "parir" has an unmistakable corporeal, animalistic quality. New words and turns of phrase are the result of new approaches to history, and their source is the speaker's very body. Tapping into the specificity of quotidian corporeal uses of language is a central aspect of ekphrastic writing.

In Santos-Febres's essays, the workarounds to represent the dynamism of languages as they are transformed for each context are best described by a metaphor drawn from performance practices. The essay's eponymous metaphor of a musical key has two senses, one that indicates a harmonic shift, the other the syncopated 3–2 or 2–3 rhythm that is the baseline for salsa. The "clave" works on Spanish, reshapes its rhythms, and changes the frequencies at which the language is audible. This particular reinvention of Spanish aims to hold the language accountable to its historical, cultural, and affective context. The phenomena that Santos-Febres names—*mestizaje*, creolization, and the Dominican and Puerto Rican dance and musical form of *bachata*—are specific to the Hispanophone Caribbean and are also representations of cultural dynamics throughout the multilingual Caribbean region. Santos-Febres makes this expansive gesture when she comments that the problems of writing with local specificity and of seeking publication for European and U.S. readerships extend beyond Puerto Rican writers to the rest of the region and other minor literatures.[20] Santos-Febres's approach is representative of Caribbean writers working *within* metropolitan languages who use ekphrases of performance as a way of working *on* those languages to put pressure on them to resonate along Caribbean frequencies.

Repetition and Writing Performance

This study focuses on the representation of performance events in Caribbean contexts, and considers performance as a range of corporeal actions, from the dance circle that permits and protects its participants to the act of walking. In each of them, the representation of performance hinges on a corporeal referent. The core of this book is focused on what Diana Taylor calls the performatic to signal a "nondiscursive realm of performance," and in so doing, to mark its distinction from the genealogy that can be traced through the concept of performativity which is a "not primarily theatrical . . . [but] discursive practice" (Butler 13) as theorized by J. L. Austin, Derrida, and Butler.[21] When I discuss performance, I refer to how embodied acts generate "a process, a praxis, an episteme, a mode of transmission, an accomplishment, and a means of intervening in the world" (D. Taylor 15). This is not to imply that to speak, to write, and to enter into discourse are not actions. Indeed, valuable examinations of Caribbean performativity are worked through in Guillermina De Ferrari's *Vulnerable States* as well as the psychoanalytic approach to identity formation through performance in Gerard Aching's *Masking and Power*. We might say, though, that the distinction between performativity and the performatic is one of emphasis: performativity's emphasis is on discourse, which impacts bodies in important ways; the performatic's emphasis is on corporeal movement, which likewise is engaged with discourse. In order to identify the distinct task that writers who engage the Fanonian circle take on by endeavoring to write about performance practices, I have chosen texts which are marked by a significant distance between the corporeal and the written, not the cases where corporeal movement and linguistic discourse merge. I draw a generic line between performance and literature in order to show how writers, as Chamoiseau phrases it, touch the distance between performance practices and writing.

The primary organizational logic is neither chronological nor geographical, but articulates the Fanonian circle's constrictions and influences. One of the main reasons that I turn to the concept of performance to organize this book is because of the term's capaciousness: the circle's shape and context constantly changes, as does the corporeal practice that takes place within it. In chapters 3 and 5, I focus on the deeply detailed textual descriptions of musical and danced events. But in chapters 2 and 4, the performances that I analyze stretch the definition of performance: in chapter 4, for example, I show how the writing of a blog, with its dependence on the immediacy of readerly response, can function as a possible enactment of the performance dynamics of the dance circle, and on that basis, I trace what happens to the "corporeal referent" in the digital sphere; in chapter 2, the storyteller's art is not confined to the proscenium stage, but exists wherever he participates in the community, from cooking a stew to organizing a burial, and the circle can be a song cycle, or the act of walking along a circular path. What delimits "performance" throughout this study is a situation in which audience and performer are protecting and permitting one another's ecstatic creativity, thereby generating the sensation of possessing oneself, to return to Fanon's characterization of the dance circle. Each chapter considers the different formations of the dance circle: in the second chapter's context of slavery and colonialism, the circle is formed under the direct threat of violence; in the third chapter, the circle is used to explore nonvisual senses and the articulation of knowledge they permit; in the fourth chapter, where performance and literary practices collide in the medium of online digital writing, bloggers set their own rules for the circle almost unimpeded; and in the final chapter, the texts end in a utopic gesture in which the outraged energy that fueled the circle bursts past the circle's protective limits.

In order to situate the *literary* representations of performance with which this book is primarily concerned, I begin with a descriptive analysis of a stage-based performance, Marissa Chibas's one-woman show *Daughter of a Cuban Revolutionary* (2007). The aim of this analysis is to clearly identify the elements of performance arts that Caribbean writers will try to draw from performance into the text. The analyses of how the performance event transforms temporality and of Chibas's demonstration of substitutability are critical to how I treat the textual representations of performance in every chapter that follows. Chapter 2, "Creole's Thinking Body," puts into conversation Patrick Chamoiseau's *Solibo Magnifique* (1998) and Marlon James's *The Book of Night Women* (2009), set in Martinique and Jamaica respectively. The project of legitimizing written creole languages has galvanized cultural works on these two islands since the 1970s. I compare these two novels based on a similar subplot that they share: the narrator's task to write down an oral performance. According to the premises of the novels, the elements of performance that the narrators have recorded constitute the text we are reading, and each text has navigated the failure to completely represent the protagonists' stories and songs. By focusing on the audience's emotive reception of the performances, these authors generate workarounds to describe oral storytelling. Further, their attention to corporeal semiotics insists upon the body's role as a site of knowledge production in the Caribbean. But throughout their negotiation of the use of vernacular Creole, both Chamoiseau and James register the difficulties of doing so in the face of pressure to standardize writing to fit the needs and limits of understanding of their metropolitan audiences.

In chapter 3, "From Spectator to Participant," I show the extent to which the constitution of the dance circle is determined by the disposition of those who form the circle, not by their performance within it, but by their supportive presence. Particularly considering the emphasis on interpretation in Fanon's explication of the circle, what happens when those participating in the circle shift their audience perspective from supporting the meaningfulness of the performers' gestures to exoticizing them, or vice versa? The three novels I analyze here, Guillermo Cabrera Infante's *Tres tristes tigres* (1964), Oonya Kempadoo's *Tide Running* (2001), and Ernest Pépin's *L'Envers du décor* (2006) reflect on the interpretive models that can either form or destroy a circle and do so by changing the senses through which performance can be interpreted. I read the moves these novels make to distort or prohibit vision alongside Glissant's opacity and analyze their reliance on the textures of tactility and kinesthesia to shift the dynamics of relation within the circle.

Chapter 4, "Staceyann Chin and Zoé Valdés: Sexilic Politics in the Blogosphere," compares the blogs maintained by two writers exiled from their respective homes in the Caribbean. While otherwise very different in their politics and orchestrations of their online personae, Chin and Valdés share a reliance on the narrative of sexile, a personal history informed by their expulsions from Jamaica and Cuba respectively as a result of their unconventional gender (King) and sexual politics. Bolstered by blog readers who make their support visible in the blogs' comments, Chin and Valdés host interactive spaces for virtual (s)exiled communities on the Web. This chapter focuses on the formal elements of blog media, especially how Chin and Valdés write in these media to make a case for a definition of community outside of the nations in which they can no longer live. I focus on their uses of the hyperlink and the temporality of blogging in their presentations of unconventional gender and transnationalism within the virtual communities that grow around their writing. Therefore, in this chapter, the primary sources are not ekphrastic descriptions of performances within novels; rather, I treat the writing on the blog itself as existing in between literary and performance practices. Like print, the reading is time-delayed and not geographically bound, but the relationship between commenting readers and bloggers is akin to the dance circle in that the blog post and its comments section are mutually dependent and propel the blogger's poetic production further. While the body's presence is absent from this textual circle, I argue that Chin and Valdés use blog media to focus on their own sexual, writing bodies, and that they generate in digital writing the kinds of workarounds that are particular to Caribbean aesthetics.

The fifth and final chapter, "Dansez et Revivez!," addresses two texts set in Puerto Rico and Haiti respectively. U.S. imperialism in the

Caribbean basin is the comparative translational link that grounds my readings of Rosario Ferré's "Maquinolandera" (1977) and Jacques Stephen Alexis's *Les Arbres musiciens* (1957). In these texts, the ekphrastic descriptions of performance create a break from the unceasing assault on the protagonists as they are incarcerated in U.S. federal prisons or coerced into laboring for U.S. corporate interests. In the breaks, the protagonists dance. Their shared dance is a rehearsal for their struggle in defense of their communities, an experiment in the social relations they want to experience together, and an assertion of their personhood in the face of every indication that they have no right to direct the movement of their own bodies. In these two texts, ekphrasis provides a break from the narrative, but the energies generated in the performance break spill out of the circle and transform the characters' actions beyond the dance circle itself. The vivid description of ekphrasis slows down narrative time (Morton, *Ecology* 44) even as it creates an "intensification of the narrative" (Webb 14). Whereas the representation of performance cuts into the linear narrative of the plot, as the protagonists suffer the corrosive effects of living in the context of diminishing national sovereignty, the momentary experience of self-possession in the dance circle informs their actions and sense of personhood once outside the dance circle. In contrast to Fanon's dismissal of performance, Ferré and Alexis claim a role for the dance circle in the evolution of revolutionary action and opposition politics.

The two main methodological frameworks for this book are, first, the intersection of performance and literary practices, and second, regional comparison in Caribbean literary studies. While few of the writers I analyze here overtly articulate that a regional aesthetic is one of their concerns, a set of shared preoccupations emerges in the representations of social performance that these writers, independently of one another, work through. I organize the chapters in this book to highlight such transnational resonances, analyze the ways that writers compensate for the differences in genre from performance to text by inventing workarounds for writing performance, and underscore the ways in which these depictions of performances require a reconsideration of how to define personhood in the wake of colonialism's epistemological violences. Tracking the descriptions of performances in Caribbean writing thus allows us to recognize a multilingual regional literary practice that is multidisciplinary at its core. To showcase this multidisciplinarity, I strengthen textual readings with analyses of the performances that the texts reference. In these cases, paratextual performance materials are a crucial source of information, and I deploy what Robin Moore calls an interart analysis, which he describes as how "one might best link the study of music with poetry, painting, and other forms of expression" (93) in order to situate oneself in the midst of various disciplines and employ their methodologies simultaneously. Side by side my analyses of ekphrastic writing, I compare lyrics, structural description of songs, and the social and historical context of the music to their representation in the texts in order to show how knowledge of the musical source material transforms textual readings. This is useful both when the music and its representation seem to reinforce one another, as well as when the information the music provides differs from its representation in these texts. I therefore frame the relationship between performance events and the literary response to them as a repetition with a difference. As a repetition in another genre, writing performance does not reproduce a performance, but to return to Wolska's proposal, it can aim to extend the resonance of that performance to other audiences. If these novels extend to their readers the performances they ekphrastically represent, in putting together this constellation of texts and analyzing their relationship to performance practices through the comparison of works produced in multiple languages and genres, my aim is also to extend the resonance of the textual representation of performance.

In offering the representation of performance as an approach to reading Caribbean literature comparatively, I draw on the centrality of repetition in conceptualizing both the Caribbean region and the medium of performance itself. Repetition, in the sense that I employ it, does not mean exact duplication—quite the opposite. Instead, I model my use of repetition on Joseph Roach's thinking about the development of performance practices in the Caribbean as part of what he terms the circum-Atlantic. Building on Richard Schechner's explication of performance as "restored behavior," in which performance is not limited to the conscious rehearsals for artistic events or the painstaking labor of maintaining rituals over time but is also present in everyday ordinary actions that are "twice-behaved,"[22] Roach links repetition to rehearsals and re-creations. Given that "no action or sequence of actions may be performed exactly the same way twice; they must be reinvented or recreated at each appearance" (46), the circulation of performance practices throughout the African diaspora reveals a series of repetitions with a difference. As I employ it, repetition stresses similarity and also emphasizes the differences that distinguish each moment of repetition from the other. Because repetition is more than the reiteration of what is already known, in attending to the incremental differences produced by repetition, this practice can instead become a form of generating knowledge.[23] That is, I propose that the activity of differential repetition as a constitutive methodology for performance is the same activity by which an island repeats itself.

Throughout this book, I attend to the connections between Benítez-Rojo's influential evocation of the Caribbean region as composed of an island that repeats itself, Roach's definition of performance, and, finally, Édouard Glissant's positing of repetition as a critical methodology for learning. In *Poétique de la Relation*, Glissant describes the function of repetition in his thinking as: "Repetition . . . is an acknowledged form of consciousness both here and elsewhere. Relentlessly resuming something you have already said. Consenting to an infinitesimal momentum, an addition perhaps unnoticed that stubbornly persists in your knowledge" (45; see French in *Poétique* 57). The "élan infinitésimal" within the practice of repetition alludes to the sense of a minute, imperceptible propulsion that shifts each instance of repetition very slightly from its previous version. For Glissant, more than simply a rhetorical strategy, repetition allows us to refine and broaden ideas because it allows for thinking to develop even before those changes can be consciously registered and articulated. In discussing the use of performance as repetition within texts as well as framing the relationship between performance events and the literary response to them as repetition in other forms, my aim is to put into practice Glissant's methodology of repetition as a means of locating knowledge.

Repetition functions as a definition of performance, a method for eliciting ideas, and a basis for a transitional imagination of the Caribbean region. In reflecting on the lack of cohesion between Caribbean peoples in spite of their shared histories, Glissant returns to the practice of repetition as a means of holding both the transnational and the local in his mind simultaneously. At the end of *Poétique de la Relation*, standing on the beach on the southern coast of Martinique from which he can see Saint Lucia, Glissant extrapolates from the connection between Martinique and Saint Lucia to envision how the path he sees between these two islands will reproduce itself between all Caribbean islands as a set of paths that, while not visible to the human eye in its totality, might yet exist:

> J'imagine depuis toujours que ces profondeurs [du volcan] naviguent sous la mer en ouest et l'océan à l'est, et que si nous nous écartons, chacun dans

> sa Plantation, par-dessous, les boulets verdis ont roulé d'une île à l'autre, tramant des fleuves communs que nous ouvrirons à notre heure et où nous mènerons nos barques. De l'endroit où je me trouve, je vois Sainte-Lucie sur l'horizon. Ainsi de proche en proche, évoquant l'étendue, puis-je réaliser cet arc-en-mer. (*Poétique* 222)

> I have always imagined that these depths [of the volcano] navigate a path beneath the sea in the west and the ocean in the east and that, though we are separated, each in our own Plantation, the now green balls and chains have rolled beneath from one island to the next, weaving shared rivers that we shall open up when it is our time and where we shall take our boats. From where I stand I see Saint Lucia on the horizon. Thus, step by step, calling up the expanse, I am able to realize this seabow. (206)

In this moment of prophecy, a historicized vision of geography leads the way to the transnational imagination: the underground rivers carved by history will guide each island's people toward one another. The necessary work, then, is not only to make visible but to "réalisé," to "make real" the regional connections that have been covered over by different (post)colonial relationships. Glissant articulates a regional transnationalism by juxtaposing local specificity with a wider regional view. This work requires the conceptual capacity to concentrate on repeated actions that, through the smallest of increments, "de proche en proche" (step by step), produce what Glissant envisions as a broad expanse, "évoquant l'étendue" (calling up the expanse). Adopting this methodology of conceptualizing the macro and micro together, *Performance and Personhood in Caribbean Literature* moves between the tradition of the Afro-diasporic dance circle and the improvisations on tradition with which performers experiment in order to speak to their specific contexts. In so doing, it surfaces the Caribbean literary practice of writing performance and explores the world of possibilities that can be made real in the circle, if only for the length of a song.

1 Performance and the Expansion of Personhood in Marissa Chibas's *Daughter of a Cuban Revolutionary*

The task of this book is to think through how Caribbean textual representations of performance broaden understandings of personhood. To explore how the genre of performance specifically can intercede in definitions of personhood, this chapter offers a performance analysis of Marissa Chibas's 2007 one-woman play *Daughter of a Cuban Revolutionary*. Throughout the play, Chibas performs much of the "backstage" work—such as establishing the scene's time and place, or getting in and out of character—and exposes otherwise unseen labor. In so doing, *Daughter* demonstrates how the means of creating theater give us a point of entry into redefining personhood. I analyze scenes from Chibas's play in this first chapter in order to work through the theories of temporality and personhood that I employ in subsequent chapters' interart analyses of the textual representations of performance.[1] I set up the elements that are unique to performance that, in the following textual readings, I will argue Caribbean writers attempt to activate in their writing: first, how performance creates a space for practicing the formation of a person as part of her community; second, the possibility of refashioning the relationship to time so as to access alternative futurities and histories. Therefore, ekphrastic descriptions of performance allow writers to focus on how bodies in motion reconceptualize community formation, reengage history from new perspectives, and manifest expansive definitions of personhood.

Over the course of the seventy-minute play, Chibas stands barefoot on a stage lightly covered with sand, enough such that Chibas's steps roll uncertain onto an unstable surface. And while she is the only performer, her presence is amplified by the full-width video screen at the back of the stage, projecting crowd scenes or white-capped waves rolling behind her. With only this setting and the props of large loudspeakers that hang from the ceiling, Chibas recuperates her family's history of involvement in the Cuban Revolution and incarnates various relatives who tell their stories through her. In the first half of the play, Chibas reenacts her parents' stories; in the second, she dramatizes her encounters with deceased or distant family members. Along this process of discovery, she moves us backward and forward through historical time. She returns to the 1957 Sierra Maestra Manifesto, to scenes of herself as a child trying to understand her parents' exilic condition, to snapshots of Havana in 1993, and to the 1951 public suicide of the uncle she never knew, Eddie Chibás, a largely forgotten political precursor to the revolution led by Fidel Castro. Each of these scenes presents a different perspective on the contemporary political fractures in the Cuban community, from 1960s Miami and New York exiles to current Cuban citizens. In analyzing how Chibas plays different characters, beginning with the people closest to her and moving ever further outward, I see both an effort to reconcile the complexities of Cubanness and a demonstration of how an expansive and relational approach to personhood can be constructed.

The play opens with an explanation of the organizing conceit: the autobiographical character, "Marissa Chibas,"[2] tells the story of her near-drowning. The encounter with death is what allows her to play explicitly with temporality; that time-travel, in turn, allows different characters to take to the scene through Chibas. The challenge to chronology and the expansion of personhood are therefore intertwined in this piece. As Chibas narrates the experience of drowning and how it triggered her capacity to become a site of communal memories, a video of breaking waves plays behind her, and the sounds of drumbeats, rushing water, and distorted voices cut into the resonance of her voice. Chibas stands unsteadily and imitates the instability of floating, her feet rolling on their outer sides, toes curling unevenly, arms held limply at ribcage height, baggy clothes billowing out. Her spine's convulsions remind us that the inverted "ah" sound of a deep intake of air is meant to symbolize water rushing into her lungs. The suffocating waves are analogized as her memories. She states: "I am also in the thrall of something within. My past overwhelms me, drags me down, calls on me to remember." She cries out "¡Cuba! ¡Recuérdate!" and begins to claw at the invisible surface above her head. Throughout the play, the gasps for air indicate the onset of a scene in which she embodies one of her family members or a younger version of herself. The rapid fluctuations between tension and fluidity that wrack her body demonstrate the effort it takes for "Marissa" to drain out of the body onstage and make a space for other persons' stories to take their place. The bodily struggle for breath signals her efforts to allow those persons and their memories to inhabit her fully. Chibas will access different pasts, different memories, and will use her own body as the site of a communal history's reconstruction, a performance of substitution akin to how Caribbean writers use the representations of performances on the page.

The way that Chibas performs the simultaneous presence of multiple subjects in the same body prompts the audience first to reconcile—or recognize as dissonant—the multiple temporalities that can coexist during the performance, and second, to rethink the concept of personhood. In this chapter, I address how some aspects of the methodology of acting illuminate the anti-Cartesian approach to personhood that undergirds my analyses of the textual representation of performance in the following chapters. The way Chibas demonstrates that "getting into character" is closer to "a character getting into her" can be read doubly: first, through Joseph Roach's theory of performance as surrogation; and second, through the Afro-diasporic spiritual practices of possession ceremonies, or *sevís*. Both theories require a fluid conception of personhood, one in which encountering another person requires that you be willing to vacate your own place in your body to make way for that other to take their place within you. I layer Agamben's idea of persons as substitutable onto this conjunction of concepts regarding personhood emerging from Afro-diasporic thought because Agamben's writing comes out of a direct confrontation with the Western philosophical tradition of the individual subject. In these three approaches, community formation, not autonomy and individualism, is the most important constitutive characteristic of personhood. I begin the chapter with a discussion of the temporality of performance as it functions in "Daughter," as the capacity to move through chronological time in a multidirectional and expansive way lays the groundwork for Chibas to demonstrate what expansive personhood looks like onstage, which is the focus of the chapter's second section. I finish with a close analysis of one scene from the play in order to tie these two concepts together and meditate on how writing can be used to extend performance. Every chapter that follows will take up the concepts of personhood, temporality, and the ethics and aesthetics of ekphrasis as a form of writing performance as I theorize them in light of Chibas's performance.

In the Suspension of "Clock-Time"

The play's organizational frame of drowning and the near-death experience triggers the process of substitution: drowning helps Chibas evacuate her body so that it can act as a conduit for the experiences of others and transform her into a repository for the shared and contradictory memories of a dispersed community. A core element of how Chibas uses the genre of performance is to point out how the experience of time during the performance itself slows and morphs. In sidestepping the telos-driven chronology of panoptical time (McClintock), Chibas moves into pockets of time in which she can be inhabited by persons whom History's grand narratives have bypassed. As such, Chibas's exploration of personhood relies on the workings of non-Western concepts of time. In a metacritical gesture, she then uses that suspension of chronology during the drowning to flash back through memory and question the narration of history. The moment of drowning and the change to her level of consciousness brought about by the deprivation of oxygen cause time to take on the fluidity and openness of the very water rushing through her. She refers to the liminality of this near-death experience as "this eternal second between worlds." At the end of the play, when she resurfaces from the water, Chibas will ascribe responsibility for her near-drowning time-travel to Ochún, the goddess of sweet waters and patron saint of Cuba, who protects people from drowning.[3] In this gesture, we can link how Chibas describes the experience of time to the West African concept of "Great Time," defined by John Mbiti as "that ocean of time in which everything becomes absorbed in a reality that is neither after, nor before" (qtd. in Russell 14). Chronological progression is exchanged in favor of either cyclical time or the overlapping of times that move at different paces. As well as the space between living and dying, Chibas's phrase "between worlds" references movement between different historical moments as experienced by the many characters who inhabit Marissa while she transitions in and out of the world of her own body. Mobilizing the time fluxes that performance permits is a critically important aspect of its textual representation. Chibas's experimentation with time as a means of interceding into how history is remembered therefore provides a model for the shifts in temporality that Caribbean writers will attempt to activate in the text when they write performance.

From the outset of the piece, Chibas challenges linear time, suspending its progress as each second is experienced as an expanded present. She develops a capacious sense of temporality that can include various historical junctures simultaneously within that present moment. In the closing narratives of each vignette, Chibas also pushes at the boundaries of chronological time by inserting the anticipatory qualities of the future into past memory. Closing the vignette in which Chibas acts as her mother, Dalia, she speaks about what will take place between 1960 and 2007 in Dalia's voice while the narrator becomes more prominent: Chibas spins on her heels and gradually turns her body in a full circle as she unwraps, removes, and neatly folds up the scarf that she has associated with her mother. Chibas falls to her knees when the monologue turns to Chibas's father, Raúl, and his death. At this moment, it is unclear if it is Dalia or Marissa who collapses at the memory. In this uncertain doubling of characters, we also witness a doubled temporality as Dalia shifts from the past tense—which characterizes the rest of her story—to the future:

> I and Raúl will leave Cuba in August of 1960 for what we think will be a short time. I will hear of my mother's death by telephone. I will declare myself a cosmopolitan woman and fight for my freedom. I will have a desperate dramatic day and take too many pills. I will go on. I will be married for seventeen years, then divorced. I will raise two daughters. Raúl will marry twice more. In his last days of life, he will ask to see me. [Chibas breathes in deeply and exhales, "Ah"] Sí, me acuerdo! I remember, I remember!

These events took place in the past and are now narrated from the 2007 vantage point of knowing how Dalia's life unfolded. But by using the future tense, Chibas situates us in 1959 so that we can experience together the estranging temporal effect of the present seen as the past's future.

At the end of every scene, Chibas shows us how one person is exploded by an overload of gestural vocabularies that belong to multiple persons. Here, the corporeal actions appear to double Dalia with the narrator as Chibas pulls off Dalia's scarf, but the first-person narration is still told from Dalia's perspective, only now older, not the same Dalia who had inhabited Chibas's body to reenact her memories before. In presenting a catalogue of important life events, some of the statements are causally linked, others stand alone as different facets of Dalia's life, and they all end with the narrator's acknowledgment of her newly recovered memory: the deep intake of breath followed by a full exhale characterizes the new presence of a character within her. This narration contrasts with the performance of memories, reenacted by the characters who displace the narrator and inhabit Chibas's body. For while the use of the future tense lends these events a sense of preordination, when characters perform rather than narrate their memories, they destabilize the relationship between the past and the present by gesturing to alternative presents that could have resulted from that past.

When Chibas stages the past by acting out how various personae bolt in and out of her, she brings into being the range of possibilities that existed in that past moment. This nostalgia, not for the past itself but for the past's potentiality to be realized into a different present, is a form of nostalgia that Jennifer Wenzel has termed "anti-imperialist nostalgia" and evocatively defined as "a longing for what never was, yet a longing that is fully cognizant that its object of desire is one of the 'ways it could have gone' but did not" (16). The workings of performance are able to make real these objects and sensations of desire within the ephemeral and bounded context of the circle, a capacity located in how performance exists in what Victor Turner characterizes as "the 'subjunctive mood' of culture, the mood of maybe, might-be, as-if, hypothesis, fantasy, conjecture, desire" (11). The collision of present and past in the subjunctive mood offers a grammatical means of articulating what is not but could be. According to this definition, the liminal aspect of performance makes available possible realities that are not tied to chronological progress.

In *Daughter*, this nostalgic relationship to the past is both driven by emotion and also a form of research; that is, Chibas dwells in the past in order to identify the circumstances that not only created the possibilities of that moment but also the elements that eventually foreclosed those possibilities. Returning to the past in a sustained and multiperspectival way allows her to experience, briefly, an undetermined future. The capacity to revisit the past and, if not change it, reorient its influence on the present is one of the most compelling reasons for attempting to textualize performance; because these performances restage the past, the authors I study throughout this book use the literary representations of performance as a return to the past to begin imagining how the past might have unfolded differently. The setting of performance itself then primes a text's readers for the temporal distentions and re-formations of personhood set in motion within the dance circle.

The possibility for reconsidering history takes place every time chronological progress is derailed and the narrator makes way for a character's reenactment of her or his own story. Just as Chibas doubles the presence of the narrator and the character in order to disorder time, as examined through the example of the end of Dalia's scene, she also begins scenes by juxtaposing the present with different pasts. Chibas's retelling of her father's story in the middle of the play uses the play's props to make this point. As Chibas and the program notes inform us, Raúl Chibas organized Havana's Civic Resistance Movement as part of Castro's revolution, which he joined in December 1956. "On July 9th, 1957, he co-wrote and signed the 'Manifesto of the Sierra Maestra' which was published that month in Cuba's national magazine, *Bohemia*. He was also made treasurer of the rebel army." After his exile in August 1960, these achievements disappear from view. These facts testifying to his involvement are accompanied by a photo that includes Raúl Chibas and Castro and, together, they demonstrate how Raúl Chibas has been wrongfully excised or forgotten from the Revolution's history. In the play, at the outset of the scene dedicated to her father's story, she plays a recording of Castro's famous 1957 Sierra Maestra Manifesto, coauthored by her father, Raúl Chibas. In this case, she gets into character by physically interrupting the Castrista narrative of the Cuban Revolution. She begins the speech with the exultant pride of her father's participation in its creation, reciting along with the loud, scratchy recording of a low, male voice first in Spanish, "Mil novecientos cincuenta y siete. De la Sierra Maestra," then in English, "where a sense of duty has united us." Raising her hands as she walks across the stage, she abandons the attempt to keep up with the entire speech. Cocking her head, she listens intently as if hearing these words for the first time and recites the last words of each sentence with the recording. Abruptly, she stops reciting and lowers herself to her knees. No longer identifying her voice with the recording, Chibas begins to interrogate it corporeally by signaling her suspicion through her bodily interactions with the torso-sized loudspeaker that represents the recording's projection: facing the loudspeaker on all fours, she looks at it with curiosity and crawls toward it. The speech rumbles on. She flattens out her body and, holding onto to the loudspeaker by the rim, pulls herself into it, nestling her head inside, while flexing her toes into the sand on the floor. When she crawls back out, she is visibly angered. She turns the loudspeaker on its head so that the sound is muffled, then rips out the cord, silencing it entirely. There is a long moment of silence; then she breaks the stillness: "I am Raúl Chibas, for the moment at least." This interruption of the party leader's voice marks the outset of the scene in which Marissa makes space for her father's story—both in her body and in the historiography of the Cuban Revolution.

As Marissa moves from echoing, then translating, then shutting down the recorded voice, Chibas creates a montage of the Sierra Madre Manifesto, a technique in which "the superimposed element disrupts the context in which it is inserted" (234), to use Walter Benjamin's terminology. According to Benjamin, this technique engages the audience's participation as one of discovery of what is represented onstage rather than a more passive act of reception. The disruption of the context is a jolt to the audience, asking us to participate in questioning Cuban historiography. For although Raúl's voice was integral to the creation of that revolutionary document, his participation has been all but erased and his voice silenced in official narratives. Chibas shows us her own methodology for investigating the official story: she goes into the loudspeaker, which here stands in for historical discourse, looks deep inside for evidence of her father's perspective and, when she doesn't find it, flips the loudspeaker over, pulls the plug on it, and interjects her father's story as a corrective. In this particular restaging of the recording, one in which the recording coexists with her caustic questioning of it, she proposes the reperformance of memory as a source that, following Diana Taylor, can be included in the archives of the Cuban Revolution and can contest the limitations of official histories. In *Daughter*, an expansive approach to personhood allows Chibas—and us—to experience time as both fluid and as having distinct periods that are juxtaposed in order to displace the chronological order. The combination of expanded concepts of personhood and temporality is what makes possible Chibas's acts of surrogation that call forth the potentiality of the past.

Personhood's Formation Onstage

A hallmark of *Daughter* is how Chibas makes visible the intensive work of identity formation as multiple and fluid. Throughout, she connects her capacity to introduce multiple characters' stories and to navigate in and out of various personae to the Afro-diasporic spiritual practices that structure the play. At the beginning, Chibas signals the importance of Ochún's guidance in navigating the dangerous waters that allegorically represent a diasporic and national set of Cuban collective memories. At its end, she closes the last full scene with the phrase, "Ashé! Ashé! Ashé!" Ashé is both the Yoruba concept of the divine energy that courses through every worldly element, and the simple affirmation, translated as "so be it," which is spoken throughout celebrations and ceremonies. Because she uses this phrase to mark the last occasion that her body vehiculates another person's voice, I suggest that we read back the practices of Afro-diasporic rituals of possession into previous instances in which Chibas represents a different character onstage. "Possession" is itself an inaccurate term, as Colin Dayan explains, because "*sevís,*" the ceremony during which one asks the god to take the place of one's own consciousness, is a mutual agreement between a person and the *Lwa*—not the expression of complete ownership, domination, and power that is usually connoted by the term "possession."[4] Judy Rosenthal's research on the Gorovodu religion practiced in Benin describes the rituals of possession/*sevís* as "paths for *becoming* Foreign Others—for thinking into what one (and one's group) is most radically *not*—and that this radical becoming, or overcoming of difference, is ecstatic, practiced because of its marvelous nature" (30). The capacity for ekstasis, or to be able to "stand outside yourself"[5] and make a space within yourself for "foreign others," has two philosophical consequences that we will revisit with each ekphrastic representation of performance. First, as Dayan shows, by inviting another to control you with your consent, "you get a sense of yourself that you did not have before" (*Haiti* 72). This practice generates knowledge by developing a consciousness about the self and, I would add, the sociopolitical context that the self must navigate. Second, the reconfiguration of a person such that Chibas can simultaneously be herself and stand outside of herself, or that she can be inhabited by foreign others and retain narrative consciousness of that presence, proposes a conception of personhood that wholly contradicts the Eurocentric ideal of the self-contained individual.

Chibas incorporates the gestural rituals of *sevís* in the liminal moments of the play, just as she does in the play's framework. In each transition from narrator to characters and back again, she marks this transfer with a tripartite action: the raspy sound of the inhale, the phrase "¡Cuba, Recuérdate!," and the full-body spasms that end in a hand gesture that claws upward as if toward the water's surface. She then changes her accent, vocabulary, catchphrases, and gestures to imitate certain key characteristics of the people she channels. Chibas's demonstration of transformation coincides with the transformation that takes place during a visitation of the *Lwa* as part of Vodou ceremonies.[6] As we see in Karen McCarthy Brown's close description of Vodou possession-performances, the signals that the *Lwa* is about take the place of the *hounsi*'s "gwo bon anj" are a characteristic choreography or posture; the *Lwa*'s particular discursive voice follows the *hounsi*'s trembling spasms. Once the seizures have subsided into the *Lwa*'s corporeal presence, the community participating in the ceremony quickly places on the *hounsi* the clothing or accessories and colors associated with the *Lwa* to complete the physical manifestation of the *Lwa*'s presence. Likewise, Chibas manifests the presence of another person taking her or his place in her body through the tight interaction of gesture, voice, and clothing: her body shudders and contorts as if drowning, or marking the struggle over who can reside in her body. Once her mother, father, second cousin, or uncle have settled in, her speech becomes marked by their verbal ticks and differently accented voices. Then, to signal the departure of her family members and the return of the narrator, Marissa, Chibas removes a piece of clothing. The rituals of *sevís* and Chibas's performance dramatize the physical and spiritual labor required for a person to make a place within herself for radical difference.

The relationship between Vodou devotees and the *Lwa* as exercised during *sevís* therefore offers a rich site for the analysis of how personhood can be opened beyond the outlines of one's body or sense of isolated self. The conception of personhood that circulates in Afro-Caribbean spiritual traditions and that emerges on the stage of *Daughter of a Cuban Revolutionary* can be defined as collective, relational, and composed of multiple and not necessarily cohesive elements. As the scholars of Haitian culture and religion Claudine Michel and McCarthy Brown state: "Human connection is the assumption in the Haitian worldview: there is suppression of unique life history in favor of a collective *personhood* from which energy is derived" (Michel 31). The self is not an autonomous individual, but is defined by its social connections. Roberto Strongman highlights this constitutive openness of the self and further remarks: "Any type of hermetic enclosing of the self is seen as potentially dangerous or associated with death. The fact that one of the most dreaded Afro-Diasporic states of being should be so similar to the Cartesian view of the hermetically sealed soul points to the contestatory and critical relationship between these two philosophical traditions" (22). Of paramount importance to my readings throughout this project is that the turn to the performing body as both a thinking body and a nonhermetic body in Caribbean literature contests the definition of universal personhood derived from Cartesianism, succinctly encapsulated by Comaroff and Comaroff as "the self-made, self-conscious, rights-bearing individual of 'modern Western society'" (52). Alternative conceptions of personhood that arise from the specificity of Caribbean experiences of spirituality, geography, and history are critical to the project of self-possession. The references to *sevís*, the methods of theatrical performance, and the liminality of a near-death experience are all sites for Chibas's exploration of a concept of personhood that is open and constituted by multiple subjectivities.

In comparing Chibas's demonstration of an actor's methods and the representation of near-death, I am influenced by the long theatrical tradition of linking death with acting, a tradition that Roach theorizes as "surrogation."[7] Describing a triangular relationship between memory, performance, and substitution, surrogation takes place at events such as funerals or theatrical events. Death and performance therefore offer moments when individuals are simultaneously memorialized and erased in similar ways. Like performances that attempt to restore behavior and always do so imperfectly, the actor as effigy is "a contrivance that enables the processes regulating performance—kinesthetic imagination, vortices of behavior, and displaced transmission—to produce memory through surrogation" (*Cities* 36). In this reading, the actor's body functions as a site of substitution. Like *sevís*, the actor's willingness to temporarily vacate her or his own body to make space for another person to inhabit it and thereby become a part of her or his consciousness contradicts models of personhood that are grounded in a fixed and contained sense of identity. The actor's transformation into a surrogate is a physical representation of the idea that persons can be substitutes for one another. Bearing in mind how Roach theorizes theatricality through the concept of surrogation, I interpret Chibas's efforts to give space to multiple persons' stories within herself as a corporeal manifestation of such acts of substitution.

While arguing that persons can be substituted for one another might seem to efface difference, I propose that substitutability gives us a way out of static configurations of social identity. Giorgio Agamben's theorization of the *qualunque* subject outlines a way of valuing individual persons not by their social class, their nationality, or other categories that the state uses to allocate wealth. That is, moving away from a theory of the individual where a propertied male is the fundamental definition of a person, we can then return to individual persons—but now with an unbounded sense of who, to echo Jacques Rancière's *Distribution of the Sensible*, counts as a person. Agamben's *qualunque*, translated as "whateverbeing,"[8] explicitly takes issue with a tradition in Western philosophy from Descartes to Hegel that defines personhood as possessing unique essences. Instead, in an effort to theorize a new mode of community formation, one that lies "beyond predicates and properties" (de la Durantaye 162), Agamben argues for a concept of personhood that is based on reciprocal substitution. In his explication of whateverbeing, Jason Kemp Winfree points out how Agamben "detaches existence from the antinomy of the individual and the universal, the ineffable and intelligibility. Outside the schema of intelligibility, where the particular is submitted to the universal, identified through its belonging to the category or concept, whatever being is exposed, that is positioned outside the membership that otherwise grants its identity" (81). I cite Winfree's explication at length because his focus on intelligibility echoes the ways that Gayatri Spivak, Walter Mignolo, and Édouard Glissant define epistemic violence, or the requirement that all persons be submitted to already-established categories and then be understood through those terms. Whateverbeing, however, sidesteps the tension between the universal and the particular by displacing transparent understanding as a mode of encountering difference and replacing it with the practical and felt operations of ekstasis and love instead.

Agamben uses the spatiality of ekstasis to make a case for substitution as a form of relation: the neighbor's space next to one's own (which one ought to be able to substitute for one another); the threshold as a space that allows one "the experience of being-*within* an *outside*" or "ek-stasis" (67);[9] and in making the case for substitutability, he argues that "what is most proper to every creature is thus its substitutability in being in any case in the place of the other" (23). To return to the language Rosenthal uses to explain *sevís*, ekstasis is the first operation in permitting the experience of radical difference, or "being in the place of the other," and rethinking individual identity on that basis. Once again, dwelling in a space beside one's own—and inviting another to dwell in one's own space—broadens the delimitations that supposedly define a self-contained and coherent personal identity. Agamben's substitutability, Roach's surrogation in performance, and the practice of *sevís* mark what might make being in the place of another possible and how one might experience what another being experiences. In contrast with empathy, whereby one comprehends another being by projecting one's own personality into that other being's circumstances, substitution and surrogation are both processes that seek to allow others to take one's own place. This capacity to stand outside oneself and invite others to take one's own place leads Agamben to conclude that the possibility for community rests in the sense that our truest selves are not atomistic individuals (24).

In thinking through the relationship between whateverbeing and community formation, Agamben specifies that whateverbeing is a general openness, not isolated to a particular affiliation. Identifying oneself solely with one category not only reduces multiplicities but also depends on an association that is extremely vulnerable.[10] For when we define ourselves as Italian, dog, or Communist, to use Agamben's examples, we also "call ourselves" those properties: the belonging is a primarily linguistic one, one that cannot guarantee exclusive and absolute belonging and which may, in fact, preclude the possibility of what Agamben deems "any real community" (10). To elaborate what is meant by "any real community," Agamben gives the example of the protesters at Tiananmen Square in 1989. Rather than align themselves with any particular identity politics, they constituted themselves as a community of "singularities [who] form a community without affirming an identity, humans [who] co-belong without any representable condition of belonging" (86). He argues that, by dint of its capacity to privilege specificity while refusing any particular identity politics, whateverbeing is endowed with a tremendous capacity to contest the state and its power. Agamben's refusal to set forth a specific agenda or elaborate a new definition of identity would seem to be in keeping with the need to remain unintelligible and, therefore, unco-optable. It is whateverbeing's substitutability that makes it a moving target for the state, as it creates a third way to personhood that avoids both a self-definition by groups that can be set against each other and a sense of absolute individualism that bears no sense of relation. In his own summary, Agamben defines the whateverbeing of the Tiananmen protestors as "want[ing] to appropriate belonging itself, its own being-in-language, and thus reject[] all identity and every condition of belonging" (86). There is no condition of belonging that can separate those whom we include among our own from those we do not.

This boundless definition of belonging is, from the outset of Agamben's theorization, held in the Latin phrase from which he derives the term *qualunque*, interpreting "libet" in "whatever" as indicating that "whatever being has an original relation to desire" (1). And contrary to the connotative indifference of "whatever" in English, Agamben insists on specificity in the reference to love: "*Quodlibet ens* is not 'being, it does not matter which,' but rather 'being such that it always matters'" (1). This emphasis on the exact specificity of a person leads us to refine the substitutability of making a place for the other in oneself as the manifestation of love. Agamben's example for how he locates this position outside of the tension between universals and particulars is the lover who is not loved for her or his properties or belonging to categories of identity, but is also distinguished by each and every one of these properties and is not an "insipid generality (universal love)" (2). I analyze how Chibas stages the stories of others alongside the language of Agamben's whateverbeing to draw out the constitutive element of love that drives her approach to representing the expansiveness of personhood in the context of a fraught and divided Cuban community.

Whereas Agamben rarely thinks through the corporeality of whateverbeing, Chibas makes whateverbeing's labor evident and asks the audience to witness the effort that it takes to make her body a site of substitutability. She likens the sensation of others taking their places in her body to being a radio, a radio that can tune in to and broadcast a wide range of ideas, opinions, and experiences that are located on different frequencies.[11] This metaphor echoes Dominic Pettman's attribution of whateverbeing to literary examples: "In *Ecce Homo*, . . . Nietzsche passionately embraces the fact that he is every name in history. In a Dionysian precursor of Joyce's H.C.E. (Here Comes Everybody), Nietzsche seizes on the potential power of whateverbeing" (148). Chibas, like Pettman's examples, seizes the potential power of whateverbeing by defining herself through an open continuity with others:

> I am a radio, I am a radio for various and sometimes contradictory voices. *Sí, me acuerdo*, I remember, *no me puedo olvidar*, I cannot forget, I am the daughter of *Raúl y Dalia*. I am the daughter who sprang from the thoughts of Eddie Chibás. I am the daughter of ocean breezes and the IRT, of *croquetas* and hamburgers, of Celia Cruz and Duke Ellington, I am the daughter whose deep roots travel far beyond homeland and geographic location, I am the daughter of *miles de balseros*, thousands of Cubans who have drowned trying to make their way to *Yuma*, I am the daughter of those who question the time when democracy and capitalism became inextricably bound, I am the daughter of those in Cuban prisons who dared demand their human rights. I am the daughter of those who fight tyranny wherever it may be, *soy hija de un revolucionario cubano*, I am the daughter of a Cuban revolutionary!

This monologue, delivered by the narrator, closes the play with a reflection on the rich multiplicity of political and cultural experiences that have inhabited her throughout the play. After pulling off the white shirt associated with Raúl, whose story has just finished, she stands in just a dark tank top and cargo pants, on a darkened stage, with a soft spotlight trained on her. At the outset, her voice is almost hollow, and she stands with her arms close to her thighs, palms facing the audience. With each clause, the volume and acuteness of her voice rises in its intensity and she correspondingly raises her arms gradually until her final posture: her triceps are at shoulder height and her hands are just above her head such that her arms are lifted in a slight curve with upturned palms. She reaches out to the audience as she shouts the last line, "I am the daughter of a Cuban revolutionary!" Coming back to the title of the play, which could initially be thought to solely define herself through her father, she now presents this relation as radically amplified from a single genealogical line to a complex collectivity.

In her description of the multiple channels that she, as a radio, receives and retransmits, she demonstrates how the concept of personhood can expand beyond its definition as individualism: because she opens herself to visitations from other subjects who each leave a piece of themselves within her in the form of recalled memory or new knowledge, by the end of the play, she can encompass ideological oppositions that are almost impossible to bring into conversation in the contemporary political sphere. She validates socialism as a viable political system, and in the next breath calls out Cuba's socialism as oppressive. As she proceeds with her last monologue, listing off the elements she has inherited, the Anglophone setting of the play provides an occasion to demonstrate how a multiplicity of sociocultural and political contexts can live together by translating between Spanish and English and between cultural references. The only point of relation between these political views is the connection between them that Chibas herself makes; she refuses to pick an identificatory label and instead describes her identity as being open to the transit of the many different ideas and experiences that move through her. By simultaneously embodying conflicting political positions and suturing the fractures between the different Cuban communities that claim Cuban identity as their exclusive property, Chibas enacts a form of relation that rejects political self-identification as its primary quality. Instead, she gestures to community without ideological conditions as its basis. A consciousness about community formation and social relation informs the personhood Chibas experiences as she performs memory work.

Extending "Daughter"

At the end of the performance of *Daughter* on January 19, 2007, Chibas raised her hands high up above her head and declaimed the last line: "I am the daughter of a ru . . . Cuban revolutionary." In producing the erroneous syllable "ru," the tongue perhaps sought the anaphora from the previous phrase, "revolucionario Cubano," and combined it with the vowel from the appropriate phrase, "Cuban revolutionary." In light of how I analyze the final monologue, the tongue tripping on translation sounds like a dense intermingling of languages, contexts, and politics. But this stutter is an accident, a part of the performance available only the night I happened to be part of the audience at *Daughter.* The element of serendipity brings the possibility of witnessing and participating in the unexpected to every individual performance event that takes place anywhere from the stadium to the circle. My writing in response to Chibas's work takes up the project that Aleksandra Wolska describes: talking and writing about a performance allows its action to "transmute and change, flowing away from nothing toward an ever-expanding material appearance" (84). It extends a version of the piece to the person hearing or reading its description. To set up what is specific to performance that writers attempt to evoke in their ekphrases of performance, the performance analysis in this last section will return to the workings of temporality and personhood, and reflect on how performances can impact their audiences.

Chibas's use of temporality in the play, breaking with chronology in order to jump across temporal distance and elongate time within different periods, as well as her demonstration of how surrogation functions for the actor on stage, is similar to how performance theorists and critics describe the experience of being an audience member. Jill Dolan references both these elements in her evocation of how it feels to be in the audience, a sensation she describes as an ecstatic experience—the ekstasis of being transported outside oneself. She reflects on the art critic John Rockwell's comments on going to the theater to identify what she calls "utopian performativity":

> "Suddenly and unexpectedly we are lifted from our normal detached contemplation into another place, where time stops and our breath catches and we can hardly believe that those responsible for this pleasure can sustain it another second." He describes an experience of utopian performativity. Such moments make spectators ache with desire to capture, somehow, the stunning, nearly prearticulate insights they illuminate, if only to let them fill us for a second longer with a flash of something tinged with sadness but akin to joy. (Dolan 8)

In Rockwell's description, he reports the experience of chronological time being displaced so that he, as part of the audience, might momentarily take leave of his normal contexts and relationships. To return to Agamben's terminology, we might think of this as evacuating our daily concerns to make place within ourselves for what is transpiring onstage or within the dance circle. While this experience of ekstasis is impermanent, Dolan suggests that it does leave behind a permanent imprint of desire for that experience. As such, going to the theater to be part of an audience is a form of participation in a public sphere that might extend utopian performativity beyond the theater to civic engagements (11) and modes of community formation.

In the second half of *Daughter*, the setting changes as Marissa narrates her first visit to Cuba in 1993, where she meets relatives separated from her by distance and ideology. While the people she encounters both in the flesh and in spirit—her deceased uncle Eddie Chibás and Arturín, his cousin and private secretary—are tied to her by blood, the change from being inhabited by her parents to people she has never met is qualitatively different in the kind of vulnerability she must summon to perform their stories. From their two perspectives, she tells the story of Eddie Chibás, the politician who committed suicide well before his brother Raúl joined and subsequently left the Cuban Revolution. However, she embeds his hope and promise into the representation of his suicide. It is this emotional quality and how Chibas uses the movement through time and the expansion of personhood to include the dead that I focus on here. In contrast to previous scenes in which she takes on a new character and tells that person's story for the entirety of the scene, here, Chibas oscillates between performing Marissa and Arturín as she stages their conversation. Chibas then transitions from the persona of Arturín into that of Eddie Chibás without the pause that normally marks her character shifts and performs her uncle's last radio address, in 1951. By bringing Eddie back from 1951 into 1993 without a break to resituate the audience and herself in a new historical moment, Chibas juxtaposes the what-could-have-been with the what-was.

Much of Chibas's reflection on her first visit to the island of her parents' birth responds to the physical condition of Havana during the "Special Period,"[12] a socioeconomic condition of deprivation and a political sensation of isolation that is reflected in Arturín's dilapidated living quarters. The narrator mentions that "there are three pictures hanging, one of Arturín's mother, one of his father, and one of my uncle Eddie. Each has the mark of the flood running across them." The decaying objects represent not only personal family histories in the pictures of Arturín's parents but also icons of Cuba's own revolutionary history in the photographs and recordings of Eddie Chibás. The detail of the watermarks that stain Arturín's apartment and the mold that encroaches on his every possession represents the state's neglect and the obsolescence of every story of Cuba's Revolution that is not officially sanctioned. It is from within the physical evidence of the Revolution's unfulfilled promises that Chibas stages a return to the Revolution's previous iterations. In *Cuban Palimpsests*, José Quiroga proposes that this expansion of temporality is also a feature of the Special Period:

> The collapse of the Soviet Union and the socialist bloc did not produce a time understood exactly as a "transition," but a period of uncertainty that still meant to connect past to future while suspending the time between the

> two. . . . Events in Cuba during the 1990s forced the state to turn the discontinuities created as a result of the socialist collapse into a narrative line that leads to an "expanded" present. Past and present, memory and memorialization are related to the project for a collective, cohesive, and *national* memory that the state produced back in the 1960s. (1, 3–4)

While Quiroga points to the official narrative that sought to bring the 1960s back into being during the 1990s, Chibas, by going back more than a decade to her uncle's unfulfilled political ambitions, seeks out a moment not of previous revolutionary triumph but of revolutionary possibility.

Chibas makes the expansive temporality of performance visible primarily through the shifts between the gestural vocabularies corresponding to Marissa, Arturín, and Eddie. In her staging of the conversation between Marissa and Arturín, Chibas remains in the same physical spot, and because Marissa in this scene is slightly hunched over, looking down at the sandy floor, the character change requires only a slight shift: with a recoiling tremor, she leans back slightly and exaggerates the hunch of her shoulders in a single beat. Both Marissa and Arturín are metaphorically drowning in memories. As the scene proceeds, the gesture Chibas establishes to signal Arturín's presence mirrors the clawing, grasping hands Marissa employs when inhaling water as she prepares to change character between each scene: Marissa's hands clutching at the air above the waterline as she recoils resemble Arturín's signature gesture of a body curved over and quivering with tension, with arms that stretch out to the audience almost above his head, fingers wiggling, beckoning, and grasping at the air. Staring at the audience that, for a moment, is asked to see him through Marissa's eyes, Arturín beckons her/us to follow him into the kitchen where he gently removes a box containing his poorly preserved archive from its hiding place. Chibas recounts, with increasing volume, this moment of discovery as she begins to walk around the central loudspeaker lodged in the sand, circling ever faster and closer to the loudspeaker until she is running. "Then a yellowed handkerchief with Eddie's initials, finally some audio tapes with large green lumpy mounds of mold on them." She takes a brief breath before exclaiming, "and one *clean* one!" Arturín's miraculous preservation of an audio recording of Eddie Chibás's last speech allows Chibas to recover her family's contribution to Cuban history, despite its systematic erasure from official histories.

Eyes wide, Arturín places his trembling index finger to his lips, then reaches out both hands, summoning the audience one last time. Giving the audience one last pleading look, he bends over the loudspeaker. Against the backdrop of the sounds of rushing air, a typewriter, and a cello, Chibas pulls out wire-rim glasses from inside the loudspeaker's cavity. She uncurves her spine beyond Arturín's capacity, raising the glasses with both hands as high into the air as possible. The dramatic gesture of placing the glasses on her face is slow and deliberate: no more tremors. Moving directly from Arturín to Eddie by straightening her posture, Chibas briefly overlaps the two personae as a drum rolls. Scrambling onto the loudspeaker, Chibas momentarily references Arturín's hunched back, then unfurls her body once more into the straight line that defines Eddie's silhouette, feet rooted firmly on the base of the speaker and neck straining toward the sky. Face firm with the corners of her mouth turned down grimly, her right arm stiff and straight at her side, she raises her left hand, index finger pointing, until it is fully outstretched above her head. Eyes squeezed closed, mouth stretched open, she presses her right fist against her forehead. An old-style radio microphone is lowered into her left hand's open palm. Their hand movements—Eddie's employed deliberately and with great control in contrast to Arturín's seemingly involuntary paroxysms—draw a comparison between the human embodiments of the different phases of revolution.

Instead of temporal removes separating the different stages from anticipation to disappointment, potentiality and resolution coexist here within the same scene on multiple levels. Just as Eddie prepares himself to speak to the Cuban people, an old film picturing crowds walking in the streets carrying banners is projected onto the screen behind Chibas. In the center of the masses is a coffin draped with a white cloth—the immediate future of Eddie's own funeral procession. The conjunction of these characters and visuals contrasts the revolution that Eddie articulated with the revolution that transpired, as represented by Arturín's decrepitude and paranoia. Watching Chibas straighten the back hunched over by age and neglect is like witnessing time reverse itself. However, the present of Arturín's fearful whispers is not simply replaced with a past moment of Eddie's defiant shouts. Rather, Chibas incarnates the past within the present in order to widen the realm of future possible action. Chibas gives us an example of how one can use performance to map out the interaction between future, past, and present.

Chibas holds one arm straight up, index finger pointed, and opens her mouth into the shape of a mute scream as the microphone swirls down. Face turned toward the microphone and chin tilted up to speak into it, the tendons bulging in the neck mark the effort to reach for the power to communicate and disseminate truth. Projected onto the screen behind is a picture of crowds in the street holding aloft a casket. It is, as we will soon realize, Eddie's casket, juxtaposing Chibas's incipient performance of the speech that ended with him shooting himself on August 5, 1951, with the images of his funeral, only a few weeks later. The images disappear abruptly and the stage darkens except for a bright white light that shines on her. Eddie Chibás declares his unwavering moral convictions, cites the problems that plague Cuba, and urges the Cuban people to overcome those failings and realize their own potential. Chibas first lip-syncs to the scratchy voice in Spanish, then shouts the English translation over the recording: "Five centuries ago, the tribunal of the inquisition cried at Galileo, liar and deceiver! Present proof that the earth revolves around the sun! . . . Five years ago I accused the minister of education of stealing the monies for school materials and breakfast and fermenting in Miami an empire of movable property. The minister and all his leaders stormed in crying liar, slander, present the proof!"[13] In the desperate desire for an alternative to an unlivable present, Chibas mines the past to resuscitate the movement that her uncle inspired for the futures that might have been. The potential avenues for social change that were available in that past moment are now foreclosed, but they can still fuel the imagination and serve as powerful challenges to the present.

At the end of her performance of her uncle's speech, Chibas's breath begins to falter. Inhaling raggedly for the last exhortations, she shouts: "Forward fellow Ortodoxos![14] For economic independence, political liberty and social justice, let us sweep away the thieves of the government: ethics over greed." Chibas holds her right hand above her head, palm open and facing the audience, then jabs her index finger into the air to punctuate her sentence. "People of Cuba, rise and go forth!" She breathes deeply, switches the microphone from her left hand to her right, and places her left fist against her forehead. "People of Cuba, awaken!" She squeezes her eyes shut. "This is the final pounding on your door!" Being in the audience at this moment, sitting in the dark together, surrounded by Chibas's shouting, straining, breaking voice is a heartbreaking experience: through Chibas's performance, we witness the presence of Eddie's passionate conviction and the physical desire for the beginning of a new political relationship between institutions and people. And yet, given the concurrence of his funeral, Chibas asks us to mourn not only for this person, but also for the possibilities, now eclipsed, that existed in that moment.

The microphone begins to rise into the air, pulled away from Eddie by an invisible force. At first, Chibas stretches to keep hold of it, then lets it go. A picture of Eddie flashes on the screen behind her as she curves her right hand into a fist and punches herself in the stomach three times. A drum pounds with each shot, three self-inflicted bullet wounds to the gut. With this choreography, Chibas reinforces the story that Eddie used his body and ultimately his life to ask his audience of fellow Cuban citizens to rethink their role in the political process. Chibas ends this scene, as she does every other, with the persona inhabiting her narrating his or her future. However, this time Eddie speaks about his immediate future in the past tense: "I died on August 16th, 1951, shortly before my 44th birthday." Chibas holds her right hand out to the audience, relaxes the grasp of her fist and lets the crumpled, balled-up paper on which his speech was written fall from her fingertips. "One year after the Revolution, Fidel will give a speech at my grave"—Chibas takes off the eyeglasses and raises her right arm to hold the glasses out to her side—"and say that the Revolution began with Eduardo Chibás. My suicide will create a political vacuum that will allow the dictator Batista to impose a military coup and the elections of 1952 will never take place. It will be the end of democratic elections in Cuba." Letting the eyeglasses drop to the ground, she crouches on the loudspeaker, clasping her knees to her chest, ending the scene without further commentary.

How long can you go without breathing? When Chibas crawls down from the loudspeaker that has been her perch for the past scene, I realize that I cannot account for the last time I blinked or breathed deeply—not since Chibas as Arturín opened her eyes wide with fear and desire, putting us in Marissa's place. Not while Chibas as Eddie turns her whole body into an instrument for projecting his voice through the theater. And not in the moments after the reperformance of Eddie's suicide, knowing that the only thing that keeps all of us within the past moment of possibility is the continuation of the scene. I hold my breath because I know that the loss of our concentration or break in our energetic attention will close the scene and therefore close out this past moment of possibility. In a very small way, Chibas's audience imitates the work she has undertaken throughout the piece: the work of ekstasis or of inviting another to take her place within our person. The audience adopts Marissa's perspective and faces Arturín's urgent gesture to join him in the secret of forgotten history. Again, following Marissa's dramatized experience, where the sense of chronological time is unmoored by the lack of oxygen reaching her brain as she drowns, the sensation of not wanting to breathe in this moment somatizes my desire to suspend history and to sustain Chibas's project of interrupting history. During this performance, as time slows and is removed from the tyranny of chronology, the audience members are corporeally impacted by—and implicated in—the performance through the transformation of their breath. In writing about Chibas's work and my experience of being an audience member and witness, I wanted to extend her piece to you, and particularly extend the sensibility of the caught breath, the many interruptions to time. In the novels that I analyze in the following chapters, we see this same desire to create an excursus in which readers can experience the interruptions to time that take place during a performance and how these interruptions to or distentions of time open up the possibility of rehearsing alternative forms of personhood and relation. How a text can extend the corporeal experience of members of a dance circle waiting to breathe together: this is what the writers to whom I now turn evoke when writing performance.

2 Creole's Thinking Body

Patrick Chamoiseau and Marlon James

Of all the performance forms, the oral performance of storytelling is the most deceptively difficult to write: in musical or dance performance events, instruments and bodies must be accounted for, but for storytelling, the temptation is to focus solely on the storyteller's rhetorical style. What is lost in this strategy of transcription is the circle that sustains the storyteller's performance. In a footnote to a discussion of writing history in *Le Discours antillais*, Glissant meditates on the role of the writer and speech in the Caribbean context, namely if the writer can open a conversation akin to that which organizes the storyteller's circle of oral performance: "The time has come to ask oneself whether the writer is (in this process) the one who hoards the written or initiates the spoken? If the process of historicization does not call into question the status of the written? If the written record is "adequate" for the archives of collective memory?" (Dash translation 64; Glissant, *Discours* 226). He leaves the question open: Can writing create an antiphonal exchange or compensate for the formal differences between the oral gesture and writing? How do writers negotiate historical power imbalances as they translate between creole oral performances and metropolitan literary traditions? This chapter focuses on the challenges of writing creole orality by analyzing the workarounds that Patrick Chamoiseau and Marlon James invent in *Solibo Magnifique* (1988) and *The Book of Night Women* (2009).

Solibo has become a classic articulation of the conflict between orality and writing; *Night Women* is a fictional slave narrative that is framed by the question of how people who experienced slavery can communicate that experience. These two novels position themselves as preserving a lost era—James, the story of a failed slave uprising; Chamoiseau, the life and art of a storyteller. *Solibo* opens with the eponymous storyteller's death, and the rest of the novel is the story of the police investigation that ensues, as well as a retelling of Solibo's stories to honor his life. While *Night Women* likewise centers on one character, it devotes more time than *Solibo* to depicting the social setting for this character's development: James describes the intrigues, hierarchies, and customs of plantation life in late-1700s Jamaica over the course of telling the story of one woman, Lilith, whose survival of slavery through both rebellion and complicity is narrated by her daughter. *Night Women* and *Solibo* are deeply invested in demonstrating the legitimacy of Creole as a form of expression; and both novels explicitly highlight the problems of the written representation of stories that circulate orally in Caribbean creole languages.

The conflict that drives both novels is, in its broadest articulation, a philosophical and physical struggle over what constitutes knowledge and who can produce it. Both narrators, who are to a certain degree removed from the action, argue for their protagonists' oral and gestural performance to be recognized as intellectual production. They ascribe value to corporeal articulations over the regimes of literacy, the latter of which are symbolized as the police reports in *Solibo* and, in *Night Women*, the British literary tradition of Fielding and Defoe. That is, James and Chamoiseau contest the hierarchies that deem metropolitan languages and philosophy superior to their creole counterparts by showing how moving bodies are sites of thought and knowledge production. These novels share in an investment in developing an epistemology with thinking bodies at its center and as such they explicitly return to the Cartesian legacies that separate intellectual from physical labor as a way of drawing a restricted line around the category of the human. In the last section of the chapter, I focus on the impact of oral performance on the development of what, following Rhonda Cobham's concept of "creole gnosis," I term a creole hermeneutic in these texts. I work from the wealth of scholarship on Chamoiseau's *Solibo*, particularly Aching's and Guillermina De Ferrari's theorizations of how this text critically stages the links between Western rationalism and personhood. I explore further how Chamoiseau and James make the case for ascribing personhood to people who are excluded from civic participation through their oral prosody and ekphrastic representation of corporeal movement.

In this chapter, I analyze the formal characteristics of Chamoiseau's and James's workarounds: the operations that circumvent the problem of writing orality while still acknowledging the continuing existence of that problem. I compare how both authors answer Glissant's question: Can one write bodily gesture, vocal tone, and the way that words become multiply ambiguous as a result of the nuances of gesture and tone? At first glance, Chamoiseau and James take divergent approaches to this question. Whereas Chamoiseau positions writing as an exercise in deficiency, James offers writing as a privileged site of self-expression; he implies that, in the face of historical trauma, it is a challenge to verbalize the body's experience, whether orally or in writing. Where the two novels intersect is in their textual modes of describing the moving body, through which they trace the foundations for a method of generating knowledge that derives its proverbs from Creole and is anchored in a thinking body. As part of the effort to describe the philosophical ground of oral performance in the Caribbean, both novels also demonstrate some of the limits to Enlightenment rationalism. I argue that they therefore set themselves in opposition to the Enlightenment project in a similar vein as Paul Gilroy's observation that "the universalist claims of the Enlightenment project . . . was, in theory, valid for humanity as a whole even if humanity was to be rather restrictively defined" (43). In their meditations on oral performance practices in Creole, Chamoiseau and James propose specificity rather than universalism and, in so doing, push against restrictive definitions of humanity.

The Stakes of Creole Literacy

From the slave-owning British and French people in *Night Women* whose world is sustained by racist ideologies to the policemen in *Solibo* who criminalize their Creolophone subjects, the epistemic violence in both novels has brutal physical ramifications. As such, the debates around language and literacy staged in both texts synecdochally reference larger questions of social exclusion. The stakes of taking up writing, moreover, differ tremendously in each novel given their historical settings: *Solibo* is set in late-twentieth-century Martinique, an island undergoing the cultural and economic influence of neoliberal globalization; *Night Women* takes place on a slave plantation between 1785 and 1819 where literacy itself is a dangerous practice for its enslaved protagonists. Whereas the narrator's qualms about writing as a suitable form for conveying the storyteller's art mark every page of *Solibo*, *Night Women* does not announce itself as the product of a project of writing the oral until the novel's very last page. Moreover, literacy and Creole have opposite signifiers. In *Solibo*, the law insists on the use of metropolitan French, giving no credence to creole expression and thereby making the use of Creole a defiant act; in *Night Women*, Creole is not only the language of communication between enslaved persons, it is also the overseer's language of command. For the novel's protagonist, Lilith, Creole is the language of protest and capitulation, of affection and abuse:[1] it is language *tout court*, not, as in *Solibo*, a symbol of cultural defiance. In this context, what is forbidden is not the use of Creole, but literacy. Both texts reject a simple binary between metropolitan and creole languages, and in reading these texts, we can reflect on the multiple valences of each system of expression: Creole as both preserving and betraying relations of affection; writing as the law and law breaking.

Reading and writing are central to the rebellion plot that drives *Night Women*, both logistically and philosophically. Nowhere is this more evident than in the way that Lilith mediates her sense of personhood through the wholly private act of reading novels surreptitiously taken from the library on the Montpelier estate, notably Henry Fielding's *Joseph Andrews*.[2] In one instance, Lilith turns to Fielding's characters to distract her from overwhelming anger at having been loaned out to work on the dreaded Coulibre plantation: "She need him [*Joseph Andrews*] every night. After working through a page, she would wipe away tears from laughing quiet-like and feel her face. The soft skin would surprise her. Something about her new days make her expecting that one day and one day soon her face would feel hard as rock. Hard from dark thoughts" (207). The dark thoughts to which Lilith refers are her fantasies of sadistic revenge against the Rogets, the slave-owning family to whom she has been sent.[3] *Joseph Andrews* presents a different fantasy, one that dilutes her anger and helps her preserve that part of her person that is not dedicated to withstanding violence. Moreover, reading prompts her to touch her face, and its continuing softness gives her information about herself: because it contradicts her expectations and her own sense of hardening from the inside, both reading *Joseph Andrews* and reading her own skin offer paths to reevaluating how she sees herself. While her daily experiences seek to deny her any independence of thought and action, these experiences of reading broaden Lilith's affective process of constructing personhood under slavery.

In a contrasting second instance, it is the clear dichotomy between the world of Joseph Andrews and her own context that moves her to action: she kills the Roget family and burns down the Coulibre house. Immediately preceding this act, Lilith had come to the conclusion that *Joseph Andrews* can no longer make her laugh because "*Joseph Andrews* lying to her, making her wish for a place and time that never goin' come. . . . Nothing in this book a nigger can use" (220). This angry dismissal of the value of literature calls forth the question of "usefulness" and writing; with regard to *Joseph Andrews* in particular, Lilith's recognition of the differences between the protagonist and herself means that she can no longer pretend to identify with the novel, but this does not make it ineffectual. Rather, recognizing the gap between them has two important results: as we will see in the narrator's own articulation of her mission in writing the novel we are reading, the existence of *The Book of Night Women* is perhaps owed to Lilith's long-term desire for a text that could be useful to someone like herself; second, in recognizing this disparity, she not only "wish[es] for a place and time" resembling the world of Fielding's white British society that is unavailable to her, she begins to fight to make that world available to herself. In including *Joseph Andrews* as *Night Women*'s intertext, James shows how the interaction with the text allows Lilith to reflect upon and act on her developing desires for violent rebellion.

Chamoiseau, in contrast to James's use of eighteenth-century British writing as a source of inspiration for uprising, offers a much more ambivalent view of literature in *Solibo*. Here a tradition of French letters is part of the official culture that must make room for popular culture. The concern elaborated in *Solibo* examines the diminishing use of Creole in Martinique at the end of the twentieth century. Published in 1988, the novel reflects on how the ever-encroaching forces of globalization create a situation of economic dependence in which local production is replaced with products imported from the metropole. The majority of the novel's characters are Solibo's audience members, individuals who have been sidelined as a result of the push to "modernize" Martinique: small-time fishermen, market workers, and sorbet-makers, all of whom are criminalized by the police investigation into Solibo's death. The novel asserts that the loss of the storyteller's knowledge and social connections is emblematic of the disappearance of Martinique's Creole practices and, by extension, its capacity for cultural, economic, and political independence. In his analysis of how Chamoiseau incorporates the relationship between oral Creole and scribal French into many of his works, Richard Burton proposes a tripartite expressive system: writing and French characterize the world of the powerful, the powerless use orality and Creole, and the writer mediates between them (470).[4] The process of creolizing standard French disrupts the traditional hierarchical relationship between high and popular culture, here represented by the linguistic dominance of Standard Parisian French over the island's informal Creole.

Historically, the context of linguistic diglossia yokes Creole with orality and popular culture in opposition to high culture and writing.[5] In both Jamaica and Martinique, the metropolitan variants of English and French respectively are the languages of the law, education, and high social status. Creole has been historically excluded from the realm of literacy, which encompasses official bureaucracies to literature. At the same time, however, because creole languages continue to be the vehicle of performance practices, they are vital to any project of historical recuperation and depiction of the Caribbean's cultural specificities. Chamoiseau encapsulates this uneasy cultural and linguistic duality in his lightly mocking portrayal of the police inspector, Évariste Pilon: "At the time of the Solibo affair, he is living with a freckled *chabine*, petitions for Creole in the schools but jumps when his children use it to speak to him. . . . [H]e lives like all of us, at two speeds, not knowing whether he should put on the brakes when going uphill or accelerate going down" (76; see French in Chamoiseau 118–19).[6] While this depiction puts Pilon's hypocrisies in a humorous light, his confusion about how to negotiate his conscious desire to vindicate Creole with his ideological conditioning to disavow it are posited as a national problem, one to which the narrator can offer no definitive solution. Chamoiseau likens this linguistic predicament to the broader political uncertainty about the future direction of the island: even when Creole is championed, metropolitan French is the automatic default for the bourgeoisie.[7]

Juris Silenieks persuasively argues that this somewhat paradoxical situation in which creole languages are integral to a sense of national history and cultural identity and yet still signify a lack of education is the result of successful colonizations in the Caribbean (524). The valorization of Creole is therefore essential to the political project of decolonization, as Supriya Nair shows in her theorization of the alignments between twentieth-century Caribbean nationalist movements and creole language politics (239). The role of literature as a pathway to Creole's broad cultural and political legitimacy is particularly stressed in the Jamaican Language Unit, a part of the University of the West Indies, Mona Campus Department of Language, Linguistics, and Philosophy, which has been working since 2002 to develop a standard writing system for Jamaican and advocates its use in state bureaucracies in order to destigmatize the use of Jamaican.[8] Rex Nettleford identifies this trajectory as beginning in academic settings in the early 1960s with the scholars of "Jamaica Talk" (16) and established as public policy in 1972 with the foundation of the African-Caribbean Institute of Jamaica (112).

The combination of literature, scholarship, and policy to promote Creole is similar to the French Caribbean's Créolité movement. In the introduction to the journal *Espace créole*, Raphaël Confiant lists the literary incorporation of Creole as an intermediary step between the development of the "Graphie-Gerec" orthography for Creole led by Jean Bernabé in the 1990s and the creation of a recognized course of study in Creole at the high school and university levels in the 1990s. In writing that "a new approach to the relationships between Creole and French has come about, thanks in great part to the Créolité literary movement which has dominated literature emerging from Guyana and the Antilles at the end of the twentieth century" (my translation), Confiant champions the innovative use of literature's linguistic potential as a key factor in contesting the prejudices against Creole more generally.

As discussed in the introduction alongside Mayra Santos-Febres's meditations on how to work around linguistic differences, the presence of Creole in the text continues to require a negotiation between writers, publishers, and readers. The success of literary innovation and linguistic activism such as Confiant's is evident in Caribbean literature written in Standard French or English, in which now, as Belinda Edmonson comments, "the use of Creole speech is de rigueur in Caribbean fiction" (94). Creole has become a more accepted—and even expected—sight in print because it can signal local authenticity. Nevertheless, Marlon James received early resistance to his use of Jamaican from a British publisher who requested that the novel be rewritten in Standard English. And although Chamoiseau has become renowned for his written expression of Créolité, speaking in a group interview with Chamoiseau and Bernabé, Confiant mentions the continuous challenges to integrating Creole into their writing: "There is also a danger that, despite our best intentions, we'll be recuperated by the Parisian literary scene as a form of exotic literature" (L. Taylor 147). He goes on to comment that, conscious of the possibility of co-optation, he and Chamoiseau have "refused to explicate the Creole in our writing" as a way of refusing to make Creole a product of easy consumption for French readers.

Night Women and *Solibo* are not written in Creole. Rather, James and Chamoiseau inflect English and French with Jamaican and Creole to various degrees. In so doing, their writing creates the kind of defamiliarizing sensation of two languages encountering and transforming one another that Doris Sommer has theorized as the hallmark of the bilingual text.[9] I refer to this defamiliarization that brings the poetics of oral performance into the text as oral prosody. As Bernabé comments,

Chamoiseau writes in "an artificial language; no one speaks the way they write. It's a constructed language, a literary language, created out of interaction and negotiation with French" (L. Taylor 147). Likewise, while James describes *Night Women* as written entirely "in dialect," he does not use the Cassidy spelling system[10] or otherwise consistently modify his orthography to emphasize phonetics. Mervyn Morris, reflecting on the rhetorical style of the Trinidadian author Samuel Selvon, coins an evocative phrase for this loose approach to writing "in dialect" in the following recommendation: "If there are enough markers to indicate that you are dealing with a creole, enough markers in the structure, then you should spell the words in a way that they will be most quickly recognized" (39). What James and Chamoiseau produce are texts that are not in Creole but rather, to adopt Morris's phrase, "deal with a creole" in their vocabulary choices and syntactical structure. Most important for my analyses in this chapter, the way that they deal with a creole is in the development of a corporeal hermeneutic proper to local Creole expression.

The opening paragraph of James's *Night Women* sets the tone for how James will use oral prosody to "deal with a creole." The structural markers that James favors in order to shift from Standard English to Jamaican primarily consist of verb conjugations, occasional spelling modifications, and the omission of articles:

> People think blood red, but blood don't got no colour. Not when blood wash the floor she lying on as she scream for that son of a bitch to come, the lone baby of 1785. Not when the baby wash in crimson and squealing like it just depart heaven to come to hell, another place of red. Not when the midwife know that the mother shed too much blood, and she who don't reach fourteen birthday yet speak curse 'pon the chile and the papa, and then she drop down dead like old horse. Not when blood spurt from the skin, or spring from the axe, the cat-o'-nine, the whip, the cane and the blackjack and every day in slave life is day that colour red. It soon come to pass when red no different from white or blue or black or nothing. (1)

As we see at the outset of the novel, only occasionally does James oralize orthography ("'pon the chile") or omit an article ("like old horse"; "is day"). The stylistic differences that stand out from what James calls "King's English" are primarily located in the verbs, where, following standard practices in Jamaican, the verbs are not conjugated according to person, and linking verbs are omitted when connecting the subject with an adjective.

In this opening paragraph, James both establishes the centrality of the body and creates "the dynamism of spoken dialect English"[11] through the rhythmic cadence that he establishes with phrasal alliterations. Here, for example, he stacks four fragment sentences together, each beginning with "not when . . . " to explain his counterintuitive definition of the color of blood and the banal nature of violence. Starting each fragment with the phrase "not when" creates a rhetorical crescendo that accompanies the reader's increasing awareness of how the meaninglessness of red is produced within the violent context of slavery as each fragment depicts blood in a different context, from the specific scene of the protagonist Lilith's birth to the multiple and daily forms of violence on the plantation. Epistemological violence against the body in categorizing it as an object underwrites the constancy of extreme physical violence against the body. In setting the scene of slavery as told from the experience of the formerly enslaved, James uses rhetorical techniques drawn from oral rhetorical styles to show how both types of violence are so mundane as to be unremarkable and so prevalent as to be part of every aspect of enslaved life. While these techniques are not specific to Jamaican, by conjoining them with the contractions specific to creolized Caribbean English, James works around the fact that he is not actually writing in Creole by making "dealing with a creole" central to our reading process.

Chamoiseau's and James's modes of "dealing with a creole" resonate with Gilles Deleuze's evocation of the minorization of language. Distinguishing minorization from code-switching that would leave each linguistic system intact, Deleuze argues for an internal disruption of such systems produced through a disequilibrium of the stutter. As Deleuze writes about Kafka and Beckett: "They don't blend the two languages, not even the minor and major language, even if many of them are linked to minorities as part of their vocation. What they do is more invent a minor use of the major language in which they experiment: they *minor* the language, as in music where the minor mode designates the dynamic combinations that are in perpetual disequilibrium" (137–38, my translation). Deleuze associates the perpetual disequilibrium created in the minor text with metaphors of movement. While Deleuze focuses on individual innovation, at play are the politics of minorizing a metropolitan language and forcibly changing it so that it can be responsive to the specificities of the (post)colonial in which it is used.

In examining the influence of Creole on the highly individual ways in which James and Chamoiseau operate in English and French respectively, the stutter, following Deleuze, reflects a dynamic interpenetration of languages and the gasping, halting vibrations that ensue in their texts. Chamoiseau's work with minorizing French has generated much critical interest as scholars have described his writing practice: Burton calls it "a distinctive *écriture* which beneath the surfaces of standard or near-standard French secretes Creole locutions" (478), while Roger Toumson refers to the same practice dismissively, calling it "créolitaire" (qtd. in Priam 28). Marie-José N'Zengou-Tayo terms Chamoiseau's minorization of language "la 'chamoisification' du français" in an essential article by the same name in which she identifies ten separate elements of diction and syntax through which Chamoiseau inflects what is primarily a French text with Creole. According to her analysis, Chamoiseau combines oral prose with more overt references to Creole in the vocabulary. *Texaco* and *Solibo* are peppered with markers of speech, such as "the 'oui' placed at the end of the sentence and the use of 'comme ça,' both of which are characteristic of Creole prose practices."[12] In terms of vocabulary, Chamoiseau invents neologisms, employs archaic French, and uses Gerec-orthography for some words that are common to both languages but the French spelling when meaning a divergent Creole definition of the word (N'Zengou-Tayo 163–64). Beyond inserting Creole into the text as individual words and phrases, Chamoiseau uses both Creole and French as a source for coining new words or presenting them anew. N'Zengou-Tayo concludes that Chamoiseau's French writing creates "l'effet-de-créole," the effect of Creole.

Like the Jamaican of *Night Women*'s narrator, the oral quality in broad swaths of *Solibo* emerges out of the repetitive cadences that structure his sentences:

> Quand mes yeux ont échoué sur ses yeux, qu'il m'a touché l'épaule (Oala, pitite?), qu'il a embrassé Man Goul en soulevant son chapeau et en réclamant une rosée pour sa gorge, j'ai commencé à percevoir sa force. Sa voix vibrait dans son front, dans ses joues, habitait ses yeux, sa poitrine et son ventre: une Force . . . sans mots ni paroles, devant l'animal Solibo était une Voix. Et quand ça m'arrive de jouer au saxo, que je veux souffler un son cracheur de feu, je ramène dans ma tête ce souvenir de lui, le do si la sol de sa voix, la cadence de sa gorge sur refrain de poitrine. Quand j'y parviens, mais c'est rare oui, le peuple me dit toujours: Charlot ho! Il était bien bel ce joli coup de saxo! (81)

> When my eyes fell on his eyes, when he touched my shoulder (heyhey, young man?), when he hugged Man Goul in greeting, raising his hat and requesting a drop of water for his throat, then I began to notice his strength. His voice

> vibrated in his forehead, in his cheeks, inhabited his chest and stomach: a Force . . . without words or expressions, before this animal, Solibo was a Voice. And when I am playing the sax, and I want to breathe into a sound like spitting fire, I bring back into my thoughts this memory of him, the do si la sol of his voice, the cadence of his throat over the refrain of his chest. (48)

In this passage, only the proper names and quotations of spoken dialogue are outside of Standard French. Instead, Chamoiseau emphasizes rhyme and rhythm in Charlot's city Creole.[13] The story, which links together disparate events such as Charlot's memory of Solibo and the exercise of his own musical art, coheres rhetorically through the structural repetition of "quand" at the outset of three out of four sentences. His descriptions of Solibo are characterized by long lists that are held together either by polysyndeton, "dans son front, dans ses joues," or asyndeton, "le do si la sol de sa voix, la cadence de sa gorge sur refrain de poitrine." But it is the digressive quality of the transcription of dialogue that lends Charlot's story the most palpable oral quality: set off by commas or parentheses, these brief references to spoken exchanges become a part of Chamoiseau's representation of performance.

Perhaps because of his own orientation as a musician, Charlot deemphasizes the importance of Solibo's creole words, both their rhetoric and content, in his depiction of the storyteller's art. Instead, he focuses on how Solibo's body functions as an instrument that not only produces a voice but is itself a force. As Charlot explains through the musical metaphor of his own profession, the voice is the melody that plays on the throat and chest when they act as instruments. In the moment of performance, Solibo becomes an airy vibration that responds to its environment, sonorously changing the air through which it passes. By setting a new vibration in motion, Solibo pushes those he touches to action. On a molecular level as well as an abstract one, the storyteller serves as agent of relation. Lest the voice be associated with the ethereal nature of the air through which sound travels, Charlot begins the description with the weight of its presence. In a series of equations, Solibo becomes a voice, and the voice is replaced by the throat: the force unleashed by the transformative power of his body is at the core of his performance. Conveying physical impact, not the syntax and vocabulary of Creole, is the writer's primary concern in describing the storyteller's vanishing art. So while Chamoiseau's main question throughout the novel seems to be whether the oral performer's speech in Creole can be converted into literature in French, the workaround to writing performance that

Chamoiseau offers here is to focus on the storyteller's corporeal interaction with his environment.

Incomplete Transcriptions

In both novels, the conceit of the audience member–writer calls transcription into question as an adequate method for writing stories that were originally orally performed in Creole. In this regard, the metaphors of translation as loss are applicable to the scenarios that occasion writing in these two novels. While the reader does not discover the relationship between the protagonist and the narrator until the last page of *Night Women*, the impossibility of preserving Solibo's performance after his death is a common topic of conversation throughout *Solibo*. There, the thematization of the difficulties surrounding writing orality risks diverting attention once more from oral performance in that, as Amy Nauss Millay suggests in her discussion of the Latin American use of this rhetorical device, "the outcome of inscribing the oral in written texts is the innovation of a discursive form that aims to subvert ideologies upheld by writing culture, and not a faithful expression of the essence of oral culture" (29). Certainly, the death of the storyteller at the beginning of the novel makes a convenient space for Chamoiseau's narrator to work through how writing can develop the same cultural significance that oral performance has historically held in Martinique. In the main, the plot is structured as a "transfer of power of the word from Solibo's orality to Chamoiseau's writing" (Aching, *Masking* 140). When evoking the storyteller's corporeality in the ekphrasis of his performance, however, Chamoiseau shifts the terms of writing orality away from the economies of translation and responds to the questions: How can a moving body be brought into the text, and what happens to it when you write about the body's self-expression?

In this section I discuss how Chamoiseau and James work through transcription as a method of representing oral performance in order to show its limitations, then turn to the descriptions of Solibo's corporeal interaction with his audience, and how a performance of funereal dirges will be remembered by those who sang them in *Night Women*. In so doing, they use the workaround of representing performance on the basis of how it impacts its audience-participants. Both writer-figures, "Patrick Chamoiseau" in *Solibo* and Lilith's daughter "Lovey Quinn" in *Night Women*, position themselves as witnesses to the storyteller and the circle of audience members. The character "Patrick Chamoiseau" in *Solibo* is physically present at the events in question in the novel, personally interacts with the story's protagonist, and uses the term "testify" to rearticulate the storyteller's stories (9). *Night Women*'s "Lovey" witnesses her mother's narration of the events that took place immediately before her own birth and describes the book she has written as "giving account of the league of women." But whereas James's narrator sets up equivalences between writing, telling, singing, and giving account, all of which are together set in opposition to having one's story told and distorted by others or altogether silenced, *Solibo* is studded with the writer-figure's metadiscussions of how best to narrate the stories he has collected as he grapples with questions of (not exactly) writing in Creole.

Chamoiseau's dismissal of transcription is evident in his relegation of this technique to the annex entitled "Les Dits de Solibo," or "Solibo's Sayings." In this postscript to the novel, the writer-figure actually transcribes a reenactment of Solibo's performance, which provides a reference for Solibo's rhetorical prowess as well as a justification for why the novel, replete with other workarounds, needs to exist to commemorate the corporealities of storytelling. In her analysis of the storytelling in *Solibo* and Chamoiseau's 1982 play *Manman Dlo contre la fée Carabosse*, Stéphanie Bérard summarizes Chamoiseau's literary techniques for evoking the storyteller's rhetoric as "sonorous methods (onomatopoeias, alliterations, marked rhythms, repetitions) and graphic methods to signal orality (choice of italicized letters, particularly for songs). . . . The typographical placement of sentences on the page is unusual: the numerous line breaks create the impression of reading poetry and not prose. Does this poetic transcription seek to render speech's musicality, its rhythmic cadence or its fractured rhythm?" (99, my translation). These are the verbal strategies that Chamoiseau describes Solibo as using to keep his audience engaged in the story. The questions that emerge are the limit of what transcription can convey.

Reading the transcription of Solibo's performance can prompt anything from imagining Solibo's virtuosity to reliving the laborious efforts to reconstitute that virtuosity. Julie Anne Huntington represents one vein of criticism, arguing that the annex creates "flurries of words that implicitly communicate the intensity of Solibo's performance, visually and audibly conveying the rhythms of Solibo's final oration" (198). I also suggest that Chamoiseau's "chamoisified" French and its lack of punctuation demand a more labored reading practice for Creolophones, although differently than for non-Creolophones.[14] The results depend on the willingness and the capability of the reader, who might render the stuttering quality of the act of transcription: the arrhythmia of rewinding a tape to hear the exact phrase, the pause to decide how to write a word that may not have an official spelling, the mechanical screech of the tape recorder as it restarts in the middle of a word.[15] So where Maximilien Laroche writes that Chamoiseau's particular engagement with orality produces his reader, I expand this assertion to propose that the text produces its readers, who each must individually reformulate her reading practices to elicit the oral aspects of the text.[16] The transcription of Solibo's performance in "Dits de Solibo" does provide a demonstration of Solibo's rhetorical agility, whether through the reader's reproduction of his style or the reader's frustration at the difficulty of that reproduction. Nevertheless, transcription is only "une tentative" (33), "a failed attempt" in conveying the storyteller's art.[17] Because it focuses on the linguistic aspects of the story to the exclusion of all other sensorial effects, transcription captures the words that can be written down but makes no place for "la parole," the spoken word, a concept encompassing all of the gestures, tonalities, rhythms, and silences that make meaning for Solibo.

Unlike James, who, in the context of slavery's total repression, does not differentiate telling from writing, Chamoiseau consistently sets up oral storytelling and writing as opposites. Working through how best to resolve this opposition, the writer-figure decides to forego his tape recorder and rely on the reperformance of Solibo's last words. After the official investigation has ended, the remaining members of Solibo's audience come together to re-create Solibo's last words so that the writer-figure can experiment with writing this reenactment. It is critical that "the oral speech is transposed into the written form starting from the memory of others, not the empirical data" (Plattner 235, my translation). However, Chamoiseau indicates that this oral repetition is no more able to reproduce the specificities of Solibo's performance than the written attempt is: "I would find a few of the survivors under the fatal tamarind: each formulated in the Magnificent's way some of the themes he used to embroider upon, the others gave the replies, and Sucette the support of his ka-drum. *Oh friends, the word isn't tame*! . . . Some lacked breath, others rhythm, not one succeeded in wedding the tone to the gestures" (158; see French in Chamoiseau 225–26). All the elements of live performance are present: the responsive audience, the interaction with the drummer, and a recollection of the words and themes. And yet, it does not compensate for Solibo's loss. For while Chamoiseau constantly indicts writing as a particularly useless form of retaining the storyteller's performance, what we discover in this episode is that a performance can never be precisely repeated, but each performance generates itself anew, to rephrase Richard Schechner's definition of performance itself.[18] The opposition between orality and writing so thoroughly discussed throughout the novel gives way to a separate problem altogether in that, if we follow Peggy Phelan's forceful pronouncement that "Performance's only life is in the present. Performance cannot be saved, recorded, documented, or otherwise participate in the circulation of representation of representations; once it does so, it becomes something other than performance" (146), we must reframe the debate from its oral/scribal foundations.

As such, embedded into the descriptions of Solibo's oral performance by the members of his audience, the writer-figure, and even ultimately the police, is the sense that what defines Solibo is a fundamental ungraspability. To return to Charlot's memory of Solibo, when Charlot describes Solibo as a voice and that voice as a force, he places at the core of Solibo's power the capacity to be whoever the person, animal, or environment with which he is in conversation needs him to be. This mode of relation, where Solibo recognizes who his other is and then transforms himself in order to engage that other, is akin to the acts of substitution discussed in chapter 1 through Agamben's theory of whateverbeing and Chibas's demonstration of acting as making space within oneself for the other. The capacity for substitutability is how Solibo describes himself and his work as a storyteller: "Solibo used to tell me: 'Oiseau de Cham, I will never drown. In water, I become water, before the wave I am a wave. I will never burn myself either, because fire does not burn fire. And regarding that tale of the long-one that you're talking about, I don't remember the incident. But it's not impossible. Each creature is but a chord which you just have to tune in to'" (44; see French in Chamoiseau 75–76). As a performer, Solibo is pure substitution, weaving himself into the contexts and landscapes he knows so well.

Oral performance is made up of rhetorical practices, the tonality and rhythm of the voice, the expressiveness of the body that houses the voice, and the relationships between performer and audience facilitated here through Solibo's self-proclaimed capacity to attune himself correctly to the vibration of any being and create a relation with that being. Indeed, considering Roger Abrahams's study of Anglophone Caribbean oral performance, every aspect of the performance is aimed toward developing that relationship. The very words of the "man-of-words" are important primarily because the rhetorically expressive style forms a community: "Creativity seemed less important than how a group managed to achieve meaning while celebrating community" (xix). It is fitting, then, that it be less important to preserve Solibo's rhetorical creativity than to galvanize the ways in which the individual members of his audience form a cohesive group through the simultaneous experience of his art. This least tangible characteristic is therefore the focus of Solibo's audience members' recollections of his performances. The ekphrases of oral performance impact the writing of *Solibo* by pushing Chamoiseau to evoke Solibo's substitutability—both in the ways that Solibo made space within himself for others, and in his audience members' attempt to attune themselves to others in their own creole practices.

Chamoiseau's representations of Solibo's oral performance are a retrospective of his life, the value of which can now be measured according to the absence Solibo has left behind. In this regard, the temporal affect of *Solibo*'s narrator is a nostalgic one, an important contrast to Lovey Quinn, the narrator of *Night Women*, whose narrative has an urgent forward movement to it, particularly, at the novel's end when she describes her mission in writing it. Here, James stresses two objectives for Lovey as a writer: first, telling Lilith's story from her perspective and with her as the protagonist; second, Lovey using the novel's penultimate paragraph to develop her momentum: "And me goin' sing the song and me mother goin' sing it. . . . We goin' sing once then no more" (416). The defiance and struggle that Lovey ascribes to the act of singing and writing result from the historical restriction of self-expression in the context of slavery. As Glissant reflects on its long-term impacts: "The alienated body of the slave, in the time of slavery, is in fact deprived, in an attempt at complete dispossession, of speech. Self-expression is not only forbidden, but impossible to envisage" (122; see French in *Discours* 405). Writing, as well as "la parole"—speech and nonverbal physical self-expression—are all strictly circumscribed so as to impress upon enslaved persons their condition of nonpersonhood. The challenge for James in *Night Women* sidesteps the debate over whether print or orality is a more fitting venue for historiography, for if we think with Glissant here, the difficulty of self-expression is as salient in orality as it is in writing.

In analyzing how James meets the challenges of writing orality, I contrast the two strategies I examined in *Solibo* as well: first, transcription, and second, the dynamic interaction between written narrative and oral performance. Throughout the novel, James prevents the description of slavery's many cruelties from becoming pornographic through Lovey's narrative presence as a witness to Lilith's motivations, thoughts, and interiority. Lilith's intellectual/corporeal experience does disappear from the narration at a critical moment when she first undergoes the formal ritual of whipping. I suggest that this is where James's narrative technique hews most closely to transcription: not of quoted speech as in Solibo, but of every excruciating detail moving between the action of the lash, Lilith's physical reaction with no access to her thinking at that moment, and the collective prurient gaze of the audience made up of Montpelier's slave and slaveholding populations (163). Rather than the Fanonian circle of protection that we will see in the community's song cycle, for example, here the audience is specifically invited to distance themselves from Lilith's vulnerability. The narration's attention fixates on the surface of Lilith's skin, noting how the lash transforms its texture. But in the complete loss of Lilith's interior viewpoint during the whipping, her body becomes object—a rare occurrence in a narration dedicated to asserting her personhood. This event reiterates an icon of slavery's violence: the first observed whipping is one of the standard elements of the slave narrative,[19] and the structure of the narrative follows the model of "Aunt Hester's scream" in Frederick Douglass's *Narrative* very closely, from the description of Hester/Lilith being tied up to the effects their screams have upon those who hear them.[20] In a rare moment in which a violent event is transcribed blow by blow, Lilith's voice disappears and she becomes a wordless body onto which others can inscribe meaning.[21]

Over the course of the novel, Lilith's perspective comes to dominate the narration of her experience of violence. For example, immediately before this whipping, Lilith is gang-raped, the first event where she is attacked and cannot successfully defend herself. Unlike the whipping, which is described in detail without Lilith's commentary, the rape is omitted from the narrative as it begins with Lilith losing consciousness and resumes with the description of how the night women care for her in the days that follow. Subsequent to the whipping, Lilith is sent to the Coulibre plantation, where she is assaulted daily; Coulibre's violence is described through Lilith's coping mechanism whereby she catalogues the various means of torture inflicted upon her and diverts attention from her own pain by tallying her own injuries and imagining herself inflicting them on the Rogets in return. In this final approach to the representation of Lilith's experience of violence, she shifts from emphasizing physical description and focuses on her thoughts in response. These three iterations of violence, first the gang-rape that is excised from the narration; second, the explicit description of the whipping from which her perspective is virtually absent; and third, the daily torture told through her psychological responses to it, mark the progression of Lilith's capacity to shape the narrative of violence such that it features not her victimization but the development of her sense of self-determination.

Indeed, the explicit aim of the novel is to introduce Lilith's version of the events that surround her, a viewpoint that the narrator implies is missing from an already-existing history when she introduces the protagonist with the defiant statement, "I goin' call her Lilith. You can call her what they call her" (1). Just as the "they"-figure calls Lilith by a name not her own, the story thus far told about Lilith is incomplete in giving account of her experience. The novel ends with this same phrase, after the revelation that the narrative has been written by Lilith's daughter Lovey, who learned of the night women from her mother. The last sentences of the novel read: "This was the first thing me write. You can call her what they call her. I goin' call her Lilith" (417), reversing the order of the first sentences so as to end on Lilith's name. In giving Lilith and not the nameless "they" the novel's last word, this final note instructs readers to reconsider the narrative as a project of historical recuperation aimed at amplifying a story about Lilith that had lacked her own perspective.

The novel's last chapter places Lilith's story in the context of a song cycle about the night women that circulates in the community. Led by Homer, the night woman who ran the Montpelier household, the other women are all unacknowledged daughters of the plantation's overseer, Jack Wilkins: Hippolyta, Pallas, Iphigenia, Gorgon, Callisto, and Lilith. Joined together by the violence that has been done to them and their shared rage, they coexist in an uneasy alliance that bursts apart in the failure of their rebellion. The community's emotional consensus about their rebellion is located within the sonority and silence of the songs. Each song distinguishes one woman, remembering her as an individual part of this collective. After writing about each woman's death at length, the narrator dedicates one sentence to the description of the song that has come to be sung about that woman in celebration, in mourning, and in judgment. In this representation of oral performance, James highlights the relation between the musicality of the song, its lyrics, and its function for creating community memory, as in the example of Pallas's song, where its description slides between the song for Pallas and the story of Pallas's death. Here, the song's rhythm and pacing correspond to the form of her death: "They beat her hard, then tie her up to a stake and burn her slow so she wouldn't pass out but feel herself burnin' to death. Her song long and mournful but when the song reach the end, it dance and the spirits jump" (415). Whereas at first, the dirgelike pace of the "long" song corresponds to the torturous slowness of Pallas's death, at its end, James contrasts its "mournful" quality with the "dance" that creates a kind of freedom for Pallas. The quickening pace of the song enables Pallas's spirit to leap out of the fire to which her material body was confined in death. The song expresses the community's effort to will into being a story for Pallas in which she succeeds in her struggle to escape an impossibly painful life and death. Similar to the strategy employed by Chamoiseau in homing in on what Solibo's substitutability provided for his community, James describes this oral performance through the many purposes it serves for those who remember the night women through song.

This last chapter and the representation of the song cycle is what the narrator explicitly calls the "time to give account of the league of women" (412), a somewhat formal, quasi-bureaucratic phrase that refers to the most complete historiography the narrator can curate. The account of the league of women includes references to the oral song cycle that has become common knowledge in this community and juxtaposes it with the written account of Lilith's memory of the events. As emerges over the course of Lovey's account of the song cycle, its purpose and its juxtaposition with the written narrative is not to achieve perfect accuracy in the chronicle but to identify what the preservation of memory achieves for this community. The community's collective choices as to how to remember each woman are placed in comparison with Lilith's version of the story, but not as a correction. For example, the reader knows from earlier in the narrative that Hippolyta died during the rebellion when Lilith shot her while defending their progenitor, Jack Wilkins. Yet the song that arises is about how Jack Wilkins shot Hippolyta himself. The narrator does not intervene to insert Lilith's version of events, but describes the song that responds emotionally to the betrayal of a father killing his own daughter. In this case, Lovey privileges the possibly erroneous stories in circulation rather than insisting on one version being the most factually accurate. By including the community's emotional response that emerges from the performance dynamic, she shows how her construction of history depends on the interaction between performance and written records. Yet again, James refuses a dichotomy between orality and writing, offering both orality and writing as complementary forms of representing another's story. The song cycle takes an expansive, polyphonic, and multigenre approach to the historical archive.

"Giving account" is James's workaround to Glissant's question of whether the written could be a vehicle for collective memory. In the oral histories of the song cycle, James does not attempt complete description, instead highlighting one evocative detail about each song that emphasizes its emotional and didactic purpose. The narration surrounding the song explains that purpose for the community, as in the contrasting examples of Gorgon and Iphigenia. Gorgon sang her own song while dying in the gibbet, and the song's wordlessness marks, once more, the unrepeatability of that performance: "Gorgon sing her song high, she sing her song low, she sing it until she run out of voice. She dead after eight days. The song about Gorgon was short and had no word, since all that need to sing she sing already" (413). Both the singers and the narrator show their respect for Gorgon with only a brief note describing the truncated song performed by the community to mark the space of her song as a gap they cannot fill. But when the community refuses Iphigenia any song whatsoever in their collective memory out of contempt, Lovey's version of the song cycle makes a place for her in the narrative: "Iphigenia thinking that if she tell massa 'bout the plot she would get British pound and freedom for sure. Turncoat nigger Iphigenia ain't got no song" (416). In order to deliver the community's summary judgment, expulsion from memory, Lovey must bring Iphigenia back into written memory. For while the reference to oral production of memory within her written account cannot translate silence, James takes a detour around the impossible task of representing absolute silence on the page by instead describing the emotional intention that supports that silence. In these instances, giving account means acknowledging the importance of silence in oral performance, even though it means betraying that intention.

Embedded into Lovey's description of the song cycle of the women's revolt is the acknowledgment that its expression is dangerous, in part because self-expression of nonpersons remains severely policed, but also because of how its subject matter interacts with the oral performance. In the songs that are sung for Callisto and Homer, for example, the act of singing drafts the singers into rebellion. Callisto's song is the only one for which the narrator includes the actual lyrics at the end of the description of her death and her song: "But she take four white man herself, and in the fields and the bush a new song rise up under the quiet, about *Callisto, Callisto, who bring backra down to so-so*" (413). The lyrics of this song celebrate Callisto's strength and how her actions transformed the "backra" slavers from omnipotent masters to "so-so," Jamaican for paleness and weakness, linking whiteness to frailty. The song raises their voices just high enough so that it can circulate yet still remain "under the quiet." Each time the song is sung, it expresses the desire for rebellion and also replicates the secrecy that is the basis from which the next rebellion will begin. The song for Callisto memorializes her legacy and reactivates the failed rebellion. Giving account, as James uses the term, not only articulates history but, in its oral form, reinstantiates it.

The representation of Homer's song, more than any other, manifests the ways in which giving account reinstantiates the rebellion that it depicts. Like Callisto's song, the song for Homer, the leader of the night women, is sung sotto voce: "Homer kill Homer and reborn herself as the struggle. They never find Homer body. Homer song get sing in a whisper like a night spirit leaping from a tree. Her song be in the dark of the eye where secrets be" (415). Unlike Callisto's song, the lyrics of which are transcribed in the text, the description of Homer's song is unspecific as to lyrics or sound. The contrast between these two approaches locates the endpoints of the spectrum of possibility in writing orality, from the explicit transcription of Callisto's song to the opacity of Homer's. Instead, the omission of precise content is crucial: When "Homer kill Homer," what the narrator eliminates are the contextual specificities of this particular iteration of the long antislavery struggle. That is, not fixing the words in print makes it possible for Homer's struggle to be disarticulated from her person and rearticulated in other times and places.[22] As such, James defines the song through its metaphorical location "in the dark of the eye where secrets be." The eye, though singular here, can be infinitely multiplied in every person whose eye holds within it the secret of Homer's song. The absence of lyrical specificity in the text allows James to imply that Homer's song can mutate as it circulates from eye to rebellious eye.

While Lovey is not one of the eponymous rebel night women, by taking up the secret act of writing, she adopts the power that their darkness metaphorically signifies throughout the novel: the drive toward self-possession. In this regard, James draws on a long tradition linking the darkness of night and Creole storytelling as a form of rebellion against colonial restrictions, as Ralph Ludwig indicates in the introduction to *Écrire la parole de nuit: la nouvelle littérature antillaise*: "Since the century of Voltaire and Diderot, light incarnates the key metaphor of analytical thinking as vehiculated by writing. . . . The night, on the contrary, has always been the site of the Creole word. It is at dusk that the creole storyteller gathers his audience. . . . The night is the universe of leisure, sensual pleasure, and the refusal to submit to the restrictions of the day" (18, my translation). In Homer's song, the dark of the eye and the night spirit signify the will to make a space for expressing the desire to overthrow slavery; furthermore, Lilith defines the indomitable urge to protect herself as "darkness" within her. Lovey elaborates further the relationship between the dark and her capacity to write: "Any niggerwoman can become a black woman in secret. This is why we dark, cause in the night we disappear and become spirit. Skin gone and we become whatever we wish. We become who we be. In the dark with no skin I can write. And what write in darkness is free as free can be, even if it never come to light and go free for real" (417). In part, darkness offers a protective secrecy for illegal acts. Foremost among what is forbidden for "niggerwomen"—James's signifier for those who accept their enslavement and collude in the system's perpetuation—is becoming a "black woman," defined in this passage as becoming "whatever we wish." The commemorative song cycle is one site where enslaved persons can express "whatever we wish" by experimenting with the articulation of the self-possession that the night women claim. In this last chapter, oral and written forms of giving account of the past are complementary. Both are sites of experimentation in seizing words to locate, express, and possess one's self outside of slavery, even when living within it.

From silence to whispered rebellion, the written representation of the oral song cycle offers a spectrum of approaches to how an enslaved person might articulate the violence she has experienced as well as the challenges of narrating such an experience. The quiet nature of these songs as the narrator describes them signals the ways in which their singers must balance competing forms of self-preservation. For those who sing these commemorative songs while still trying to survive slavery, the desire to defend the rebellion comes into conflict with the survival strategy of total self-effacement. The account of the league of night women that Lovey gives in this last chapter attempts neither to subsume the songs into a written form nor to produce a totalizing account. Moreover, as in the example where Solibo's audience who attempts to reperform his last performance, the examples in *Night Women* show that when the community sings the night women's songs, they fail and succeed, quite differently than when Lovey writes them, to repeat the performances they reference. More at issue is how the songs and the memory they form sustain a community and an idea of freedom well beyond their failed rebellion. In this, José Esteban Muñoz's gloss of Miranda Joseph identifies the ways that performances are not confined to the present:

"Performance is the kernel of a potentiality that is transmitted to audiences and witnesses and that the real force of performance is its ability to generate a modality of knowing and recognition among audiences and groups that facilitates modes of belonging, especially minoritarian belonging" (98–99). In their ekphrastic representations of oral performance that I analyze in the chapter's last section, James and Chamoiseau demonstrate the impossibility of exactly reproducing the performance in the text, just as they expand on what remains from the performance: nothing short of the transformation of the audience into a community of belonging that is joined together by a commonly shared idea of what knowledge is and where it is generated.

Toward a Creole Hermeneutic

Through their different approaches to representing the stories of others, the narrators of *Night Women* and *Solibo* continuously return to the problem of how to account for what is silent or what relies on gestural communication.[23] These particular concerns echo the unresolvable dilemma that Glissant comes up against when thinking through the relation between writing and Creole: "The written requires nonmovement: the body does not move with the flow of what is said. . . . The oral, on the other hand, is inseparable from the movement of the body. There the spoken is inscribed not only in the posture of the body that makes it possible (squatting for a palaver for instance, or the rhythmic tapping of feet in a circle when we keep time to music), but also in the almost semaphoric signals through which the body implies or emphasizes what is said" (122; see French in *Discours* 404). The impasse presented to James and Chamoiseau by the incompatibility of writing with the body's corporeal forms of meaning making that are integral to the Creole language results in, as discussed in the previous sections, an attention called to the failures in transcribing oral performance and a focus on the narrated memories of audience members. In this section, I propose that in order to represent the importance of oral performance in literature, they take a detour away from the storytelling circle itself and, in its stead, reflect on how the epistemological grounds for Solibo's performances and the central metaphors in *Night Women* are located in moving bodies.

In addressing Chamoiseau's use of performance in *Solibo*, literary criticism of the novel sometimes seeks to draw the genres of performance and literature together.[24] I am wary of subsuming the live arts into the domain of the text, in the fear that arguing for equivalence between literature and performance will sideline the work that is specific to theater practitioners and performers. Instead of merging the two genres, I propose that James and Chamoiseau situate their texts as legacies of oral performance by using literature to do something that creole storytelling often does not: fully explain how assuming that corporeal experience and expression is a form of thinking that guides how we ask and answer questions about the world. As Ludwig's writing on creole oral storytelling as a nighttime activity indicates, keeping communication in the dark challenges the metaphors and practices of Enlightenment philosophy; it also shields the storytelling circle from accusations of having articulated such challenges in a context in which it is illegal to do so. The Creolophone oral story and proverb are meant to be allusive and to protect their most dangerous meanings.

The novels, however, explicate how oral performance operates in Creole. Furthermore, they use their explanations of the meanings of oral performance that might remain hidden in their oral form to describe a creole hermeneutic that serves as an alternative to western rationalism. I borrow extensively from Rhonda Cobham's theorization of a "creole gnosis" in thinking of this mode of investigation as a hermeneutic in Creole. Cobham defines creole gnosis as a "sanctioned code for articulating Caribbean systems of belief and knowledge" (868), themselves based on the persistence of African cultural practices, and in "Mwen na rien, Msieu: Jamaica Kincaid and the Problem of Creole Gnosis," she identifies the problem of creole gnosis: that it is often disavowed or silenced. In representing how Creolophone storytellers ask and answer questions from a creole worldview, James and Chamoiseau offer a hermeneutic that is distinct from a Eurocentric philosophical perspective and is derived from metaphors expressed in Creole. In so doing, these texts propose two concepts: a sense of temporality that is not limited by chronological time, and a thinking body.

Locating knowledge in physical experience makes it necessary to contend with a particular historical problem in the Caribbean. In *Caliban's Reason,* Paget Henry provides a clear explanation for the difficulties surrounding the concept of the thinking body. Given the need to justify the political ideology of slavery, rationalism—and the political rights it confers—is established as the purview of the mind, while the body is consigned exclusively to labor and stripped of the possibility of reasoning. As a result, "Euro-Caribbean texts of the tradition repeatedly recognized the dancing, dramatic, oratorical, religious, and musical capabilities of Africans but never their philosophical capabilities" (75–76). Further reminding us of the dynamics of colonial power embedded within the speech/writing debate as it plays out in certain contexts, Omofolabo Ajayi contends that the disregard for nonverbal communication, which has its roots in Judeo-Christian traditions, produces a "'disembodied body' as the Western opposite of the more holistic verbal/non-verbal communication system where the body, as one such system of communication, is valued, or even regarded as sacred" (qtd. in Stanley Niaah 136). That is, to take Henry's argument one step further, within this binary construction, corporeal movement cannot actually be recognized as a knowledge system in its own right. As such, recognizing the philosophical dimensions of Afro-diasporic performance traditions and identifying those performances as corporeal forms of epistemological production, as is offered by the representations of performance in these two novels, is a route to claiming full personhood.

Turning to oral performance in order to argue for expanding the political category of personhood brings us back to a complex problem regarding the role of art for Afro-diasporic peoples. Gilroy's explication of this historical problem in "Masters, Mistresses, Slaves, and the Antinomies of Modernity," in *The Black Atlantic,* dovetails with Silvio Torres-Saillant's caution against accepting the popularity of Caribbean performing arts as a substantive replacement for the success of political movements. As part of a reflection on the construction of the Enlightenment project, Gilroy marks out the problem of art in two phases: first, "art was offered to slaves as a substitute for the formal political freedoms they were denied under the plantation regime" (56) and then, as a consequence, "art became the backbone of the slaves' political cultures and of their cultural history" (57). Not coincidentally, the separation drawn between art and life that Gilroy identifies in Enlightenment thought made the articulation of a political culture inaudible as politics when housed in artistic expression. In their written explanations of how oral performance vehiculates political thought, Chamoiseau and James attempt to make the demonstration of political thought within performance practices legible—if not audible—to their readerships.

Both writers, Chamoiseau more overtly than James, position their novels as narrating history from a marginalized perspective,[25] creating a space for Solibo's audience to tell the stories that do not fit into the genre of the police inquiry, and for the much-maligned Lilith to defend her story of survival. The interpretation of the scene of Solibo's death is reoriented from seeking a murderer to identifying why he became nonessential; likewise, the Montpelier revolt shifts from a "failed rebellion" to recognition of the night women's assertion of personhood. Locating thought in the body results in, to recall Wilson Harris's phrasing, "a different reading of texts of reality" (183) as represented in these novels. Just as using Creole expression in the text claims space for a distinctly Caribbean form of expression, the description of a thinking body challenges Western philosophy from a Creole perspective.

Chamoiseau and James offer metaphors for doing philosophical work that situate understanding the world as located in a corporeal experience of the specific geography and history of Caribbean space. The descriptions of Solibo remind us that the Creole language and its oral site of production is where this form of generating knowledge is produced; as we will see, they focus on how Solibo's active body morphs as it moves through the world, and in so doing, transforms conceptions of time and space. The witnesses to Solibo's last performance earnestly attempt to evoke Solibo's capacity to disappear into the environment during the police procedural, the *procès-verbal*. Inevitably, their descriptions of Solibo's disappearances—both during his performance and in his death—come into sharp contrast with the answers that the police inspector seeks. For example, in response to the routine question as to whether or not he had seen Solibo on the day of his death, the character La Fièvre responds with the reflection: "You can run into the wind which comes from the horizon, but never into the horizon" (193; see French in Chamoiseau 133). La Fièvre's response rejects the very premise of the question by referencing Solibo's constitutive unattainability, and in that rejection he indicates the need for a very different kind of question. In interpreting La Fièvre's questioning answer, I turn to Carolyn Cooper's work on metaphor in the context of oral performance where she argues that, in order to value what she terms "oracy," we must stop privileging abstraction: "At the very least, [revalue] making of metaphor as a kind of literal-minded process of abstracting. The metaphorical is to oracy what abstraction is to literacy—a way of generalizing" (*Noises* 82). I therefore take La Fièvre's metaphor of Solibo as the horizon and all of the audience members' contestatory answers as generalizing a way of asking questions that are more suited to contextual specificities, or the elaboration of a Creole hermeneutic.

My analyses here rely on criticism that has researched the anti-Cartesianism of *Solibo*, particularly Aching's "Turning a Blind Eye" in *Masking and Power* and De Ferrari's "Lurking Shadows" in *Vulnerable States*. As indicated in their chapter titles, both Aching and De Ferrari use Glissant's concept of opacity, which I discuss further in chapter 3, to analyze the novel's alternatives to the visual regime of the state and its demand for transparency. Aching draws on Slavoj Žižek's observation that the state uses an "ideological mask of cynical reason" in response to popular carnivalesque strategies (130) in order to show how the police, Martinican men who draw their power from and act on behalf of the state, mobilize metropolitan French, writing, and the legal system—all aspects of cynical reason—alongside practices of physical violence inherited from the plantation systems of control to extract from Solibo's audience members "'rationality' and full visibility under the law" (145). The cynicism of reason emerges here because this confrontation between reason and popular culture is staged as a cover for violent subjugation. This physical violence has an attending philosophical dimension, which De Ferrari demonstrates by identifying two ways in which Chamoiseau's novel rejects the Enlightenment rationalism. First, within the novel, Solibo's oral performances resist "the lessons of European universalism" (62); second, the novel's use of multiple genres pushes against the idea of reading one single solution for the mystery of Solibo's death since "each genre proposes a notion of the real that is valid only within its own conventions" (31). The physical and philosophical implications of the contest between Enlightenment rationalism and a Creole mode of interpretation are both central to the redefinition of thinking that I argue James and Chamoiseau propose in their descriptions of oral performance: instead of Enlightenment values that separate the body from thinking, in *Solibo* knowledge is redefined as a body's experience of the specific space it inhabits, and in *Night Women* what might be thought of as the body's instincts are reclassified as a form of kinesthetic intelligence.[26] Through the reference to oral performance and corporeal movement, both novels imagine what "thinking from the body" could look like.

The experiential measurement of temporality is the clearest way that Solibo's Creolophone audience pushes against a philosophical system that makes no room for kinesthetic intelligence. The police will only accept answers that use standard chronological time to describe "how long did you sit there listening to his solo?" (97). Yet in their answers, each of Solibo's audience members broadens the meaning of time well beyond the limited sense that Inspector Pilon employs. Even as a frustrated Pilon shakes his watch in their faces, they ask, "What is time?" (97). Time as they experience it bears little relation to the relentless ticking of Pilon's watch. Confronted with the increasing prevalence of imported French goods and the obsolescence of various traditional trades, each of these characters finds that the loss of one's livelihood destructures any sense of time's passing. Both factory and farm workers point to Martinique's dependence on France as the reason for their detachment from a sense of time. Without labor to structure it, time loses its definition altogether, just as the setting of oral performance interrupts panoptical time and creates a sense of time that corresponds only to the beats of the storyteller's engagement with the audience. As the briagadier-chief Bouaffesse comments; "Could be they aren't completely wrong. When I was unemployed after Algeria, and I sometimes found myself by a ka-drum, ten thousand years could go by and you could have even cut my balls I wouldn't have moved, you know!" (98). Both the performance and the obsolescent workers exist outside of the metropole's chronological time and point to a Creole logic for describing an experience of time that is more expansive than Inspector's watch.

The form of generating knowledge that Solibo's community has learned from him emerges when contrasted with the police's investigation protocols during *les auditions*, when the inspector and his lieutenant question each suspect individually. Through these sets of unintelligible questions and answers, Chamoiseau stages a direct collision between two competing hermeneutics. I start from De Ferrari's analysis that "[as] the examination of Solibo's death places us squarely within a Eurocentered philosophical predicament that privileges scientific knowledge, Western logic, and the written word, the failure of the Enlightenment to understand the Afro-Antillean oral culture that Solibo represents becomes evident" (35). In *les auditions*, Solibo's Creolophone audience members insist one after another upon the intellectual value of asking questions according to a Creole rhetorical practice. When the witnesses to Solibo's last performance are asked to account for his death, they showcase how "oracy" uses metaphor as a form of generalizing from the specific to the systemic. Each of them in turn argues against the disembodied intellect of the police protocol and points back to information that has been gleaned from corporeal experiences of the specific space of Fort-de-France—its markets, its cemeteries, its bars, or the mangroves on its outskirts—by asking: What do you know of the world in which you actually live? Do you use the knowledge your own body generates and accumulates as it moves through that environment? Solibo's Creolophone witnesses assert that knowledge is derived from an investigation into corporeal experiences; through this assertion, they outline a Creole hermeneutic that centers the body as a site of knowledge production.

The insistence on the local, cultural specificity of place emerges consistently throughout the interviews, as when one of the witnesses, Pipi, responds to the inspector's questions by asserting that the best way to make sense of Solibo's life and death is to navigate the world as Solibo did:

> Sans vouloir te conseiller (tu es une maître-pièce de la policerie, et je le sais), chercher qui a tué Solibo n'appelle aucune vérité. La vraie question est: Qui est Solibo? Quand maintenant tu ajoutes: Et pourquoi Magnifique? . . . , je suis content. Je suis content parce qu'ici, il faut sarcler les vraies questions. Questionner la terre-là, la mer-là, le ciel-là, la manière de ce morne, le nom de cette rue-là, l'horizon où parfois des pays inconnus pointent leur ombre. . . . Eh bien, j'ai appris cela de Solibo: apprendre à questionner, plus de certitudes ou d'évidences, mais la question, toute la question. C'était ça, Solibo. Tu comprends le "Magnifique"? (185)
>
> Don't want to tell you how to run your investigation (you're a masterpiece of policework, and I know that), but to look for who killed Solibo can get at no truth. The real question is: Who is Solibo? . . . When you add: And why Magnificent? . . . , then you're talking. Because that's where we must plow up the real questions. We must question this earth, this sea, this sky, the curve of this hill, the name of that street, the horizon on which unknown countries sometimes cast their shadows. . . . Well, I found this out from Solibo: to learn to question, no more certainties or evidence, but the question, the whole question. That's what Solibo was about. You understand the "Magnificent" part? (127)

As Pipi elaborates how to ask questions about Solibo and where to focus one's attention, it becomes evident that a constant attention to the specific materiality of the Martinican landscape is at the foundation of Solibo's Creole knowledge base. In listing off the objects that require attention, Pipi's repeated demonstrative pronouns localize each individual object and highlight its individual physicality—in contrast to the assumption of the police that you can use the same set of questions to obtain any answer you might need. Moreover, the form of asking questions itself has a material dimension: acquiring knowledge is represented by "sarcler," to dig deep into the earth, reaching down beyond the root of things. Integral to the form of generating knowledge that Pipi has inherited from Solibo is a constant engagement of the body with its surroundings.

Attending to the specificity of Martinican landscape according to Solibo and his audience requires an understanding of space as an entity that changes according to use. Just as Solibo is capable of transforming his physical body, the examples given by the last witness to be interviewed, the shopkeeper Richard Cœurillon, upend once stable notions of how space functions:

> Fais-toi raconter par les békés anciens ces histoires de nègres-marrons que pièce chien ne pouvait pister. Des nègres dissimulés dans une forêt grande comme une niche de colibris, mais que rien ne parvenait à localiser. Les vieux chasseurs et les békés d'antan les appelaient *guerriers*! Solibo Magnifique était de cette catégorie-là. On ne peut pas assassiner ces gens-là, inspectère. (196)

> Get the old békés to tell you stories about the maroon blackmen that no dog could track down. Men hiding in forests small as a hummingbird's nest but whom no creature could locate. The old hunters and the békés of bygone days called them *warriors!* Solibo Magnificent was of such a category. You can't kill these people, Inspekder. (135–36)

With this set of stories, Cœurillon calls upon historical precedent to illustrate that the investigation's central question, who killed Solibo, is unanswerable because Solibo could not have been murdered in the first place. Each of these examples, including the overarching figure of the maroon, defies what is usual or expected. They stand out as counterintuitive, from the hunting dog that cannot identify its prey, to the juxtaposition of "grande" with a tiny object that undercuts the expectation of a large space altogether. The forest, which is apparently small, seems impenetrably large to the slave catchers when the warrior enters it: the basic properties of space are revealed to be unstable, flexible according to the storyteller's need. While Pipi's take on the Creole hermeneutic is to inquire into specific Martinican locales and question how the body engages with these places, Cœurillon's reflections build on Pipi's insights by pointing to exactly whose body moves through those local spaces and how their individual presences make distinct impacts on those spaces.

The derision expressed toward Solibo's Creolophone audience during "les auditions" makes clear that, in the eyes of the law, the audience members have nothing of value to offer. The reorientation of the body as a site of knowledge production is thus a form of self-defense, a way of asserting one's individual value. Identifying and asserting one's individuality is even more important for James's night women, who struggle for recognition of their very personhood. The night women's physical rebellion is paralleled by their struggle to articulate a philosophy that can combat a dominant ideology that does not recognize them as persons. The turn to the body as a site of knowledge production is for

James's narrator, just as it is for Solibo's audience, an important method for undermining this governing philosophy. With *Night Women*'s most arresting image, "Every negro walk in a circle. Take that and make of it what you will," James's narrator uses the corporeal activity of the itinerant enslaved, who make meaning with each reiterated step, as the metaphor with which to reflect on Lilith's ideological self-liberation. Interspersed at five separate instances throughout the novel, this phrase introduces different lines of thought that correspond to critical turning points in the plot as well as to different articulations of the experience of slavery—always through embodied action.[27] The paths ground into the earth by the circles traveled by the enslaved offer a set of open-ended interpretations for how to use the thinking body's praxis as a way of reconceptualizing the experiences of slavery.

The descriptions of slavery brought into being by the invocation of the circle sometimes lay out the sociological organization of the plantation and sometimes indicate what actions or events might transform that way of life. The first instances present slavery as repetitive and eternal, drawing on the cyclical connotation of a circle to underscore the unchanging nature of the plantation kept unchanging by a regime of violence. In the reader's first encounter with this phrase, before it has become a recurring motif, the circles are naturalized:

> Every negro walk in a circle. Take that and make of it what you will. A circle like the sun, a circle like the moon, a circle like bad tidings that seem gone but always, always come back. Woman work round the sun and sleep round the moon and sometimes work round both, especially if it be crop time. Other times woman wait on the moon, especially if it fat with blood and rise low over the Blue Mountain. That be the season of the Sasa, the Asaase Yaa or the Ogun and the other forgotten gods. (32)

While first a one-dimensional outline of the sun and the moon, the circles quickly become an introduction to the seasonal structure of slave life on the plantation. The demands of the plantation harvest intervene in the normal division of labor and rest, but their actions are also governed by an interpretation of nature's cycles according to an African religious system that endures despite the cultural losses incurred during the Middle Passage. These residual practices refigure the harvest from crop time to the low, red harvest moon and indicate the concurrent presence of two natural cycles: that which is organized by the labor of slavery and the other which is autonomous from the demands of the plantation. The signifiers of this second moon are bodily: blood and fat indicate its presence. It is in this oblique way that the corporeal is a necessary part of an interpretive system that James's narrator proposes as a counternarrative to slavery's structure of time on the plantation.

Broadening out from the first reference to the circles as yearly harvest cycles on the plantation, the second iteration uses the circles to represent a slave life predetermined to end in bondage. The counternarrative that is possible in the interpretation of the harvest disappears from view when James takes the longer view of generational time and the inheritance of bondage:

> Every negro walk in a circle. Take that and make of it what you will. A road set before every negro, from he through the slave ship or him mother pussy, that be just as dark. Black and long and wide like a thousand year. And when a negro walk, light get take away from him so he never know when he hit a curve or a bend. Worse, he never see that he walking round and round and always come back to where he leave first. That be why the negro not free. He can't walk like freeman and no matter where he walk, the road take he right back to the chain, the branding iron, the cat-o'-nine or the noose that be the blessing that no niggerwoman can curse. (118)

This reflection on the inescapability of violence begins the chapter in which Lilith loses her status as exempt from brutal punishment and is gang-raped and whipped as a consequence of having spilled hot soup on a guest at the Montpelier house. From the thousand-year trajectory to "no matter where he walk," both time and space are organized to conspire against her attempt to redirect her own path away from her oppression. According to the narrative arc, for the generalized "every negro" that is the subject of this passage, the entry into slavery can lead to only one end: the body's instrumentalization and subjection to torture. The litany of "never," "not," and "no" that marks the passage rhetorically shuts down any possibility other than violence when operating within the temporal scale of a lifespan. The consciousness of slavery's unchanging nature as experienced by the enslaved population of the Montpelier plantation is understood as the exhausting and unceasing itinerancy without directionality, the corporeal practice of "walk[ing] round and round."

James's circles can function as symbols that permit broad commentary on the organization of a slavery-based society and the cultural practices that define it. While the previous examples stressed their immateriality, the circles also have a strong material presence. Their matter is specified in each separate example, whether the circle becomes the moon at a specific time of year or the shackle that presses against the subject's neck. The doubly-signifying circle, both symbolic and material, is produced by a deeply ambivalent language. With the phrase "take that and make of it what you will," James's narrator demands that the reader recognize her own interpretation as uncertain, unfixed, and only one of many possibilities. Indeed, the image of James's "every negro" walking in a circle, tracing a different meaning with each repetition of the circle's path, corresponds precisely to a multiply-signifying language that presents ideas in a nonlinear way. That is, the body's circular path here maps onto a linguistic pattern of circumlocution.[28] In this mutability, the "every negro walk in a circle" formula draws on the capacity of oral expression to modify text to context. George Lang, who contrasts orality with the fixed quality of print, states: "Whereas a print document can constitute proof of some misdemeanor or planned revolt, speech is uttered and disseminated at the discretion of the speaker, who can tailor expression to fit the audience, text to context. The pointed thrust of a seditious tale can be blunted on the spot; a proverb can be deflected into another gist" (*Entwisted* 126). For Lang, the capacity for meaning to shift as needed depends on the corporeal aspects of oral expression, not necessarily on the words themselves. In refusing to fix signification and thereby leaving interpretation pointedly unwritten, James's central metaphor imitates this aspect of orality. Equally important in signaling the orality of the novel's leitmotif is the corporeal quality that James invests in each iteration of the circle figure: even the abstract circle is filled with the materiality of an itinerant body whose feet scuff a path onto the earth's surface.

James imitates orality's malleability in the text not merely by showing the variability possible in the trace of the circle, but by anchoring these shifting meanings in variations of how the body experiences temporality. While both the examples of agricultural time and slavery's inheritance of violence conclude in historical or philosophical interpretations of the abstract circle, these interpretations are reached by considering how the body registers the passage of time or how ritual structures of time are aligned with the body's own cycles. That is, intellectual work is attentive to the body. This is most evident when the sense of temporality reduces precipitously from the *longue durée* of yearly and life cycles to the single instant of illumination. This change in approach to the circle is introduced at the outset of the chapter in which Lilith takes the dramatic action of murdering the Rogets and burning down the big house on the Coulibre plantation. The chapter begins: "Every negro walk in a circle. Take that and make of it what you will. But sometimes that circle start squeeze in on itself and get smaller and smaller and smaller like a mark, or a head. A head so small that the negro have one chance to stomp it with her foot and stomp it good. Lilith know. She learn and she learn it good. Plenty things be a sin, but every sin come with temptation and chance" (218). Lilith rejects her conditioning, refusing to believe that each action will result in an ever more brutal response. She adopts instead a malleable sense of temporality, choosing to regard each instant as having its own distinct existence in which her action is possible. This shift in perspective begins in the body; the phrase "Lilith know" follows the description of her stomping foot, and it is attention to her foot that makes Lilith intellectually aware of the very slight and temporary shift in power. The contrast in sensation between the foot's action when tracing a long-suffering path and a single stomp signals her potential moment to rebel. Kinesthetic intelligence, in this case, precedes verbal articulation.

The insistence on the body's intelligence in each iteration of the metaphor of the circle places this theme at the center of the narrator's project in writing *Night Women* because the extended metaphor functions as a set of excurses in which the narrator, Lovey, addresses her readers directly. Part of this project engages colonial intellectual production by taking up writing and shaping English to include her own Creole turns of phrase. But she also flatly rejects key tenets of colonial philosophy, namely the division between thinking brains and laboring bodies. Lovey rejects the designation of enslaved persons as pure instruments of labor. She demonstrates the capacity for Lilith's body to produce thought, thereby throwing into question the colonial definition of intellectual work as disembodied. It is through the attention she accords to her body's interaction with her environment that Lilith is able to devise a concept of temporality that allows her to defend herself against her abusers. James locates the potential for seizing rebellion by distending time in his juxtaposition of the long cycles that form the large, multigenerational circular paths and the instantaneous pinpoint. Lilith must change her perspective from a long view of the phenomenon of slavery to a moment of interpersonal struggle in which the power dynamics are temporarily reversed. If she ignores knowledge of the cycle of violence, which indicates that any rebellion will be met with brutal consequences, and instead focuses her energies on the possibility of an instant, she can take action. Resistance requires a sense of the present where one act is lifted out of the linearity of cause-and-effect relationships, isolated from the pressing weight of the future, and given its own life cycle, or circle. By violently upending the hierarchies of slavery, even if only momentarily, Lilith acts on a belief in her full personhood. She refuses to accept that she is a lesser form of human, and in the strongest instance of her rejection of that ideology, she relies on knowledge generated in her body.

In a 1994 interview with George Yancy, Angela Davis commented about her experience with philosophy departments in the United States: "It's clear—especially in philosophy departments where faculty and students struggle to legitimize philosophical knowledge that is produced in places that aren't considered essentially philosophical—that there is an ongoing struggle to legitimize alternative sites of knowledge production" (23). In working through the ways in which a specific body's interaction with its environment is posited as a starting point for producing knowledge, I argue that James and Chamoiseau engage in fiction the project of legitimization that Davis outlines in philosophy departments. This engagement is most evident in the debate surrounding language politics, since, as James comments, "What struck me was that even in 2007, people still refuse to have stories told by the people who experienced it, in a language that breaks standard English" (James, interview by Lydon). These linguistic interactions of breaking Standard English and chamoisifying metropolitan French call our attention to the continued need to broaden the philosophical grounds by which people are allowed to create and contribute knowledge. As the conversations between La Fièvre, Pipi, Cœurillon, and the police in *Solibo* corroborate, demonstrating a corporeal basis for epistemology strikes at the very heart of the dynamics of uneven power distribution in contemporary Martinique just as it does for Lilith on the Coulibre plantation. Because what constitutes knowledge serves as that basis for determining who has the right to personhood and its attending privileges, the meditations on the capacity for writing to represent oral expression in these novels seek to make a space for the articulations of thinking bodies.

3 From Spectator to Participant

Audience Formation in Guillermo Cabrera Infante's *Tres tristes tigres*, Oonya Kempadoo's *Tide Running*, and Ernest Pépin's *L'Envers du décor*

As we have seen in Chamoiseau's and James's novels, observing how witnesses of a performance event are impacted by it is an important tool for writers to describe the significance of performance. Two reasons this strategy works particularly well for Caribbean representations of social performance are that first, audience members form the circle with their bodies, presence, and attention; and second, any audience member is a potential participant, to return to Marlene NourbeSe Philip's encapsulation, "you crossing from looking to dancing and back again to looking" (152). This chapter focuses on the role of audience members in creating the dance circle's protection for experimentation, or more precisely, through their narration of the performance events as Fanonian circles. In thinking about how an audience can move from spectator to participant, I start from Anne Bogart's suggestion about the qualities of the theater, that "you have to make room for the audience—not only room for their bodies, but also room for their imaginations. Theater, at its best and most true to itself, invites the audience to play an active role" (76). The active role that the audiences play in these three texts, I suggest, is that of temporarily becoming the kinds of interpreters that the performers need in order for their dance and music to exceed exoticizing stereotypes of Caribbean cultures. Although these spaces, with their stages that formally separate audience and performer, are not evidently configured as dance circles, their descriptions feature the dynamics of audience-participant-performer relationships where those who hold the energy of the circle support and accompany performers' experimentations. In these unexpected Fanonian circles, audience-participants respond to their own intellectual/corporeal responses to performance events as a way of textually representing Caribbean performance practices.

This chapter considers audience formation in Oonya Kempadoo's *Tide Running* (2001), which takes place on the island of Tobago in the 1990s; Ernest Pépin's *L'Envers du décor* (2006), set in early-twenty-first-century Guadeloupe; and Guillermo Cabrera Infante's *Tres tristes tigres* (1964), which presents a portrait of pre-Revolution Havana's entertainment culture. One of the features of the ekphrases of performances in these novels is that their narrators use references to tactility, particularly viscous textures, and their own kinesthetic experiences to describe how they interact with the performances. By accounting for the sense of balance or "the sensations of movement and perception of the position of the parts of one's own body" (Reynolds 212), kinesthesia can mark how the vibrations of unexpected rhythms throw a person off balance. This chapter traces two consequences resulting from the concentration on the inner corporeal movement of audience members: first, the change in physical perspective corresponding to changing balance likewise transforms one's perspective in interpreting the performance environment; second, the ways in which kinesthesia itself draws attention to "movement itself as a way of knowing, a medium that carries meaning in an immediately felt, somatic mode" (Sklar 70). As the narrators depict a form of audience that is informed by kinesthesia, and experience performances in which the visual is obscured or distorted, they practice a form of personhood that I elaborate by thinking with Glissant's theory of opacity.

By modifying the visual and underscoring the brief eruptive ekphrastic descriptions of performance in which vision is set aside, these texts point to an upending of post-Enlightenment hierarchies of the senses. To briefly review the rise of what Martin Jay calls the scopic regime and its consequences for knowledge production, the Enlightenment's economy of the senses links objectivity and rationality with disembodied vision. This follows the Cartesian mind/body opposition in which, as Elizabeth Grosz summarizes it, "the mind [is placed] in a position of hierarchical superiority over and above nature, including the nature of the body" (6), and moreover, the optimal body was one that allowed the mind to work without the interruption or interference of the needs and sensations of corporeal matter (Jones 5). Although the history of the senses as it is conceived in European philosophy from the Stoics onward is characterized by nuanced debate about the significance and interpretation of each of the senses (see especially Robert Jütte's *The History of the Senses* and Daniel Heller-Roazen's *The Inner Touch*), the nineteenth-century development of a racialized hierarchy of the senses in the disciplines of anthropology and philosophy simplified those debates. David Howes's research on anthropologists in the era of contact shows how they "constitute[ed] themselves as rational Europeans and their subjects as sensuous savages. . . . Sight and hearing were traditionally linked with intellectual activity and civilized behavior in European culture, while taste, touch, and smell were associated with animality. . . . [I]t was imagined that 'primitive' peoples, would show a predilection for the 'lower' or 'animal'—in short, 'primitive'—senses" (4).[1] This nineteenth-century racialization of the senses in anthropology and philosophy is a direct legacy of Enlightenment prioritization of vision, which, as Omise'eke Tinsley states, links "invisibility and privacy . . . to oppression, while access to visibility and publicity is aligned with empowerment. . . . Enlightenment vision relegated entire continents to darkness and subhumanity" (25).[2] These challenges explicating how the visual can be used for domination are embedded into the suspicion of the visual arts in Kempadoo, Cabrera Infante, and Pépin—critiques that motivate their evocative, if momentary, explorations of kinesthesia. The representation of thinking bodies that are interpreted as such within the dance circle poses an epistemological question by asking what can be known when we reprioritize the senses we use to interpret performance.

In these novels, the suspicion of the visual, which is often mentioned in association with the tourism industry, stems from the power of the image to circulate stereotypes and the power dynamic assumed in the one-sided dynamics of distanced observation. The attitude that Robert Jütte ascribes to the figure of the flâneur, that of "a born spectator, the universal onlooker who never feels that he is being looked at by others in return" (198), indexes the desire to survey without being subject to evaluation in turn, a desire that Michel de Certeau has theorized as the "scopic and gnostic drive" of the no longer extant World Trade Center viewing platform: "When one goes up there, he leaves behind the mass that carries off and mixes up in itself any identity of authors or spectators. . . . His elevation transfigures him into a voyeur. It puts him at a distance. It transforms the bewitching world by which one was 'possessed' into a text that lies before one's eyes. It allows one to read it, to be a solar Eye, looking down like a god. The exaltation of a scopic and gnostic drive: the fiction of knowledge is related to this lust to be a viewpoint and nothing more" (92; see French in Certeau 140). The sense of removal from a responsibility to the persons who make up the masses reveals the desire to move through the world without being affected by it. As Certeau intimates, it is a perspective that enables a kind of fiction of untouchability more than an actual nonmutual relationship.

Kempadoo's Sunday *fête*, Cabrera Infante's famous *el chowcito*, and *L'Envers*'s impromptu dance floor created by spontaneously pushing aside the furniture in an unlicensed restaurant: each of these performance spaces has the potential to serve, like Fanon's dance circle, as a sanctified space for protected experimentation—but only with the assent of the participating audience. As such, these moments of performance demonstrate a shifting mode of relation, oscillating between a circle of copresence between participants to a site of potential commodification based on the audience members' interpretive disposition. Nevertheless, in these often dark, cramped, and improvised spaces, rather than sit back and admire the spectacle, audience members must experiment with their senses to find different ways of interacting in the dance circle. In this regard, the spaces and the performance events on which I focus in this chapter are overtly set against commercial stages, from the famous Tropicana Club in Havana to the beach resorts that dot the island shores of the Caribbean. In eschewing such spot-lit stages, the representations of performance events that I analyze here turn to the interior of the body to find new modes of engaging one's environment. As Susan Leigh Foster writes about kinesthesia, "one's history of engagement with the environment profoundly affects how one sees, and consequently what one sees" (54). What can be seen and known differently once one's corporeal relation to the world has been kinesthetically reoriented? This question guides my readings in this chapter.

In the Dark: Oonya Kempadoo's *Tide Running*

Oonya Kempadoo's *Tide Running* (2001) evokes what one can know of another person, particularly in the context of self-interest and self-deception. Like her 2013 *All Decent Animals*, it has at its center a young Indo-Trinidadian woman in a romantic relationship with a white European man who finds herself at a remove from the society she considers her own upon her return to Trinidad and Tobago. Particularly in *All Decent Animals*, whose protagonists are involved with Carnival in Port-of-Spain, Oonya Kempadoo might draw on her own education in the fine arts, both in college in the Netherlands and while working with Peter Minshall in Carnival before beginning to write fiction. This interest in the visual arts is also featured in *Tide Running*, with Kempadoo's veiled references to the sculptor Luise Kimme and the protagonist's profession as photographer, but it is the brief and evocative writing about dance in *Tide Running* that is the focus of my readings. Describing a Sunday *fête*, Kempadoo emphasizes the darkness of the rumshop and fishing shed where the *fête* takes place and the loudness of the music reconfigures the senses of the participants as the text concentrates on their kinesthetic interactions. The primacy of the tactile and auditory and the momentary loss of vision in Kempadoo's description of the performance event provide a literalization of Glissant's concept of opacity as well as the temporary reorientation of social relations.

The plot of *Tide Running* revolves around the limits and possibilities of knowing other individuals within the context of postcolonial globalization. The two protagonists, Cliff and Bella, represent two different forms of globalized identity, and Kempadoo depicts their relationship as vacillating between camaraderie and transactional exchange. Cliff is an Afro-Tobagonian young man who has never left Tobago, and Bella is an Indo-Trinidadian woman who has traveled the world for her work as a photographer. After having chosen to settle herself, her British husband, Peter, and their child, Oliver, in Tobago, where her social circle consists primarily of expats and hoteliers, Bella strikes up a friendship with Cliff. Cliff quickly becomes a mainstay in the family's life, both as her lover and as a playmate to Oliver. In the second half of the novel, Cliff is arrested for stealing from Bella's home. From Cliff's perspective, he was doing nothing more than borrowing from friends. In the misunderstanding or abuse of the limits of friendship, the novel ends with Cliff's incarceration. Despite Cliff's protestations that he was doing nothing more than borrowing as one would from friends, he ends the novel incarcerated with no hope of release. Through Cliff and Bella's relationship, *Tide Running* explores the collision of class, race, gender, and the tensions that emerge around the effort to create relations across difference.

Bella's identity position is that of the "foreign-local," a Trinidadian expression that, as Rosamond King explains, "refers to Trinidadians and Tobagonians (or their descendants) who do not live in the country full-time but who know enough about the place, language, and culture to qualify as *somewhat* local. . . . *Foreign-local* insists that seeming opposites can coexist in the same body at the same time but paradoxically also insists that those opposites remain fundamentally both separate and different" (2). Because the novel's chapters alternate between Bella's and Cliff's perspectives, from the outset Cliff voices the paradoxes surrounding Bella's "foreign-local"-ness: "Dem people is from Foreign. De lady is a mix-blood, like she from Trinidad but a time I hear she call out to the boy and she don't sound Trini" (19). Kempadoo marks the differences between their narrative perspectives by writing Cliff's voice as accented, whereas the chapters that adopt Bella's perspective are written in a more formal register. The power differential between them runs along a second axis: aside from Bella's "foreign-local"-ness in Trinidad and Tobago, Kempadoo somewhat schematically makes Bella and Cliff represent the ethnic and social schisms that differentiate Trinidad and Tobago. As a small satellite island to Trinidad's regional economic powerhouse, Tobago is far less significant both politically and economically, a marginalization that Kempadoo telegraphs in the text early on, when Cliff's younger brother Ossi remarks that "when them Trinis come over to Tobago, they look like they come from Foreign" (17).[3] Foreign marks a whole host of qualities, but for Ossi, Cliff, and their peers in Plymouth, it signals class through easy access to the U.S. brand-name clothes, food, and household goods that saturate their media.

The novel's scopic regime reveals the dynamics of the power differential between Cliff and Bella's family, particularly given Kempadoo's dual-narrator structure that makes evident the divergences in how Bella and Cliff interpret their interactions. For example, chapter 6, "dem people," begins with their perspectives of the same event: Bella and her family having a day at the beach. First, Cliff dedicates two paragraphs to observing them, noting every nuance of their interactions (36–37). When Bella picks up the narrative, she allots only a single sentence to Cliff, "He's still out there, a silhouette on the boat" (37), reducing him to a two-dimensional postcard figure. Whereas Bella has the luxury of a simple glance, Cliff must carefully gauge their personalities and how they interact in order to successfully cultivate a friendship with Bella and her family. This power imbalance is exacerbated by the trope of photography that partially structures their relationship, in which Bella is the professional photographer, and Cliff, one of her subjects. In *Tres tristes tigres* and *L'Envers du décor* as well as *Tide Running*, the visual arts of photography and painting—and even vision itself—are used to signal the power to objectify as well as the inaccuracies of the stereotypes such objectification produces as when Bella dismisses her own images as "false pictures" (102). The prominent place of visual culture in these texts makes the argument for displacing visuality within the textual representation of performance events.

The conflicts in the novel's plot arise in part because of Bella's desire to qualify as entirely, not somewhat, local and therefore seeks to downplay the ways in which she is different from Cliff. The yearning for connection across difference, to know others, and the question of how such encounters can be structured and managed courses throughout the novel: photography is used bluntly to symbolize unbridgeable distances between persons whereas the multivalent trope of the Caribbean sea offers the possibility of connection through shared kinesthetic experiences. The text begins with Cliff's reflection on what he calls "that sea feeling," a feeling that the sea's rhythms give meaning to his own: "Is the same sea that does reach everywhere. When I look at the silva-line on the sea, it more far away than the skyline on the land. That's cause the sea so big. If I could'a never see it at all, nowhere 'round me, it go be like you lock me up. Drain something out'a me and leave a hole in me chest. I breathe in and let it out in time with the next swell'a water under me" (5). A kind of communion with the sea—seeing its vastness and bearing witness to its powerful activity over time—forms Cliff's core, and he synchs up his breath with the sea's breath, the slow exhaling "spluff" of its waves (3). Part of the meaningfulness of the sea is its sense of limitless reach and its possibility for carrying Cliff along with it to spaces and experiences beyond himself. For Bella, the sea as a place of connection derives from the sea's roiling activity that has the potential to strip individuals of the social differences that separate them on the shore: "An embarrassing-simple pleasure, being beat-up by the sea. Raised a pride in me to see such a thing. Something shared by people so different, a similarity so human and fine" (90). The fact that her husband and Cliff have the same reactions to the sea is a signal of a commonality that can serve as the basis for her friendship with Cliff. The sea and its potential capacity for easy connection goes unfulfilled—but the source of its connection, the shared kinesthetic sensation of the body engulfed by rough waters, presages the mode of relation that will be enunciated in the moment of performance. This leitmotif of a commonly felt kinesthetic response is replayed in the detailed description of the Sunday *fête*.

The hallmark of the *fête* is the darkness among the dancers and the interpretive adjustments that must take place when vision is blocked. Reading this literal darkness with Glissant's articulation of the concept of opacity shows us how we might learn to rely on sight differently. Opacity is "an epistemologically-grounded world vision that allows each subject the right to her or his own unknowability" (Murdoch 885), in which the centrality of interpreting and producing the world is foregrounded. Opacity is therefore one facet of a broader lifelong philosophical project for Glissant that he conceptualizes as *la Relation*, in which he describes the violent cross-cultural encounters that have formed a world system that privileges specificity, a "totality structured in a way that eradicates the hierarchical opposition between center and periphery" (Britton, *Glissant* 12). As a "creolized totality that contains difference without subsuming it to the same" (Lionnet 1508), opacity names an alternative to Eurocentric methodologies of acquiring data and demanding complete transparency from its objects of analysis. Central to establishing racial hierarchies that relegate broad categories of peoples to the category of the subhuman, or as a means of denying persons the right to full personhood, transparency and universality are strategies of encounter deployed in projects of colonial domination, as Glissant identifies them at the outset of *Discours antillais*: "We demand the right to obscurity [*l'opacité*]. Through which our anxiety to have a full existence becomes part of the universal drama of cultural transformation: the creativity of marginalized peoples who today confront the ideal of transparent universality, imposed by the West, with secretive and multiple manifestations of Diversity. [Note: The West is not in the West. It is a project, not a place]" (2; see French in *Discours* 14). What Glissant rejects here in championing opacity is the demand for understanding, if understanding begins with the violent demand for non-European peoples to translate their worldviews, philosophical grounds, and cultures into terms that can be evaluated along Eurocentric metrics and values, and results in the reduction of their "full existence."[4]

Like many postmodern theories of identity, opacity proposes that comprehensive and absolute truth about a person or collective is an impossible question. Here, aspects of one's own self are always opaque to oneself, let alone to another, and allowing oneself the space for unknowable complexities is not only an act of interpersonal generosity but also a necessary corrective to the assumption that rigorous research questions will always yield the most accurate knowledge. Opacity and Relation, like Agamben's whateverbeing, undergird forms of personhood defined by their fluid interplay. As Celia Britton explicates Glissant's opacity in comparison to Jean-Luc Nancy's work, opacity "is based neither on opposition nor on identification" (*Community* 37), and a sense of collectivity is "originary to the individual subject" (*Community* 36). This collectivity is literalized in practices of *sevís* and ekstasis, where the core values of consent and respect allow you to be fundamentally unknowable instead of requiring that other persons translate themselves into terms that are familiar and comprehensible to you. Instead of requiring a one-to-one translation between cultures, opacity values the specificity that is untranslatable, and locates itself in "the remainder that is left over whenever I try to convert an element from one system to another" (Prieto 116). In this sense, opacity is equally germane to the project of interart analysis, where two forms of representation collide within an ekphrasis, as it is to the ways in which individual characters are portrayed as encountering one another in a context of domination and uneven power.

Within the emphasis on visual evaluation that characterizes the majority of *Tide Running*, the ekphrastic representation of the dance circle that literally takes place in the dark creates an excursus for a thought experiment: if transparent access to knowledge of an other is impossible and, moreover, a form of ontological violence, what models for knowing another person does obscured vision facilitate? The Plymouth Sunday school *fête* at the Paris rumshop and the fishing shed offers a rare opportunity to set aside visual observation and experiment with the tactile.

> She disappear gone in the thick black center'a the shed. Oiling-down with the big lump'a bodies. In there does be clampy, man tie 'round woman, bumsey and breast pasting you down. Girls don't mind what on they bumper. Pusspiration running high, hot and sweaty. *Hold a gyal and give she, gi' she jukie-jukie. Hold a man and give he, gi' he jukie-jukie.* The bass in there does pump up you blood, thunder you chest. Battie-rider short pants riding, pum-pum shorts rolling, pedal-pushers pushing. (40–41)

The dark closeness of the dance space, as Cliff narrates it, demands different sensibilities: the visually impenetrable darkness of this particular dance floor means that the stereotypical modes of evaluation and hierarchization are unavailable. Each character, usually so clearly and visually marked by her or his degree of Foreign-local or foreignness throughout *Tide Running*, disappears in the dance circle's collectively-formed "dark center." From Cliff's perspective, momentarily outside of the circle, by not minding "what on they bumper" or who their dance partners might be, women and men discard any utilitarian criteria for their partners' class or appearance. In the dense mass of bodies that are undifferentiated by status, the sensorial apparatus to which everyone has access in this moment is touch.

After citing the song lyrics, Kempadoo describes the internal aspect of tactility, the kinesthetic effects of music's vibration as heartbeats and circulations are reorganized along the beats of the bass. Reading with Merleau-Ponty's *The Visible and the Invisible*, Paterson describes this activity as "the kinaesthetic body responding to the movements, texture and rhythms of its surrounds, the dehiscence (the bursting forth of the massy body into the material world) [which] suggests that flesh has a resonance, a vibration, a texture of its own that responds to the textures of the world" (161–62). In the description of bodies dancing together, the resonance of flesh with the textures that surround it has both a cutaneous and an internal response: on the skin's surface, sweat binds the dancing bodies to one another, oiling and pasting them together in Kempadoo's viscous vocabulary of what bodies produce together. The way that bodies in this dance circle respond to the textural quality of the music is defined a kind of reciprocity between dancers: the "clamping" and "tying round" gestures place their bodies in a contact of mutual possession, and bass pumping their blood at the same rate aligns all of their bodies along the same rhythm. In the dark, the dancers engage in a kind of temporary nonhierarchical mode of encounter where instead of acquiring knowledge about what differentiates them, what is legible is their shared internal and external transformation to the music.

Viscous textures permeate Kempadoo's ekphrasis of performance; this texture is in part a direct result of the denseness of the physical space, characteristic of social dance spaces throughout the Caribbean as in dancehall, where, as Sonjah Stanley Niaah writes, "No space is ever too small to stage an event, as the more persons there are bursting at the seams of the venue, the more successful the event is" (60). This physical "oiling-down," "pasting," and "pusspiration running" has, I argue, an affective dimension of close connection, a dimension Eve Kosofsky Sedgwick suggests in her definition of desire in *Touching Feeling*: "I will be using 'desire' . . . not for a particular affective state or emotion, but for the affective or social force, *the glue*, even when its manifestation is hostility or hatred or something less emotively charged, that shapes an important relationship" (18). The intimate reciprocity physically and affectively generated on the dance floor is grounded in a mutual vulnerability, for, as is well established, to touch is also to be touched—albeit differently—by the other. Whatever you learn about the other, you open yourself to the other learning about you. As such, touch changes the power dynamics between researcher and her object of inquiry, and, as is salient to both the characters in *Tide Running* and *Tres tristes tigres*, the dynamics of capture between a photographer and her subject. Thus when Jennifer Fischer writes about touch performances that "where vision affords an all-knowing transcendent perspective, touch implicates the beholder in often unpredictable ways" (173), one of the consequences is the transformation of beholder into equally beholden. The coimplication of touch requires that the drive for an "all-knowing perspective" be suspended and replaced with the felt recognition of the depths of what cannot be seen. As vision loses its clarity and the hierarchical relationship of surveillance loses its characteristic distance in this brief Fanonian circle in *Tide Running*, the thought experiment of literalizing Glissant's theorization of opacity with its implicit rejection of transparent vision opens a space for considering how touch might temporarily allow for nonhierarchical forms of encounter.

However, as we see in this same event, touch in no way guarantees mutual vulnerability, and "feeling" in particular can function as a code word for a generalized exotic sensibility that is an important part of how some tourists expect to interact with Caribbean spaces.[5] Cliff cannot give up the distinctions between himself and Bella, for if he allows himself to see her and her family as much more than walking legal tender, he risks losing the monetary benefits associated with befriending them. Kempadoo reveals Cliff's ambivalence through his relationship to the music playing in the rumshop. Whereas the volume of the music can disrupt exploitative social formations, Cliff uses the music at the club to orient himself away from the collective dancers, as when he sings his own version of Buju Banton's 1995 "'Til I'm Laid to Rest."[6] In an interart analysis of *Tide Running*, I cite the lyrics of the song's chorus side by side with Cliff's version to highlight how Cliff productively mishears the source:

Lyrics on *Til Shiloh* liner notes	Cliff's lyrics
Til I'm laid to rest	——
Always be depressed	Always be de best,
There's no life in the West	there's no life in de West
I know the East is the best	——
All the propaganda they spread	Propaganda dem'a press,
Tongues will have to confess	times will have to confess
I'm in bondage living is a mess	I'm in bondage, living is a mess. (40)

Cliff's version eradicates the political overtones of Banton's lyrics by skipping over the reference to the Rastafarian repatriation project and by omitting the last stanza, where Banton calls upon his listeners to "organize and centralize, come as one," intimating the need to form a communitarian alternative to a destructive capitalist system.[7]

Cliff's productive mishearing marks a pivotal moment in Kempadoo's representation of performance, the moment where Cliff is able to regain his leverage at the *fête* and reject the suggestions made in the Banton lyrics. Here, Cliff only sings along the lines that he deems appropriate to his situation, as in "I'm in bondage, living is a mess." Both versions associate this physical confinement with a spatial stasis and they both long for the opportunity to move out of their insularity. But the African East to which Buju Banton looks is off the map of Cliff's consciousness. Indeed, his misquotation of the first line, "always be de best" instead of "always be depressed," brings forth a contradiction in his self-identification: he does not deny that he is currently living on the bottom rung of a hierarchical society, but by articulating himself as "de best," he indicates that his desire is not, as it is Banton's, to reorganize the system of wealth distribution but only to elevate his own status such that it might correspond with his sense of self. Cliff reorients the lyrics so as to find in them a rallying cry for his desire to transform his class status within an exploitative hierarchical system. In Kempadoo's ekphrasis of the dancers at the *fête*, a tension emerges between Glissant's opacity, with its built-in safeguard for what is specific to and unknowable in each person, and the Fanonian circle, with its drive to explicate the meaning of a dance circle to the reader who is positioned outside of that circle. These dance circles are contingent in part because of their logistics, but also because they require the audience to participate in creating the energy, texture, and feeling of permissive protection that constitute such a circle. And, in Kempadoo's novel, as in Cabrera Infante's representation of *el chowcito*, the narrating audience member who witnesses as he participates is ambivalent in his commitment to setting aside the usefulness of distanced vision and of becoming the audience that might allow the performer to move outside of stereotyped encounters.

The Feeling of Family: Guillermo Cabrera Infante's *Tres tristes tigres*

Kempadoo, Cabrera Infante, and Pépin all embed critiques of the visual into their novels by relying on the classical idea that touch is the most trustworthy sense because its proximity allows for personal verification. Abandoning spectatorship in favor of the vulnerability of participation relies on accessing information through the liquid textures of bodies sweating close to one another; in turn, it allows the audience-participants to interpret the performance event they experience beyond expected stereotypes. In Cabrera Infante's *Tres tristes tigres* (*TTT*), the spectacular nature of the Havana nightlife places vision as the predominant source of information and mode of interpretation at the center of the novel. But slightly off-center is a site that Cabrera Infante situates as exceptional in every way, including the dominance of the visual. Narrated by the professional photographer Códac, *el chowcito*, or the after-after show where performers go to unwind once their night's work is done, offers an alternative to the economic transactions that undergird the performances at the famous Tropicana Club by structuring performance engagements according to what we might call "the feeling of family." So what defines *el chowcito* is not a space that has been dedicated to it but the presence of the people who feel connected to each other through their shared love for their artistry. The feeling of family thus is what transforms the proscenium stage in the nightclub into a site for the protective permission of the circle. Cabrera Infante's exactingly detailed description of the relationships between audience members and performers who take the stage to improvise together makes the narration of *el chowcito* in *TTT* an example of a Fanonian circle in its extension of permission and protection for experimentation.

Throughout his career, Guillermo Cabrera Infante was invested in moving across different artistic genres as evidenced by in his obsession with filmmaking and the capacity to bring the moving image into exchange with the written word. Born in 1929 in the Oriente province, he moved in 1941 to Havana, the city that would become the setting of much of his fiction. While he opposed the Batista regime and was part of the cultural wing of the Castro government from 1959 to 1965, he officially exiled himself in 1965 and moved to London in 1966, where he lived until his death in 2005. His degree was in journalism, and in addition to a prolific career as a novelist, he was a film critic, wrote screenplays, and translated his own work and others, including James Joyce's *Dubliners*. His wide range of activities indicates a lifelong interest in how art can be translated from one genre or language to another. As Justo Ulloa and Leonor Ulloa write of Cabrera Infante's career, "[He] has produced a hybrid genre that seeks to provide a place in history for those revolutionary Cuban writers like himself who are no longer in favor with the political left" (141). Throughout his career, his work has been lauded, from the 1960s, when he was included among the Latin American Boom writers, to his receipt of the Miguel de Cervantes Prize in 1997.

Cabrera Infante's masterpiece *Tres tristes tigres* (*TTT*) was first published in 1967. An impossibly wide-ranging novel, *TTT* has been read as being about the word and the instability of language (Rodríguez Monegal, Levine), the city as a main character (Winks), or the fragile stratagems of a people facing adversity, as David Gallagher puts it in his challenge to those who criticize Cabrera Infante as being nostalgic for the Batista regime (69). Cabrera Infante himself has written on numerous occasions about what compelled him to write the novel, offering up different stories of the novel's origins, all of which might be encompassed as the driving impulse to respond to what was lost in the wake of the Cuban Revolution.[8] One such story surrounds the 1961 censorship of the short film *P.M.* directed by his brother, Saba Cabrera Infante, that attempted to evoke "a view of Havana after dark, the camera peeping into the small cafes and bars and dives patronized by the common Cuban having a last time before the political night closed in" (*Mea Cuba* 484). In this story, Guillermo Cabrera Infante writes that *TTT* came about as he tried to create *P.M.* "por otros medios," that is, by other means, or to translate the phrase literally, using other media. Another story is that *TTT* had its first iteration as "Ella cantaba boleros" (She sang boleros), a short story published in October 1961 in *Lunes de la Revolution*, a literary journal originally run by Cabrera Infante.[9] The short story was a response to the deaths of his mother and the famous Cuban singer La Freddy, which, on a personal and national level, signaled to him the end of a Cuba he had known and treasured. In *TTT*, "Ella cantaba boleros" eventually becomes a series of eight vignettes about La Freddy's fictional counterpart, La Estrella, "the star," that are dispersed throughout the novel. Connecting all of these stories of origin is the urgency to write about and re-create the world of pre-Revolutionary Havana nightlife with the knowledge of what Cabrera Infante thought of as its disappearance.

A five-hundred-page novel divided up into many vignettes and narrated by a huge cast of characters who work in the nightlife, *TTT* is held together by the eponymous tigers and their friends: the actor Arsenio, the movie critic and writer Silvestre, the wordsmith Bustrófedon, and their friends, the *bongosero* Eribó and the photographer Códac.[10] They cruise the city at night looking for art and meaning, more often than not finding themselves at the famous Tropicana Club, spectators to the moneymaking spectacles of mediocre but beautiful singers such as Cuba Venegas. Compared to the heartrending performers who populate *el chowcito*, such as La Estrella, Cuba Venegas's musical mediocrity is an offense to the narrators, and she comes to symbolize the success of untalented performers who rise to fame because they can fulfill the exotic expectations of the tourists whose presence is critical to the major clubs' and casinos' financial health. Because the Tropicana Club then sets the standard for the club circuit, sites like *el chowcito* that counterbalance that standard take on an outsized sentimental importance in the novel's imaginary. Echoing Gallagher, I would suggest instead that what Cabrera Infante wishes to preserve in *TTT* is not Batista's

Cuba; it is instead a world where there was room for unofficial play, even if individual ingenuity needed to find its expression when circumventing the constraints of a corrupt and violent system. The death of Bustrófedon is a symbol for this relation between pressure and release: his wordplay and wisdom are presented as the result of a tumor physically pressuring his brain. Similarly, at *el chowcito*, the low production values make smoothly functioning performance events impossible and create the necessity for improvisation and unpredictability that are one source for the Fanonian circle's virtuosic performances.

TTT is dedicated to portraying the ways in which the participants and performers in "la farándula nocturna de La Habana" play off of the nightlife's main stages in a way that is reminiscent of Certeau's theorization of tacticians and strategists in *The Practice of Everyday Life*. In contrast to strategists who seek to replace repressive institutions and social organizations with more enlightened ones of their own conception, the participants of the dance circles seek no established locale or institutional permanence. By using "cross-cuts, fragments, cracks and lucky hits in the framework of a system" (38; see French in Certeau 62), they evade fixity, which in this case results in the evasion of artistic cooptation. The ephemerality and invisibility of the tacticians' mode of using urban space are forms of self-protection. Kempadoo's *fête*, Pépin's impromptu dance spaces, and especially *el chowcito* lack the sense of physical separation with which Fanon endows the dance circle in the evocation of "hillocks and riverbanks": these performance spaces must create zones of protection within the dense urban environments into which they are integrated. Probing at the city's fissures and seeking in its wounds the moment and space for spontaneous outbursts, these tacticians create spaces within the urban *quadrillage* where experimentation with corporeal resistance is permitted and protected.

The best way to get at what is distinctive about *el chowcito* is to use *TTT*'s own dichotomy in which *el chowcito* is compared to the famous Tropicana Club, mainstay of the tourism scene and commercial entertainment. Cabrera Infante opens the novel with a scene set at the Tropicana. This four-page prologue is a transcription of how the Master of Ceremonies, "El Emsí," opens the evening's performance at the club, starting off the novel's linguistic playful virtuosity with a splash. In his rollicking introduction to the show, the city, and the novel, he imports vocabulary and references to French, Brazilian Portuguese, and English, which he refers to as the language of "Chakespeare" (*TTT* 20), all of it in his idiosyncratic take on Cuban *choteo*, "the local language of sexual humor" (Levine 23), as he touts the club and its acts. The majority of his speech, however, is dedicated to identifying his audience members as he greets them, selecting out noteworthy individuals for special mention. In El Emsí's speech, the Tropicana is a place for spectacular performances, but it is also a space to see and be seen. Among the values that El Emsí's presentation highlights are wealth, fame, and their correlated factor, foreignness.

In the world of the Tropicana that Cabrera Infante describes, the "good neighbours" (20) quite literally come first, a fact El Emsí addresses directly when he finally turns his attention to the Cuban audience members:

> Cubans, countrymen, it is now time for us to give a warm hand to our clientele in the courtyard, who have welcomed with the proverbial generosity and typical courtesy of the Criollos, so typically ours, typically Cuban as these palm trees which you see at the end of the salon and these *guayaberas* (with a black tie, eh?) which is the typical dress of the elegant *habanero*, with that typical hospitality as always—our typitality, ho ho ho!—you have allowed *us* to present to *you* first our international clientele. (5; see Spanish in *TTT* 21)

"That typical hospitality as always" articulates the Cuban audience's training as colonized subjects under the purview of the United States' Good Neighbor policy, in which economic and cultural imbrication supposedly replaced military intervention with the same goal of ensuring that U.S. business interests were protected. The Tropicana's practice of ranking visitors first signals this long-standing political tradition. In this speech acknowledging the impact of the "ENORMOUS American audience of glamorous and distinguished tourists" (4) and with no less than six references to the "typical," El Emsí selects out the Tropicana's visual signifiers that will satisfy their visitors' expectations of Cubanness: "those palms . . . and those *guayaberas*." The stage at the Tropicana is dotted with palm trees to bring the evocation of the picturesque landscape into the interior space, and the *guayaberas* are provided by audience members themselves: that is, while they have come to enjoy the show, the Cuban audience members are also part of the Tropicana's set.

El Emsí on the one hand identifies the cultural expectations associated with the generalized Cuban audience, and on the other, calls out by name the members worthy of attention, thus dividing up the audience. He tracks all this social climbing and gauging not only verbally but also by literally shining a spotlight on the wealthy, famous, and therefore most valuable patrons at the show that evening. As in *Tide Running*, the presence of the photographer-narrator in *TTT* emphasizes visual evaluation as the means for producing this stereotyping system. For example, when el Emsí comes to the end of his announcements, he notices the photographer: "Lights! Lights! LIGHTS! (*Coño!*) Just a minute *amigo*, please, it's the ladies' turn now. But—hold it!—if it isn't our great Great Photographer of the Stars! *Sí, el Gran Fotógrafo de las Estrellas!* Not a great astronomer but our friend, the Official Photographer of Cuban Beauties. *El Gran Códac!* Let's greet him as he deserves. *Un aplauso!* A round of applause for the Great Códac" (7; see Spanish in *TTT* 23). While the bilingual reiterations and joking undercutting errors are part of El Emsí's rhetorical style, Cabrera Infante here foreshadows Códac's role in the production and circulation of stereotypical images of what Cuba has on offer for its visitors.[11] Vision dominates scientific inquiry because it is the easiest sense for which to produce a permanent record and, by standing in for the medium of photography and its use for U.S.-based commercial interests, Códac evokes photography as an instrument of imperial domination. Photography and the visual in this case are used to reinforce relations in which "Europeans had a monopoly over the scientific tools for measuring, testing, and recording, while their subjects often had (or at least were expected to present) only their immediate corporeal being" (Howes 4). In both *Tide Running* and *TTT*, the nuance and potential resistance to commodification *within* the art of photography is not addressed, and photography functions principally as a blunt instrument of (neo)colonial capture.[12]

At the Tropicana Club, the spot-lit visual display of wealth and conspicuous excess creates hierarchical evaluation of classes. However, at *el chowcito*, institutional permanence and economic capital do not determine worth; here, value is reassigned from a strictly capitalist system on a nightly basis. We are introduced to this space in the first "Ella cantaba boleros" vignette (70–80), as it takes place at the Las Vegas club after the after-show has finished. Their obligations to the club's patrons concluded, dancers and musicians congregate to perform with and for one each other. The status of commercial success is not applicable here as there is neither an economic incentive for artists to perform nor an imperative to conform to external expectations or commands. In his description of the values on which *el chowcito* is built, Cabrera Infante through the narrator Códac insists on *el chowcito*'s refusal of the socially sanctioned value of economic productivity:

> El chowcito era el grupo de gente que se reunía a descargar en la barra, pegados a la victrola, después que terminaba el último show y que descargando se

> negaban a reconocer que afuera era de día y que todo el mundo estaba ya trabajando hace rato o entrando al trabajo ahora mismo, todo el mundo menos este mundo de la gente que se sumergía en las noches y nadaba en cualquier hueco oscuro, aunque fuera artificial, en este mundo de los hombres rana de la noche. (73)
>
> (The *chowcito* was the group of people who got together to get lost in the bar and hang around the jukebox after the last show was out to do their own *descarga*, this Afro-Cuban jam session which they so completely and utterly lost themselves in that once they went down they simply never knew it was daylight somewhere up there and that the rest of the world's already working or going to work right now, all the world except this world of people who plunged into the night and swam into any rock pool large enough to sustain night life, no matter if it's artificial, in this underwater of the frogmen of the night.) (58)

In this explanation of what makes *el chowcito* special, Cabrera Infante uses two sets of contrasts: first, the world of commerce operates in the daylight, whereas *el chowcito* purposefully creates darkness for itself; second, he resignifies the connotations of artificiality, such that instead of the more common association with the superficial, its artifice references an environment deep enough for its inhabitants to be fully submerged within it. To return to the contrast with the Tropicana, it is the refusal to convert experience, sentiment, and relation into monetary value that is the hallmark of *el chowcito*.

Three physical qualities stand out in this description of *el chowcito*: its relative darkness, its status as a hole-in-the wall or "cualquier hueco oscuro" of the city's *quadrillage*, and the aquatic textures evoked by the reference to "los hombres de rana." Though less evident than the viscosity of the Sunday *fête* in Kempadoo's description, the liquidity of the environment requires total immersion in the physical and affective rules that govern relationships within *el chowcito*, and it is these distinctions that will make the textual Fanonian circle possible. These three elements allow its participants to temporarily escape the drive toward monetization that undergirds the intersection of money, status, and tourism in the Tropicana's performance environment. As an example, when Códac first encounters La Estrella, even though the cheapness of her clothes is part of his extremely thorough physical description, it is not until they have both left *el chowcito* that he actually computes: "I gave her a sharp look and saw that she was as poor as hell" (64; see Spanish in *TTT* 78). That is, the visual markers of status are momentarily superseded by *el chowcito*'s value system in forming his interpretation. In celebrating the rejection of economic exchange as the driver for interpersonal relations, Cabrera Infante risks reinscribing the fetishization of La Estrella's destitution as a sign of her Afro-Cuban authenticity. However, what I underline is less the cliché of the starving artist and more that *el chowcito* creates an environment in which interpretation of performances privileges an emotional connection between audience and performer over the visual signifiers of "Cuban typitality" that permeate the Tropicana.

To recall Fanon's description of the dance circle, its meaningfulness exists whether recognized by audiences or not. However, its interpretation as either "deciphered as in an open book" or as "unorganized" and random depends entirely on the audience members' disposition. The ekphrastic descriptions of performance events at *el chowcito*, as at Kempadoo's *fête* and the impromptu dance spaces in *L'Envers du décor*, are marked by a multivalent set of interpretive possibilities, a vacillation along a spectrum from generosity to exploitation that resonates with the way that José Piedra describes the multivalent quality of hip movement in Caribbean dance forms: "The rumba hips, exaggerated, voyeuristic, exhibitionist, deified, and prostituted as they might appear to be, might also be a signifier of both acceptance of our bodies and defiance of foreign impositions, and even further: a substitute for the silenced or muffled voice, and not just for women and through women" (107). When assessed according to the uneven power relations driven by economic exchange, the dancing body can be misread as prostituted. By crowding out and literally dimming the power relations that govern the interpretation of performances on other Havana stages, *el chowcito* encourages the interpretation of rumba hips as exercising their own self-possession in defiance of foreign control.

While watching the *rumbera* Oliva dance and La Estrella sing, Códac's training as a photographer of stars and socialites kicks in. As Aching has demonstrated, Códac will subject La Estrella to extreme visual violence, the first salvo of what will become Códac's ongoing efforts to assimilate La Estrella into the world associated with the Tropicana, or what Aching terms "a culture industry's demand for static, exportable icons of national culture" (106). Like Cliff at Kempadoo's *fête*, Códac quickly eclipses the interpretative modes that are possible at *el chowcito* in favor of a reversion to his training in image-production. I want to also suggest, through my reading of Códac's ambivalent audience engagement with

Oliva, that Cabrera Infante writes into his ekphrastic representation of *el chowcito* its transitory and contingent function as a dance circle:

> Como la música se iba cada vez que se apagaba la vitrola, la rumbera se quedaba en el aire y daba unos pasillos raros, largos, con su cuerpo tremendo y alargaba una pierna sepia, tierra ahora, chocolate ahora, tabaco ahora, azúcar, prieta ahora, canela ahora, café ahora, café con leche ahora, miel ahora, brillante por el sudor, tersa por el baile, en este momento dejando que la falda subiese por las rodillas redondas y pulidas y sepia y canela y tabaco y café y miel, sobre los muslos largos, llenos, elásticos y perfectos y su cara se echaba hacia atrás, arriba, a un lado, al otro, izquierda y derecha, atrás de nuevo, atrás siempre, atrás golpeando en la nuca, en la espalda escotada y radiante y tabaco, atrás y alante, moviendo las manos, los brazos, los hombros de una piel de increíble erotismo, increíblemente sensual, increíble siempre, moviéndolos por sobre los senos, al frente, sobre los senos llenos y duros, sueltos evidentemente, parados evidentemente, evidentemente suaves: la rumbera sin nada debajo, Oliva, se llamaba, se llama todavía por Brasil, ya sin pareja, suelta, libre ahora, con la cara de una niña terriblemente pervertida increíblemente inocente también, inventando el movimiento, el baile, la rumba ahora frente a mis ojos: todo el movimiento, toda África, todas las hembras, todo el baile, toda la vida, frente a mis ojos y yo sin una maldita cámara (76)

> But as the music stopped every time he switched off the jukebox, the dancer remained in the air and made a couple long delicate steps, her whole body trembling, and she stretched out a leg sepia one moment, then earth-brown, then chocolate, tobacco, sugar-colored, black, cinnamon now, now coffee, now white coffee, now honey, glittering with sweat, slick and taut through dancing, now in that moment letting her skirt ride up over her round polished sepia cinnamon tobacco coffee and honey-colored knee, over her long, broad, full, elastic, perfect thighs, and she tossed her head backward, forward, to one side, to the other, left and right, back again, always back, back till it struck her nape, her low-cut, gleaming Havana-colored shoulders, back and forward again, moving her hands, her arms, her shoulders, the skin on them incredibly erotic, incredibly sensual: always incredible, moving them around over her bosom, leaning forward, over her hard full breasts, obviously unstrapped and obviously erect, the nipples, obviously nutritious, her tits: the rumba dancer with absolutely nothing on underneath, Oliva, she was called, still is called in Brazil, unrivaled, with no strings attached, loose, free now, with the face of a terribly perverted little girl, yet innocent, inventing for the first time movement, the dance, the rumba at that moment in front of my eyes, all of my eyes and here I am without my fucking camera. (62)

At its core, this textual representation of the Fanonian circle foregrounds an environment in which performers' improvisation lead to performances that are recognized by their supportive audience not as self-exoticizing or unorganized, but as a virtuosic reinvention of forms.

Part of what drives Oliva's improvisation—and Códac's ability to notice her reinventions—are the low production values of *el chowcito*: the accident of the music's instability creates the circumstances for Oliva's adjustments and forces her to pace her rhythms differently. Oliva's response to the interruption of her music is to incorporate the suspense of that interruption into her movement, thus distending the audience's experience of time. In *distentio*, Ricoeur elaborates Augustine's solution for how future and past can occur within the point-like present moment "by entrusting to memory the fate of things past, and to expectation that of things to come" (11) such that an amplified experience of the present can include "the idea of the distended relation between expectation, memory, and attention" (9). Augustine's example of this threefold present that incorporates the vestiges of a long past and the portents of a long future is the resonance of sound. Here, in the jerking interruptions to the smooth passage of chronological time, Oliva calls attention to the presence of the past in the Afro-diasporic history of the rumba. However, as Melissa Blanco Borelli argues in her work on Cuban *rumberas* in Mexican cinema, the *rumbera* "cannot completely decide for herself how she wants to be seen because her body pertains to an economy of visibility within which it is assigned loaded signifiers: they supersede her" (218). For a moment here, when Códac assents that he perceives "toda Africa" in her movement, he has been jolted out of his spectatorship and instead participates in Oliva's resignification of her movement away from the economy of visibility as the sole system of interpretation.

The sensibility of the distended present is available to the reader through Códac's narration, which itself is marked by a progression toward a more fluid orientation to temporality. At the outset of his attempt to fully capture Oliva's dance in his vivid description, he strings together each isolated visual impression of color and movement with the conjunctions "ahora , , , ahora . . . ahora . . . y . . . y . . . y . . . ": each point-link instantiation of the present is separate, as if a series of frames divided by the clicks of a camera's shutter, stilling her moving body into distinct images as a camera would. But then, when he turns to describing her inventiveness, he jettisons the conjunctions. Casting aside distinctions between past and present along with the conjunctions, he speeds up the rhythm of his own language to join Oliva's, and his increasingly syntactically wild verbal account of the performance reflects the need for a new way to process and interpret what he sees, one in which meaning is generated in the transitions. So when Códac describes Oliva as representing an entire gender and continent, it is not that he seeks to essentialize either the idea of Woman or Africa, but that her constant motion makes it impossible for him to pin her down and to ascribe to her any one attribute. The oscillations and shifts between, for example, perversion and innocence, are so rapid that she incarnates the contradictions between her multiple personae simultaneously. In order for Oliva to produce this rich multiplicity of meanings, she requires an audience attuned to the African diasporic cultural forms that her body references, an audience who is capable of reading her body as expressing intellectual/corporeal meanings. Her rhythmic defamiliarization of the rumba, in part due to *el chowcito*'s contingencies, solicits Códac's increased attention and transforms his mode of interpretation from the camera's framing into a more expansive mode through which Códac is able to recognize in her dance a history of transculturation.

Oliva's performance asks of *el chowcito* to become an audience that is more participatory than it is observational, one that is more akin to a dance circle than the Tropicana. And later on in the novel and in Códac's oblique reference here as well, the narrators will comment that Oliva, "la rumbera sin nada debajo" (76), leaves Havana to become a dancer on the tourist circuit in Brazil. Her performance here could easily be interpreted as a risqué sample of exotica. But if this space serves as a temporary dance circle, it is because the audience is not disposed to reduce her to an exploited sex object. At the end of the evening, Cabrera Infante gives us a sense of the source of this disposition in the words of a waiter who addresses the group as "familia." Here, the narrator stresses the sincerity that exists in this artificial space: "No decía la palabra por decirla, decir familia y decir otra cosa bien diferente de familia, sino que quería decir familia de verdad" (78); "and he really meant it, family, he didn't say the word for the sake of saying it, saying family and really meaning something quite different from family, but family was what he meant, really" (63). By focusing on how the verb "decir" permits linguistic dishonesty in many social situations because it signifies both "to mean" and "to say"—and by implying that the two rarely coincide—Códac attempts to take his cue from the waiter that in *el chowcito* there is an absolute correspondence of words to meaning, between what people feel and what they express. This honesty is more commonly seen in the performers: "La Estrella's impulse to transform trivial or well-worn basic material—her *bolero* repertory—into a new statement in which sentiments become emotions, clichés wisdom, and ugliness a more profound beauty" (Winks 135). In the waiter's speech, we witness the ideal of *el chowcito:* performers offer vulnerability and candor to their audiences, and in a pact of mutual respect and support, audience members will participate in their performances rather than treat them as pure spectacle.

Particularly in Códac's last comment, "yo sín una maldita cámara," we see his frustration at having to use narration as a workaround for photographic documentation, his anger at the suspension of his primary role as an instrument of image production, and his continuing desire to be in a superior position of spectating power over the performer rather than audience-participant.[13] As such, Códac rejects the possibility offered by *el chowcito* to embrace opacity's call for being in relation to another person without demanding that they make themselves fully available for scrutiny. The transformation of the senses in this moment only temporarily destabilizes the use of vision for the capture of static images and to establish a power differential in which the personhood of the photographer's subject is diminished to object-hood. In general, as Christopher Winks rightly comments, Códac represents the "racist commercial machinery of stardom that, while it benefits a beautiful mulata like Cuba Venegas with more looks than voice, eventually undermines La Estrella's talent" (134). Moreover, throughout the novel, vision and sound are set at odds, surfacing most notably in the damaging conflict that surrounds La Estrella's failed rise to fame. I propose that Cabrera Infante both celebrates the ways "the common Cuban" enjoyed Havana after dark, as he writes about *P.M.*, and embeds into that celebration a deep suspicion of specularity. For in this rapidly eclipsed moment at *el chowcito*, where Códac is able to briefly engage with a performer in ways other than racist commodification, the emotional contagion he experiences and the disorientation it generates permits him to participate in the performance *beside* Oliva, using the interpretive matrix of the Fanonian circle by identifying the long histories of resistant ritual in her dance.

"Lâcher le Jus du Malheur" and Ernest Pépin's Conversions

Both *Tide Running* and *TTT* feature performance events where the shift in interpretative modes, from the visual to the tactile and kinesthetic, is contested and temporary. Pépin's use of performance to explore the senses in *L'Envers du décor* does not revert quickly to the status quo, but instead narrates a protagonist's progressive and permanent transformation. As such, the tone of these ekphrases is markedly different in its utopian orientation, and the spaces in which the performances take place do not have the same cramped sensation as they do in Kempadoo's and Cabrera Infante's writing. Here, a protagonist anchors himself in a community, and on the basis of that relation, fundamentally reorients not only his sense of self but also his very ideas about the formation of personhood. Pépin's driving metaphor for this conversion is the liquid that flows through the protagonist's body: sweat and tears remove the malignant pus from within him as the very matter that constitutes his physical interiority changes and therefore permits him access to new ideas, new interpretations of the environment that surrounds him, and new ways of being. As in *Tide Running* and *TTT*, it is the experience of participating in performance events that creates the conditions for experiencing movement as a way of knowing.

Ernest Pépin (Guadeloupe, b. 1950) has consistently been concerned with Guadeloupe's cultural production and its relationship to economic justice. He has balanced prolific, prize-winning literary production with active engagement as a public intellectual throughout his career. Since 1985, he has held various positions in the General Counsel of Guadeloupe, including director of cultural affairs. His first literary publication is a poetry collection, *Au verso du silence* (1984), and his second chapbook, *Boucan de mots libres*, which won the Casa de las Américas prize in 1991, is a bilingual book in which Nancy Morejón translated Pépin's work into Spanish. His novels *L'Homme au baton* (1992) and *Tambour-Babel* (1996) were both award-winners, and since then he has regularly alternated between publishing novels and poetry. The main concern that drives *L'Envers du décor* is identifying how Guadeloupe's cultural heritage can become a greater part of Guadeloupeans' daily lives. Throughout the novel, the protagonists discuss Guadeloupe's colonial histories and debate how to best address those histories as they move into Guadeloupe's future.

The title *L'Envers du décor* implies a binary between the picturesque and its opposite, and the novel itself indicates how this binary might resolve. Structured as a series of exchanges between the two protagonists, the Frenchman Jean-Paul LeBon and Anadine, an Afro-Guadeloupean matriarch figure, the plot primarily follows Jean-Paul's trajectory. His story begins with the decision of Jean-Paul and his then-wife Sylvie to leave their dreary lives in the outskirts of Paris for the exotic islands, choosing Guadeloupe without much forethought. In a gesture that encapsulates how they think of their relation to Guadeloupe, they open a fine dining restaurant and name it *Le Christophe Colomb.* When the restaurant fails, Sylvie leaves Jean-Paul, and he becomes a homeless beggar, living in complete destitution until Anadine rescues him. This loss of economic privilege sets off a set of experiences—namely Anadine's mentorship, camaraderie with a community of Haitian clandestine workers, and participating in pan-Caribbean performance events—through which Jean-Paul transforms how he imagines himself from a latter-day European discoverer to a champion of Afro-Creole cultural traditions. The novel attempts to shift the terms of the debate about Guadeloupe away from the picturesque entirely. As Anadine protests, "Je ne suis l'envers de rien du tout. Je suis moi!" (167, "I am not the inside out of anything at all. I am myself!"). In my readings, I analyze how participation as an audience member to performances is critical for Jean-Paul's transformation into a person whose self-definition does not hinge on its belonging to—or exotic difference from—a European norm.

Given the political relationship between France and Guadeloupe, Jean-Paul has the right to reside in Guadeloupe without being categorized as an immigrant or ex-pat. And yet, like Kempadoo's Bella, he is dogged by a sense of separate difference, to return to King's characterization of the "Foreign-local." To get at that paradoxical and ill-defined sensibility of being somewhat local, both Pépin and Kempadoo use Afro-Creole characters (Cliff and Anadine) as the standard-bearers for the local, depict the tourism industry as absolute nonbelonging, and employ characters (Jean-Paul and Bella) who navigate between the two extremes. In the chapters set in high-end tourist resorts in *Tide Running*, Bella encapsulates the criticism that the tourism industry in the Caribbean is a second iteration of colonialism, comparing its power dynamics to slavery: "Now tourism is the trade, the new crop" (116). Tourism in the Caribbean often functions as an externally controlled monocrop,[14] and "from an economic perspective, the move toward the creation or expansion of tourism within many island states can often merely shift the burden of dependence on larger metropoles from one form of production (e.g. agriculture) to another (e.g. experiences)" (Duval and Wilkinson 62–65). In referring to the dominance of the tourism industry in the Caribbean region, the fictional protagonists of these three novels are keenly aware of the role that tourism plays in perpetuating metropole-periphery relationships of economic power, as signaled in George Gmelch's observation that tourism began its precipitous growth in the region just as the sugar industry began to decline (7) and Ian Strachan's work in *Paradise and Plantation*, in which he argues that "like the plantation that gave birth to it, Caribbean tourism is rooted in export, the export of paradise to North America and Europe" (112).[15]

In these texts, however, criticisms of tourism are a vehicle for articulating questions about development more broadly. As in *Tide Running*, concerns targeting tourism "from Foreign" in *L'Envers* are an outlet for expressing resentment of the wealth and power disparities within the boundaries of the nation. Pépin, through the voice of Anadine, links up tourist attitudes about Creole culture with French economic and social policies that drain Guadeloupe's resources, specifically calling out the BUMIDOM[16] and the VAT[17] and characterizing these uneven exchanges as "On enlevait nos boyaux pour mettre de la paille" (129; They took out our guts and replaced it with straw). While Anadine is derisive of the political equality promised by 1946's departmentalization, her overt goal is not political independence from France. Instead, the approach that Anadine and Jean-Paul ultimately adopt to address what she metaphorically refers to as the socioeconomic disemboweling that results from belonging unequally to the French nation is a small-scale project of cultural renewal within their community. The formation of spaces and personal involvement that can sustain regular literary and *léwoz* soirées, evenings of theatricalized music and dance anchored around *gwoka*, is seen as a different engagement with Guadeloupean culture than the production of the picturesque that dominates the representation of the tourism industry in the novel. The postcard, Jean-Paul's ex-wife's Sylvie's second career as the painter of stereotypically traditional Creole scenes and landscapes, and the illustrated guidebook that is the tourists' "bible" (48) make vision the sense by which visitors confirm their expectations.[18]

Pépin explicitly contrasts the stasis of the visual arts and the kinesthesia of being an audience member to a musical event that takes place through the novel. Jean-Paul's exposure to performance events eventually undermines the simplicity of the stereotype. Toward the end of the novel, Pépin describes at length a Kassav concert from Anadine's perspective. In the 1980s, a group of Martinican and Guadeloupean musicians formed the group Kassav and pioneered the musical style that they called *zouk* after the "Martinican Creole word refer[ing] to a party at which the greatest freedom of expression is permitted. . . . [T]he hot, loud, and intense tempo of *zouk* encourages its listeners to jump-up in the streets, especially during Carnival time" (Berrian 44). Anadine describes how the whole audience dances in response to the live performance in terms of individual movements, how audience members are joined together by their shared responsiveness, and the transformational exchange between performers and audiences. Dancing together with Kassav playing music is, in Anadine's description, about transforming oneself and one another. She observes about herself that, despite her old bones (124), she is able to get down into the rhythm, and moreover, that her dancing transfers those rhythms into the ground connected to her feet: "je cadençais la terre." The most common use of "cadencer" is to describe how a person gets her own body into the rhythm, but here, Anadine uses the cadence of her rhythmic action to get the earth and herself in sync. The corporeal transfer of rhythm becomes a way of merging those who dance together: "Gibbon [*sic*] ansait, explosait ses jambes (mais c'étaient nos jambes!)" (124; Gibbon danced, exploded her legs [but they were our legs!]). The parenthetical integrates the audience response into the description of the movements of the vocalist Marie-José Gibon. Audience and performer are so synched that they have become momentarily substitutable for one another. Pépin's three-page description of the concert is set at a cultural center where Kassav is on a proscenium stage, and the audience faces the musicians. While it is not in the formation of a dance circle and lacks the crucial potential for anyone in the circle to jump into the middle, the momentary sense of communion between performer and audience shares with the circle the sacred nature of the performance event.

Pépin's ekphrases of performance in *L'Envers* are moments where dance and kinesthetic awareness create apertures in the definition of personhood, such as the characterization of the relation between performers and audience as so close as to be substitutable, and the possibility of accessing new ideas through movements that transform one's inner constitution. Anadine recognizes that her response to the music prompts revelatory ideas within her: "It was at that very moment, while listening to a solo, that I understand that we had invented the drum to knock on heaven's door. Beautiful knock! A serious knock! The arts center vibrated with our bodies. We were united, soldered together by the drummers' hands" (124). The drum's vibrations travels both vertically—as a petition to God so that he might alleviate suffering, a petition that began with the onset of slavery and continues through to this moment—and horizontally through the dancers who, by dancing on the drummer's rhythm, amplify the rhythm's resonance. Anadine's thoughts likewise move along both a long historical trajectory of struggles for self-possession and the present challenge that Jean-Paul faces. While Anadine can only know what takes place within herself, in checking in on Jean-Paul, she notices evidence of an internal conversion. Here Pépin returns to a motif he uses throughout the novel for conversion, the change in substance of the liquid that flows through the body, as Anadine comments: "son corps était en sueur et plus il transpirait, plus je voyait qu'il était en train de lâcher l'eau sale de la peine" (123; his body was sweating and the more he sweat, the more I saw that he was in the process of releasing the dirty water of sadness). The release, both physical and affective, is the result of his danced engagement with Kassav's musical performance.

One element that links the performance practices in which Jean-Paul participates to the dance circle just as in *el chowcito* and the Sunday *fête* is that they present the possibility for something unexpected to take place, in contrast to the visual arts, which are used in these texts to confirm stereotypical audience expectations. For Jean-Paul, retraining his initial colonial perspective is a hard-won challenge. Even after he has lost all his wealth and is wholly dependent on Anadine, his imagination of how he can interact with the landscape is limited to Eurocentric discovery narratives. When, for example, Anadine has put him to work clear-cutting the overgrowth on an abandoned lot, "he felt like one of the first colonizers" (51). But while he fantasizes a way in which he might retain his privilege, a small group of Haitian itinerant laborers pass him and, shocked to see a white man chopping cane, comment among themselves; "Since Dessalines, they had never see that!" (51). The oddity of a white man suffering in a cane field prompts a long debate among them about whether they, as the most marginalized and debased group of people in the region, should feel dissimilarity from Jean-Paul based on their racial difference or whether his current backbreaking labor should bind them together in solidarity. By helping Jean-Paul with his task without requiring payment for their services up front, the Haitian men model a possible path for relation. In their gesture of fraternal solidarity, they introduce Jean-Paul to a form of labor that is not driven by capitalist exchange: the Afro-diasporic *coumbite*, the traditional practice of cooperative labor and mutual aid among Haitian peasantry (Frank 112). His imaginary is broadened by this alternate mode of social relation.

In making the encounter with the unnamed Haitian men central to Jean-Paul's story, Pépin has occasion to call attention to one of the divisions that striate the region: the discrimination against migrants from other islands and the prejudice against Haitians in particular. Anadine, who is in all other ways an almost saintly character, voices this deeply held suspicion as she reveals that her fight for justice is limited by the borders of Guadeloupe. But Jean-Paul's relationship with Guadeloupe is not grounded in cultural inheritance as Anadine's is, nor does he share her xenophobia against Haitians. As such, he is in some ways more open to the heterogeneous and regional circulation of ideas that his participation in a dance circle with the Haitians opens up for him. After they have finished clearing the plot, the unnamed Haitian men take Jean-Paul back to an informal restaurant run by Choucoune, a Haitian woman with whom he will later have a tragic love affair.[19]At Choucoune's, they push the tables and chairs off to the side so that they can dance to the *compas* (*konpa*). For Pépin to choose this musical genre as the first experience that removes Jean-Paul entirely from his colonial mind-set is itself notable as this genre has a Pan-Caribbean formation of its own: although strongly associated with Haiti, it was heavily influenced by the Dominican *merengue* at its inception. The *compas* was a creolized musical form throughout its development, and it formally creates spaces for extensive musical quotation, that is, it is structurally capable of including a multiplicity of historical and cultural references.[20] Even while referencing a national musical form, Pépin alludes to the necessity for political connections between island nations to reflect the already existing cultural connections. As such, Pépin embeds a sense of regional history into Jean-Paul's Guadeloupean education.

Pépin names Jean-Paul's conversion and revelations—and the dance circle that the Haitians form around him to protect his exploration—"the miracle of the *compas*." In this improvised space,

> il sentit son corps se dégonfler en lâchant tout le jus, tout le pus de ses malheurs. Il devint léger, léger et voilà que, lui aussi il s'élevait dans l'air avec la virtuosité d'un oiseau foufou. Ses compères haïtiens avaient l'habitude des métamorphoses. Simplement, ils ne savaient pas que les Blancs aussi pouvaient entrer dans le corps d'un oiseau. Légèrement surpris, ils accompagnèrent les arabesques de Jean-Paul en battant des mains. Le miracle du compas se manifestait là, devant leurs yeux. Choucoune, elle-même, admirait ce Blanc qui dessinait des volutes, des boucles, des lassos au gré de son ivresse. (54)

> he felt his body deflate by letting go of all the juice, all the pus of his miseries. He became light, light and there it was that he lifted himself into the air with the virtuosity of a crested hummingbird as well. His Haitian brothers were accustomed to metamorphoses. They simply did not know that white men could also enter into the body of a bird. Lightly surprised, they accompanied Jean-Paul's arabesques by clapping their hands. The miracle of the *compas* was manifesting itself right there, before their eyes. Choucoune herself admired this white man who drew spirals, bows, lassos as his drunkenness bid him.

Together, a *compas*, a dancer, and a group of friends who urge the dancer to express whatever the music makes available to him convert Choucoune's informal restaurant into an unexpected and unlikely dance circle. Up to this moment, Jean-Paul has conceived of himself as a self-contained individual, having never experienced personhood as open in the model of African diasporic religious structures, wherein one welcomes the presence of collective and individual others and, consequently, takes on new attributes.

Experiencing music alters Jean-Paul's normal mode of relating to the world around him, beginning with the reconfiguration of his own body. His emotions take on corporeal form, first as dense liquids that keep him earthbound; then as the pus of misery dissipates, his body floats lightly above the earth. The verb "lâcher" used to describe this process is the same one that Anadine uses about Jean-Paul at the Kassav concert. After linking Jean-Paul's emotional change to the change in his body's constitution, Pépin describes Jean-Paul's dancing by comparing his movement to the animation of usually static objects. Beginning with the arabesque, either referring to curvilinear intertwined visual ornamentation or the ballet posture that features one horizontally extended leg, he then turns to similarly curvaceous but static objects—volute, boucle, and lasso—incorporating into dance and movement things that are not generally supposed to move. This animation in itself is not unusual. Pépin adopts the spectators' perspective to highlight that what is unexpected about this dance is the dancer's race. The practice of ekstasis is one that is wholly new for Jean-Paul, and he requires the circle of protection and permission around him to encourage his choreography, which is physical, emotional, and psychological labor all at once. Holding Jean-Paul's energy, Choucoune and the Haitian men he has just met create a circle with their handclaps, amplifying the CD recording with a live sound that affirms their presence and solidarity.

Unlike *Tide Running*, where vision is momentarily disabled by the darkness of the performance space, or *TTT*, where the narrator recognizes that the performance he witnesses will always evade photographic capture, the rebuke to the visual is more subtle in this text. Indeed, at first it seems that becoming a bird might offer Jean-Paul another opportunity to fantasize that he has a colonial mastery over the space, this time through "le survol," the survey. However, what and how Jean-Paul sees has been fundamentally thrown into a different balance by his dancing. Instead of a stable viewing platform that imbues the distanced viewer with a feeling of authority, as Certeau theorizes it, he takes on the attributes of the "foufou," the smallest of the hummingbirds that are indigenous to the Antilles, and he is endowed with a bird's-eye view and a bird's speed—a defamiliarizing perspective: "C'était un magma d'arbres, de fougères et de choses sauvages. Le tout en grande dévalée" (54; It was a magma of trees, ferns and wild things. The whole in a great downward tumble). Describing what Jean-Paul ascertains as the *action* of a tumble, Pépin replaces vision with kinesthesia as the sense by which Jean-Paul accesses information. We return to the question that guides this chapter: What can you know when you change how you access information and your mode of interpreting it? Here, Jean-Paul has access to a blur of activity, with the uncertainty of whether the motion is that of the land itself or his own; without any stasis that might allow him to visually capture the landscape, Jean-Paul must experiment with sensing a landscape that is made unclear—or opaque—by the speed at which it is seen.

Jean-Paul's kinesthetic experience, both his danced movement and the changes to his interior matter that this movement enacts, are important not only because they transform Jean-Paul himself, but also because their disorientations prepare him to interpret performances he witnesses as an audience-participant from a new perspective. For him to dislodge himself from narratives of colonial discoverer, it is necessary for Jean-Paul to be thrown off-balance. Once unsettled and in motion himself, he is able to undertake the process of becoming an audience-member to the performances he will witness. Indeed, as he flies out of Choucoune's home, he gazes upon the sea, but now, he sees it not as the fixed image of a picturesque landscape, but as dancing:

> Et il fut ébloui lorsqu'il survola la mer de la Côte sous le Vent. Soulevant ses jupes à la manière des danseuses de gwoka, voltigeant ses pieds en de grands tourbillons, creusant et recreusant ses reins dans une transe continue. La mer avait des mains. Ses mains étaient des îles! Et les îles pensives méditaient sur leur sort, se demandant pourquoi elles avaient tant de mal à se donner la main. (55)

> He was blown away when he flew over the sea of the "coast under the wind." Lifting its skirts in the fashion of the *gwoka* drum dancers, acrobatically fluttering its feet in great whirls, digging and digging in its hips in a continuous trance. The sea had hands. Its hands were islands! And the pensive islands meditated on their fate, asking themselves why they had such a hard time giving each other a hand.

The sea as a dancer brings together both local specificity and a pan-Caribbean political consciousness. Here, Pépin shifts from the *compas* musical style that guided Jean-Paul's dance at Choucoune's to *le gwoka* (big drum), a Guadeloupean musical style that since the 1980s has symbolized Guadeloupe's cultural autonomy and specificity.[21] Pépin chooses terms that signify both Guadeloupean specificity and regional characteristics: while the *gwoka* drum is strongly identified with Guadeloupe, it can also be found under slightly different names throughout the Caribbean; "la Côte sous le Vent" is the name of a region of Guadeloupe on the island of Basse-Terre, but is also a more generic designation for the leeward, or west coast of Caribbean islands. These references to local specificities that repeat themselves throughout the region are points of departure for the meditation on regional political and social cooperation that Jean-Paul is able to interpret in the sea's movement. For it is in the gesture of raising up and whirling the skirt to the *gwoka* beat that the islands, or the sea's hands, are able to recognize their mutual coordination and broadly consider other ways in which they might follow the lead of their shared dance.

Because of its detailed description and explication, ekphrasis can have a pedagogical role in the text, indicating through the audience's physical responses and epiphanies how a reader should interpret the textual representation of performance. In the three ekphrases examined in this chapter, the shift away from spectatorship and the distortion of the visual prompts the reader to ask what you can know when you give up stereotyping in *Tide Running*, exoticization in *TTT*, and the privilege of a colonial perspective in *L'Envers*. The attention to kinesthesia tracks the change in the audience's sense of balance that results from participating in the dance circle and the new ideas and perspectives to which the audience participants have access while in the circle that they themselves create. Like the mutual reciprocity of touch that has constituted the aesthetic focus of my readings, the circle and audience rely on each other completely in order to permit access to the audience members' kinesthetic transformation: the dynamic of a circle of permission and protection leads the narrators to change their interpretive mode from vision to kinesthesia and tactility, and the participation of the narrators as audience members helps sustain, even if for only a moment, the dance circles' safety of darkness, feeling of family, and miracle of the *compas* in these three texts. Fanon defines the dance circle as a site of permission and protection and in these ekphrases of contingent and vulnerable performances, it is its mutually dependent nature that emerges as the circle's core.

4 Staceyann Chin and Zoé Valdés

Sexilic Politics in the Blogosphere

Can a dance circle exist without the copresence of persons to form it? Just as the dark and densely textured spaces examined in chapter 3 stretch the concept of the dance circle to include spaces where performer and audience are not configured in a literal circle, this chapter looks to social media interactions for examples of the circle's permissive protection. Here, the dance circle stretches to sites where moving bodies are separated by time and space but are connected by digital networks. I analyze the online presence and interactive literary engagements of two Caribbean writers, Zoé Valdés and Staceyann Chin, in order to think through the text-based form of online writing as a site for the dynamics of the dance circle. The blog posts that I have selected for analysis vividly describe bodies in motion, but they are not examples of ekphrases of performance; rather, I propose that we consider that the circle is formed through the interactions between bloggers and their commenting readers, who, by lending their attentive and vocal support to the blogger's experimentations, function as audience-participants. This reading of responsive relationships that develop the comment sections of blogs into spaces for community formation depends on one of the early promises of an interactive Web: that it can connect people who would otherwise be separated by physical distance, creating communities through reading and responding to one another on a single website.

Of all the Caribbean writers who maintain blogs, I bring Valdés and Chin into comparison because one preoccupation of both blogs is exile propelled by sexuality, or "sexile." A neologism coined by Manuel Guzmán to identify the nexus of exile and unconventional gender, in sexile, the reasons that prompt exile also often lead to exclusion from the immigrant community.[1] Because their immediate circulation is not limited to a shared geographic space and because, for their commenters, online media can be largely anonymous, blogs are ideal media for navigating sexile. Through the conversations on Caribbeanness and unconventional sexualities on their individual blogs, they take up the spirit of M. Jacqui Alexander's question about economics, sexuality, and the Caribbean nation-state: "Why has the state focused such a repressive and regressive gaze on me and people like me?" (5). Valdés, Chin, and their blog communities create a space for criticizing state repression by queering Caribbean communities. Using the dynamics of live performance events, Valdés and Chin in concert with their readers radically redefine relation and community in the construction of blog-spaces as dance circles.

The phenomenon of sexile has been associated with the Caribbean region since the early 1980s following the Mariel boatlift, possibly the single most populous gay migration.[2] Recent efforts by Mariela Castro to reduce institutional homophobia in Cuba have quieted the narrative surrounding sexual discrimination as an important push factor for migration from Cuba. The region's reputation for cultural and institutional homophobia nevertheless continues to circulate[3] and is an important piece of Chin's and Valdés's narratives of their emigrations from Jamaica and Cuba, in which sexual discrimination ultimately made the lives they wanted to lead untenable.[4] The sexual discrimination they have experienced is, in many ways, not comparable as Chin identifies as a lesbian and Valdés does not. Rather than sexual practices, to place them in comparison, I draw on Rosamond King's inspired phrasing "unconventional gender," which she defines in *Island Bodies* as "any behavior, identity or disposition that transgresses or threatens the heteropatriarchal order" (22). A rejection of the state's constraints on personal freedom is, in both cases, aligned with transgressive sexual expression, and the trope of sexile is a starting point for creating Caribbean communities that are not physically anchored in the nation.

Staceyann Chin (1972–) grew up in the Montego Bay area of Jamaica, went to college at the University of the West Indies, Mona, and emigrated when she realized that protecting her physical well-being conflicted with her desire to be completely and uncompromisingly open about her sexuality. In 1997, she moved to Brooklyn and developed her career as a poet, touring and performing on Broadway with Def Jam Poetry. She has published four poetry chapbooks and written and performed three one-woman shows. In 2009, Chin published *The Other Side of Paradise*, a memoir of her childhood that was critically well received and commercially successful. Her memoir, a Jamaican "antiromance" in Donette

Francis's phrasing (161), follows the sexile trope closely by ending with the decision to migrate after being threatened with rape for being a lesbian. Although the memoir ends when she leaves Jamaica, her work does not treat the United States as a site for the unmitigated celebration of sexual freedom, as her poetry is sharply critical of U.S. class politics and racism.[5] As Kelly Baker Josephs notes, sexual politics, along with imagery drawn from the Caribbean and United States, are fused together, as "it is her immigration that enables her art, both in form and content" (47). In this regard, sexile gives her the platform to mount challenges against the places from which and to which she is exiled.

In her online writing, Chin creates a space where she and her commenters can express their intersecting desires and identities. Chin's use of digital media has always been one of cross-posting as dissemination. All of her blog posts were also cross-posted at MySpace in the late 2000s, and from 2007 she has gradually migrated her social media presence to Facebook. As of 2013, staceyannchin.com no longer exists as the host of her personal website, but I concentrate my analysis of her digital writing on the now-defunct *Cyberjournal* because of the effort and investment required by readers to visit and engage with her blog on her website.[6] Since 2011, she has written commentary for the *Guardian* as well as a series of pieces for the *Huffington Post* on the journey to motherhood for a single lesbian, performed poetry, given readings to promote *The Other Side of Paradise*, and written a new play, *Motherlode*. On *Cyberjournal*, she gives shape to this intersection of identities and continues to explore how the changing geographic and cultural contexts of migration to Brooklyn and her global travels complicate her self-representation.[7]

Zoé Valdés (1959–) is an immensely productive writer of fiction and nonfiction, filmmaker, and art gallery owner best known for her second novel, *La nada cuotidiana*, one of the quintessential texts about Cuba's Special Period. Published in 1995, the year that Valdés went into exile, *Nada* tells the semi-autobiographical story of a young woman growing up under, and becoming disillusioned with, the Cuban Revolution. Her work is the subject of polarized critical debate, varying from its evaluation as purely commercial and devoid of literary merit, to a creative engagement with genre parody, humor, and, as Isabel Alvarez Borland analyzes evocatively, "the recovery of a world lost to exile through the sensorial re-creation of the image" (346–47). Because of the subject matter and timing of her rise to literary fame, she is the pioneer of both what Esther Whitfield calls "Special Period fiction" (2), and the "new Cuban boom" which repeats the commercial marketing structure of the 1960s

Latin American Boom (55). As part of this group of Special Period fiction writers, Valdés is most often compared to the novelist Pedro Gutiérrez and the blogger Yoani Sánchez. All three portray post-1990 life in Cuba as "a dreary, enervating routine of food shortages, transportation troubles, and narrowed opportunity" (Rohter). But where there is little room for nostalgia in the presentist style of dirty realism that Gutiérrez cultivates (Birkenmaier 483), Valdés's blogging dwells in nostalgia in order to imagine alternative Cuban futures with her readership.

Valdés reads her relation to the Cuban state through its historical institutional homophobia as she merges her anticommunist politics with an articulation of sexual freedom in the face of what she characterizes as the Revolution's social conservatism and prudery. On her blog, Valdés revisits her relationship to Cuba from different points of her memory and her current experience; throughout, she consistently equates sexual repression with an absence of political freedom, pointing to this equation as the cause for her exile. The story Valdés tells of exile is that she left Cuba due to political and artistic repression.[8] While an equation between the legislated discrimination of homosexuality in the majority of Caribbean islands and Valdés's account of her relationship to the Cuban state does not hold, the state's categorization of Valdés's erotic writing as "sexually deviant"[9] and Chin's evocations of her lesbian sexuality exist along the same spectrum of threats to the nation's sense of moral order. The far-flung communities that Chin and Valdés foster in their online writing are comparable in that they mobilize frank discussion of sexuality in order to unsettle the status quo of the state's restrictions.

Valdés proposes that her blog can foster an imaginative space for reconceiving Cuban identity and community that is decidedly unaffiliated with other major movements. A vocal anti-Castrista, she nevertheless has no affiliation with the leaders of the Miami exile community, and she has openly derided Yoani Sánchez's political opposition to the Revolutionary regime from within Cuba. Instead, she has been in Paris since 1995 and aligns herself with the European literary festival circuit and Europe-based protests against the Cuban government. The community discussion that she permits on her blog, zoevaldes.net, follows her own ideological parameters. Although the commenters on her site are primarily friends and fans, there is the occasional dissenting commenter who challenges her positions on Cuban politics. For disagreeing, Valdés summarily dismisses them from her online space. In so doing, Valdés deepens the fault lines that have fractured the Cuban community since the late 1950s and creates a space that is narrowly circumscribed to dissident voices.

While Valdés and Chin both ground their narrations of exile in unconventional gender, the similarities in their politics end there: Valdés conjoins sexual deviance with anticommunism and locates this intersectionality in Cuba and not in Paris, whereas Chin reflects on the intersections of queer politics with race/color and class in both Jamaica and the United States. As a result, Chin emphasizes the far-flung geographical spatial capacities of the blog and focuses on radical queer politics, whereas Valdés tends to exploit the temporality of the blog and concentrate her sense of space on the island of Cuba as she constructs a definition of Cubanness that contests the communist state. They share, however, two poetic blogging practices: the hyperlink and audience/reader interaction. Throughout this chapter, first focusing on Chin, then on Valdés, I analyze their use of the formal characteristics of blog media as the impetus for their literary experimentation. Through the hyperlink, they consciously develop a form of interrupted reading that models, on a micro scale, the formation of diasporic communities, staggered and disrupted by migrations. Their writing solicits readerly interaction, and they integrate their readers' voices into their own blogging to highlight the blog's antiphonal quality—a quality that likewise characterizes live-performance dynamics. As I do throughout this book, I use Fanon's evocation of the dance circle to define how performance dynamics work in the context of the blog: "The circle of the dance is a permissive circle; it protects and permits" (57). The blog as a performance space is a circle composed of audience-participants who both permit and protect the performers' creative experimentation that emerges therein. Within these circles, Chin and Valdés counter their exclusions from the nation by creating alternative circuits of relation.

Blogger-Reader: A Web 2.0 Dance Circle

In his concise list of blog media's constitutive elements, Adrian Miles defines a blog as composed of short entries that support comments and that are individually written and self-sufficient.[10] The wide variety of blogs that fit this definition can be divided into three types: (1) personal, which function as public diaries; (2) topic-driven, where the blog's author(s) focus on a theme of varying specificity or breadth in which the author has particular interest or expertise; and (3) filter mode, which compiles hyperlinks to the best of the Internet from the blogger's point of view. While Chin and Valdés oscillate between all three modes, I will focus on longer-form essays and poems that display their dexterous use of blog media's formal elements. The formation of blogs through individual entries allows the blog hosts a great deal of flexibility in posting on a wide variety of topics without necessarily creating cohesiveness between them. Therefore, when returning to a single topic over a series of posts, blogs offer "a surface, a space, a site for potentially endless re-inscription" (Rettberg 114). The following analyses show that Chin and Valdés use blogs' capacity for reinscription in order to rearticulate the subject position and voice of Caribbean sexile. In its endless, noncohesive, and potentially contradictory returns to the same themes, the blog takes on the methodology of performance: repetitions with a difference that enable the slow and incremental transformation of knowledge.

I include this study of blogging as part of the broad investigation of how performance impacts Caribbean literature because I see blog media as drawing from both performance and literary practices. Focusing on the commenting feature of blogs, I compare the blog to the dance circle. Blogs have none of the live corporeal presence that most commonly defines performance environments and permits the engagement between performers and audiences. But blog media's formal elements do allow bloggers and their readers to engage in the "adaptive action of continuous feedback," which, as Lindemann argues, approximates the interactions between performer and audience on the blog (359). A relationship between blogger and reader is similar to that which exists between performer and audience in the dance circle in that immediate reader/audience responsiveness is a constitutive quality of both artistic forms. Just as the audience members form a protective circle around the performer who is then free to improvise on traditional forms and experiment aesthetically, a community of blog readers takes on an antiphonal role for bloggers, from encouraging continued writing to offering feedback when the blogger blunders. Every post contains an anticipatory quality, an undercurrent of desire for a "yes" to the question, "Is anyone out there?"[11] Readers' page-views and comments are therefore the "krak!" to the blogger's "krik?," and the presence of the comments section at the end of each and every post asks readers to justify the blogger's raison d'être and fend off the loneliness of the blogger's offline isolation.[12] The responsive interaction that commenting blog readers bring to blogs' comment sections therefore resonates with the participatory presence of audience members in a performance environment.

Reader participation is a constitutive element of blogging to the extent that Axel Bruns and Joanne Jacobs have proposed the term "produser" for blog readers, combining "producer" and "user" to reflect the contribution of blog readers to the production of a blog (5–6). Every writer is vulnerable to her readers, but while in the print publication world there is significant lag before the writer's work passes through the editorial gauntlet and into readers' hands, the blogger knows immediately whether any given post has attracted traffic or not, incited commentary or not, was linked to by other bloggers on Twitter and other social media or not. The pop culture bloggers Tom Fitzgerald and Lorenzo Marquez of www.tomandlorenzo.com comment movingly on how the visible presence of a responsive audience changed their lives: "When you have a blog that suddenly becomes 'talked about,' and when you feel like you're drowning out in the real world, that blog becomes your lifeline and the people who read and support you become, in many ways, more important to you than even your friends and family. Because those wonderful strangers are demonstrating something that even your closest compatriots sometimes fail to: they believe in you." Like the dance circle which breaks away from the "real world" to create the possibility of different social relations and new realities even if only temporarily, the online relationships of people who have never met face to face nevertheless create a kind of closeness that feels more substantive than physical copresence. This relationship, which can lead to a direct or indirect source of financial support, sustains bloggers in their writing projects, both on- and offline.[13] The temporal sense of immediacy builds audience responsiveness into the blog form that is closer to the performance event than it is to the print publication cycle, both by creating the constant anxiety that no one is reading and by providing the blogger with assurance of having a responsive readership. Audience encouragement is so critical to the continued existence of any blog that I would add an element to Miles's definition of the blog form: the need for readership.[14]

But the absence of publishing houses and editorial staff that is crucial to the conversational relationship between bloggers and readers calls into question the place of blog media as a literary form. The ephemeral aspect of the media, the brief and episodic features of posts, and the fact that the vast majority of blogs are self-published and thus often endure no editorial vetting process, distinguish it from print-based literature. In *Blog Theory*, Jodi Dean uses Walter Ong's concept of "secondary orality" to argue that blog posts are not literature because, as media, they are in between orality and literacy. The basis for my work on blogs, likewise, is that digital media lie between performance and literary practices. However, I disagree with Dean's suggestion that the collision of oral and literary practices impoverishes the written form and that, as a result, blogs should be excluded from the category of literature. For Dean, the rhetorical tools that structure orality, such as repetition and using personal experience as evidence, are evidence that blogging loses the analytical or exploratory aspects of creative writing.[15] In contrast, I locate the intersection of orality and literacy in digital media in the performance dynamics of responsive relationships between blogger and reader. Moreover, in analyzing Chin's and Valdés's blog writing for example, it becomes evident that they craft their poetry and essays for their blogs with the limitations and possibilities of the media in mind. Rather than lying outside of literature, then, I argue that the formal elements of blog—particularly the hyperlinking capacity, temporality, and capacity for readerly interactivity—present creative challenges for writers.

Outside of Dean's rhetorical analysis, the concern that blogging is not an appropriate site for literary production derives from the sensation of unpolished, unedited immediacy—a direct and unmediated connection between blogger and reader. In an interview by Nicholas Laughlin, Marlon James encapsulates this sentiment when he responds to the question "Do you think of your blog as a literary work?" with the answer: "No. A searching exercise yes. A playground for thoughts to grow certainly. My amateur attempts at journalism, probably." For James, the media's temporality creates a forum for amateurish exercises and underdeveloped ideas. However, writing the story as it proceeds does allow for crafting a stronger relationship between writer and reader. The poems Chin produces on *Cyberjournal* can create precisely this impression, as they occasionally seem like the result of Chin's juxtaposition of unconnected thoughts, written as if recording thoughts tumbling from her mind simply as they fall. Combinations such as:

I wish I could drive.

Downtown Decatur
I forgot my vibrator

shit

in "Up and Down," the first post published on *Cyberjournal* on October 29, 2003, set the tone for Chin's interactions with her audience: humor, politics, and a deep investment in corporeal experience. "Up and Down" is emblematic of Valdés's and Chin's blogging production in that Chin signals what it looks like to write on a blog, to truly engage with the media—as opposed to only using a blog to publish writing that could just as easily be printed elsewhere. Like much of Chin's blogging, "Up and Down" reflects on what blog media has to offer: its sense of presentist immediacy and its community-building capacity.

"Up and Down" is a meditation on the promise and failure of blog media. Chin calls attention to the ways in which these media, touted for their constant availability, become unavailable. This first post inaugurates and christens the new website, but it also picks up from another older, previously discarded blog. Commenting on the new space and the loss of the previous incarnation of her blogspace prompts reflection on the instability of the media: "no luxury of a continuance / a thought carried over / a brooding given from one frame to the next." Any illusion of total accessibility is belied by confessing the instability of her own blogging experiences: the sites go up and down, and with each inscrutable technological failure—"each time these hosts and servers and what nots / fuck up / I start again"—written words disappear and the writer begins seemingly anew, a fresh first blog post even as it is *in medias res*. Archives stored online disappear, connections are interrupted, and the ideal of immediate access is unstable.[16] While the Internet promises to overcome physical distance in connecting writers and readers, it is subject to the temporal frustrations incurred as slow connection speeds prevent pages from loading at a reasonable pace. Particularly salient in connecting readers residing in nations with unreliable fiberoptics infrastructure, the economics of bandwidth can disrupt this form of connection; as corporate interests drive legislative efforts to end Net Neutrality, the digital divide seems likely to grow over time, not shrink.[17]

The unstable immediacy of the media is the subject of Chin's anxiety about writing on the blog, but also appropriately mirrors the themes of constant movement and transformation that ground Chin's narration of self in the blog form. As Dean describes it: "Blogging is not told as a story but presented in moments as an image, reaction, feeling, or event. [Blog posts] are immediacy saved, conversations preserved" (47). This reflection on writing the blog concords precisely with how reading the blog functions: taken as a whole, the blogger's persona emerges, but posts do not necessarily connect to one another or provide stylistic unity. As Chin moves through the post, she enunciates the purpose that blogging serves for her as a writer: to chronicle her current intellectual community by noting who she is reading and meeting—complete with hyperlinks that invite her readers to share her reading list, to reflect on her present state of being and her present actions, and to catalogue these passions and projects as they exist in the moment, knowing that they will change, morph, and disappear as her previous blog had and the blog she inaugurated with this post eventually did.

For several years, Zoé Valdés's purpose for blogging was stated in the right-hand sidebar of her blog under the heading "Aviso a los lectores," the text of which was drawn from a post entitled "Información a los lectores. Information aux lecteurs." There, she begins by outlining the blog's origins:

> Como les he informado con anterioridad empecé a hacer un blog hace cuatro años en la calma más absoluta, concentrada en mis temas favoritos, buscando un espacio de encuentro con ustedes, de pensamiento, de intercambio de ideas, y también de divertimento.
>
> As I have already mentioned to you, I began to write a blog four years ago in the most complete calm, concentrating on my favorite themes, looking for a space to meet you all, to think, to exchange ideas, and also to have fun.[18]

The shift in pronouns in this description encapsulates the relationships on Valdés's blog: first comes "my themes," then she turns to "with you." Direction comes from Valdés and trickles down to her readers. However, immediately after this paragraph, which focuses on an openness of exchange, she contrasts her original blogging concerns with problems in the blogosphere that have emerged throughout the past four years. She asserts that some commenters on her blog have used that space to wage a defamation campaign against her including slanderous accusations of plagiarism, unauthorized use of material she has published on her blog, and attacks against her person and her work. She identifies the source of these attacks as "un plan // de los servicios secretos castristas, de linchamiento social y político," a strategy of social and political lynching on the part of the Castro secret service. As such, Valdés's introduction to her blog presents a space of open exchange and participation—but only within the context of having to construct defenses against politically motivated destruction. Any vulnerability she offers her readership is explicitly protected by a technological fortress mentality, complete with martial metaphors of attacks and defenses.

"Información a los lectores" is a measured description of her approach to blogging, with bullet points of evidence and a line mentioning that this "aviso," or warning, has been written under the advisement of legal representation. It encapsulates a sentiment and approach that Valdés articulates in the comment sections of individual blog posts and that is most prominent in an addendum she wrote to "Memoria del ciclón Flora," a 2008 blog post in which she rebukes a commenter for participating in a campaign of defamation against her. The original post consists of a photo-portrait of Valdés at age ten and a two-paragraph vignette of her recollections of living through hurricanes. It is followed by a header in all caps, "ACLARACIÓN SIN DEMORA," or clarification without delay, and then a response to a comment that she had already scrubbed from the comment section. The "aclaración" is as long as the post itself and blends a response to the criticisms articulated by the unnamed commenter with a generalized warning to that commenter and anyone who might use the same line of attack:

> Alguien que entra desde Cuba en esta bitácora, y que sé muy bien quién es, aunque enmascare su nombre, y que me llama por los graciosos calificativos de "puta, tortillera," etc, (podría añadir "maricón" y "travesti," esos me gustan hasta el orgasmo, yo soy muy maricona, todo lo maricón me hechiza) me sugiere que cambie la foto que puse de cabecilla en este blog porque ahí yo tenía catorce años. . . . La próxima vez publicaré tu nombre y tu IP. No lo hago ahora porque de este lado hay una ética y un respeto, que por cierto, yo siempre tuve con los demás cuando vivía en Cuba, como podrás muy bien recordar, porque de ese respeto y de esa ética mía te has beneficiado ampliamente. Si no te gusta mi blog o te trae malos pensamientos, perdón, o cargos de conciencia, no entres. Así me ahorras borrar tus comentarios inmundos.
>
> Someone who is coming onto this blog from Cuba, and I know perfectly well who it is, even if they disguise his or her name, and who calls me by the gracious epithets of "whore, dyke," etc, (they could add "fag" and "tranny," I love those to the point of orgasm, I am very faggy, everything fag enchants me) suggests that I change the photograph in my blog header because in that picture I was only fourteen. . . . The next time I will publish your name and your IP address. I am not doing it now because, on this side there is ethics and respect, which I would note, I always employed with others when I lived in Cuba, as you could do well to remember, because you have benefited greatly from my respect and ethics. If you don't like my blog or it brings you bad thoughts, or rather, a weight on your conscience, then don't come onto it. That way you'll save me the trouble of erasing your repulsive comments.

In contrast to "Información," here Valdés jumps from self-defense to reminiscence to the threat of doxxing anonymous commenters, or publishing their private identification. The two articulations of the same idea—"Información" as a general statement, "aclaración" as a personal and specific response—demonstrate blogging's spectrum of spontaneity: from the seemingly off-the-cuff recording of ideas and emotions, to commentary that evidently has undergone a meticulous drafting and editing process.

In this spontaneous defense of her person, politics, and blog, Valdés articulates the nexus of anti-Castrismo and unconventional gender that is characteristic of how she deploys sexilic politics on her blog. As she presents it, her space is invaded by a Cuban Castrista who, along with petty criticisms, insults her for an expression of sexuality that is not state-sanctioned. Valdés is married, and a mother, but she also writes erotically charged and sexually explicit novels. This, combined with her insistence on circumventing Cuban institutions to market her work, places her outside the bounds of acceptable economic behavior in a socialist country. Both her critics and, ultimately, Valdés herself express this deviation from the norm in queered sexual terms: "whore, dyke." These interactions shape her editorial approach to blogging where writing is publicly visible, but participation is closely controlled and individually vetted. In contrast, Chin discusses homophobic environments in the United States and in Jamaica but rarely mentions the state as a particular antagonist. As a result, the approaches both bloggers take to their relationships with commenting readers create very different senses of crafting online spaces: Valdés constructs a safe space for her commenting readers and herself in direct and loudly voiced opposition to the Cuban government—a space that requires constant defense; for Chin's *Cyberjournal*, the intersection of oppressions that she experiences are primarily offline.[19] *Cyberjournal* was therefore a space where Chin's poetic reflections on sexilic politics were amplified by her commenting readers' responses about their experiences. In both spaces, bloggers and commenters contribute to the tenor of the online space through its mutual use.

Staceyann Chin's Amplifications in the Remix

One impulse for the creation of *Cyberjournal* was to allow audience members with whom Chin connected during her live spoken-word poetry performances to extend their connection. So while Chin's blog posts on *Cyberjournal* and elsewhere feature a range of personal reflections and topics, her practice of mentioning her current touring location offers live audience members a specific commenting space in another venue to respond and react to her work. In all of her social media platforms, commenting readers engage widely with Chin's writing. In *Cyberjournal*, which, given its 2013 disappearance, I treat as a past-tense event, some commenters only stopped by to corroborate their presence at her live shows, but more often, they took up the topics Chin articulated in specific blog posts and amplified them with their own experiences. Together, Chin and her commenting readers mobilized the blog to push against homophobia. As such, in Chin's use of the digital setting, new strategies of writing—and reading—emerged: blog media and its temporality of presentism produced, in Chin's blogged poetry, a sense of the wide range of thoughts, geographic spaces, and interlocutors that shaped her world. These many references and influences reflected a heterogeneous writing experience and created a practice of interrupted reading where the heterogeneity of Chin's references entered into, interrupted, and remixed the poems themselves. In discussing Chin's blogging production, I focus on how audience members are converted from many different points of contact into commenting readers, the interactions between Chin's poetry and that of her readers, and the strategy of the remix: all elements that lead me to propose that amplification characterizes Chin's approach to digital writing.

Upon arrival at the no longer extant www.staceyannchin.com/v2/index.html, the screen went entirely black with a graffiti-style header of Staceyann Chin's name and, on the left, a silhouette drawing of Chin in action: feet in an open stance, arms pumped and fists clenched, wearing wide-leg pants, a tank top, and her hair in a natural hairstyle. Once the sound applet loaded, Chin's voice would stream through computer speakers, moving from a shout to soft laughter at the end of the question: "Am I a womanist or a feminist? The student needs to know if I do men occasionally and primarily, am I a lesbian?" The website's opening statement centered Chin's own queerness as a topic for personal and theoretical exploration and the digital networks of the blog and website, now transferred to social media sites equipped with more extensive networks of readers, provided the site for extensive conversations on the creation of queer diasporic communities.[20] Clicking on the *Cyberjournal* link allowed the reader to access the blog by bringing up a new window. This screen loaded up the text of the most recent post on the left side and a calendar of the archives on the right, so that visitors could navigate to any post in the archives along with its accompanying comments. *Cyberjournal* was one part of her personal website, where she promoted her work and represented in a multimedia forum the intersection of her personal history, political activism, and art.

While many blogs incorporate audiovisual media alongside text, *Cyberjournal* featured only text.[21] Chin's use of the hyperlink function therefore is one of the most important techniques for surfacing the digital traces of her diasporic relationships. Hyperlinks, "a word, phrase, or image that you can click on to jump to a new document" (Christensson), embed into one post the presence of other posts and invite readers to interrupt their reading experience of the post itself. In his 1997 study of hypertext writing, George Landow proposes that linking "dispers[es] or atomiz[es] text" and that it "bridg[es] gaps between text—bits of text—and thereby produces effects similar to analogy, metaphor" (215). When she embeds links within her poetry, Chin indicates where she finds resonant kinship for her own writing and asks readers to visit those sites. If readers choose to follow the links she provides, the post will be expanded beyond Chin's words to include the connections located at other URLs. So while the navigational features of the hyperlink make it primarily an author-driven function, the decision as to whether or not to embed the link into one's own reading of the post—and then how to juggle one's reading between two or more posts—is entirely reader-driven.[22] Users can leave their initial reading to enter a space about which they know nothing and then return to the already-familiar page, or they can transfer back and forth between them and braid the multiple sites together in a unique way.

The interruptions that are built into digital reading environments have led to the Internet being criticized as diminishing literacy.[23] In "Digital Clutter: Why How We Read Matters," Nicholas Carr argues that the Internet creates an environment of skimming superficiality, citing Steven Johnson: "Online, you can click happily from blog post to email thread to online *New Yorker* article, sampling, commenting and forwarding as you go. But when you sit down with an old-fashioned book in your hand, the medium works naturally against such distractions; it compels you to follow the thread, to stay engaged with a single narrative or argument." Carr's nostalgic characterization of "old-fashioned books" as containing a single narrative that works against distraction does not accurately reflect a large body of fictional frame narratives such as *The Arabian Nights*, works by writers like Dickens and Balzac who were initially read in serialized form, or heterogeneous novels like *Tristram Shandy* and its postmodern successors that create fragmented reading experiences.[24] Beyond an overgeneralization of novelistic reading practices, Carr's objection to "commenting and forwarding" hits on the aspects of Internet reading that take the reader out of a solitary engagement with the text. Carr assumes that superficiality results when readers follow links away from an initial website. This diminished attention can be one result of following links. However, in analyzing Chin's use of hyperlinks in her blogged poetry, I propose that readers can also use links to reflect back on the website where they began and, by juxtaposing the various links, use the sampling technique of which Carr is so critical in order to unearth the profound connections between different texts.

Chin's use of hyperlinks in her poetic blogging expands readers' relationships to her work by inviting them to pursue her poetry's political and affective contexts; the amplifying power of the hyperlink is evident in her intimate poem "Atlanta," posted on December 7, 2004. "Atlanta" describes her state of being in all of its corporeal and emotional sensibilities at the moment of writing, and the wide-ranging paths of her memories and personal connections. In the last section of the poem, Chin settles into the present moment of writing with the refrain "tonight." Using the present continuous tense, she breaks from the activity of writing to embed into the poem the action of reading: "tonight /*I am reading your article/thinking I should have said so much more / (maya you made me stunning)*." The now-dead link sent readers to an interview Chin did with Maya Trotz at jouvay.com where Chin discusses the impact of her distanced relationship with Jamaica.[25] Trotz comments on Chin's sexile: "You are speaking for the many Jamaican friends who are afraid to speak out about their sexuality, but you can since you are on a plane off the island in the morning."[26] Chin nuances this status by conjoining economic concerns with freedom of sexual expression: "You do a lot cause you in foreign." Chin comments bluntly on the importance of remittances to the Jamaican economy, whereas her physical distance results in her being, as Chin says, "out of touch with the politics of the poor." This reluctance to separate citizenship from justice, whether gendered or economic, evokes one of Chin's mottos, "All oppression is connected!"[27] The amplification of "Atlanta" to include Chin's conversation with Trotz through this hyperlink embeds into the poem the complexities of sexile.

In "Atlanta," Chin uses the Internet's linking capacity to model how she negotiates physical distance. The interview at the link makes explicit that, while physical absence from Jamaica offers Chin some protection, the Internet can still extend the possibility of her connection to those Jamaicans who have access to it. The theme of the poem itself is interpersonal reconnection: Chin evokes the solitude of an artist's life while on tour and, concurrently, she remembers her family's dispersal and the queer community she has constructed in her travels. In the first section of the poem, Chin describes the biological family that was never whole and is in the process of being reconstructed, and in this section, she names her chosen family composed of friends or lovers.

Rushnie
and Samantha
and Chris
Lebo
Mackie
Kano

you are all laid
thick beneath my tongue

tonight
Atlanta was witness.

Despite their distance, the friends that constitute her global community are "laid thick beneath her tongue": they sustain the very muscle that powers sexual pleasure as well as performance poetry. This poem and Chin's blog more broadly map out what Gayatri Gopinath defines as a queer diaspora: "Rather than simply doing away with home and its fictions of (sexual, racial, communal) purity and belonging, queer diasporic literature instead engages in a radical reworking of multiple home spaces. The queer diasporic body is the medium through which home is remapped and its various narratives are displaced, uprooted, and infused with alternative forms of desire" (165). "Atlanta" tracks the way that Chin forms community through her travels and consolidates that far-flung community on the blog itself. In the face of the impersonal anonymity and evacuation of physicality that the Internet can encourage, Chin's writing refocuses our attention on the vulnerabilities of her own body—a move that can connect her to an individual reader. "Atlanta" provides an example of how she assumes intimacy with her readers.

Perhaps because "Atlanta" is about Chin's reliance on the digital space of the Internet for creating a community when copresence is not possible, Chin compensates for absence with an evocation of her body's corporeal sensations. Considering the sensual relationships that can develop through Internet LISTSERV communities, Juana María Rodríguez describes the linguistic workarounds that participants create to make the body present in its absence: "In these exchanges, rather than discursive disembodiment, the body becomes a discursive fetish, continually described, adored, coveted precisely because it is absent. Elaborate descriptions of the senses—touch, sight, smell, taste, and hearing—become the medium through which arousal is cultivated and maintained. Here the bandwidth of language expands beyond the narrative to do the sensory work usually associated with the activities of the body" (142). Chin likewise centers us on her body at the moment of her writing. The anonymous hotel room in Atlanta becomes specific through her corporeality:

> no regrets
> tonight
>
> only hope pulsing proud
> of you and the dirt tracks you have carved
> from rock
>
> and the rhetoric of class
> chiseled
> granite inside this generation's chest
>
> I had a massage today
> and I loved the soft oil
>
> sliding
> civil down my naked ass
> over my hips
> my body is my own tonight.

Chin infuses into this seemingly random time and place the specificity of her corporeal experience in the present moment. Even memory has the materiality of carved rock and chiseled granite. In contrast to the hardness that characterizes her familial narrative, when articulating the pleasure that her naked and vulnerable body takes in its self-possession, her words luxuriate in the soft, sibilant alliteration. By articulating what the body feels like at the moment of writing, she both makes use of and challenges the immateriality of cyberspace with language that does not allow us to forget the physicality of a queer diasporic body as it moves through the world.

In this poem, Chin claims her body's expressive sexuality and connects it to a familial network, a queer diaspora, and Jamaica—if only obliquely: the self "carved from rock" alludes to "the rock," Jamaica's nickname. In combination with the complex questions of community and exile raised in her interview with Trotz, Chin models full personhood and unconventional gender in the context of national spaces that legally validate only a narrow range of sexual identities. Invested as it is in evaluating the consequences of an existence lived across multiple locations, the hyperlink to Trotz's interview that Chin enables within the poem adds the crucial dimension of sexile into the queer Caribbean diaspora that she maps. Contrary to Carr's assumption of interrupted reading as superficial skimming, an interrupted reading practice of Chin's "Atlanta" amplifies the poem and reflects Chin's interrupted experience of writing. The digital home of Chin's blog can be accessed and updated at any moment from any geographic location. Chin pauses time in her narrative to point to an explanation of the dynamics of sexile, an addition that is both central to the present story and located elsewhere. "Tonight" is the insistent refrain of the last section and, in this instance, signals Chin's conscious decision to set the past aside, to actively negate regrets and recriminations, and to replace them with an expression of hope. This insistence on "tonight" is about locating her body's sensoriality in one moment of experience. In the midst of her tribute to the ties of friendship and family that sustain her, she separates a space for her individual body and shares it with her cyber audience in the present moment.

The sampling of other sites that is so important to my reading of "Atlanta" is a long-standing tradition in poetic creation, as in the historical avant-garde's use of collage in poetry and the visual arts. A form of citing influences and highlighting networks, the hyperlinks that enable remixes and samples are a staple of blogging. Mark Amerika's redefinition of the "remix" is useful here in separating it from the assumption that it entails superficiality in writing and reading. "Becoming a Remixologist: Art, Theory and Sound Practice" draws on Guy Debord's *Méthodes de détournement* to present the imbrication of aesthetic theory and practice as it takes place within the remix of objects culled from an open source web. Further building on snippets of phrases taken from Alfred North Whitehead's "Theory of Feelings," Amerika presents the affect of remixing: "My latest micro-track of DIY remix philosophy that reads in part: A feeling is an expression in the concrescence of a remixologically inhabited language space. . . . Each expression of feeling sinks into the components of some more complex feeling of a later phase and each phase adds its element of novelty." Remixing, then, uses not just the snippets of words and phrases or images but the feelings generated in their earlier iteration to build on that sentimental base even as the elements that produced it are recombined and recontextualized. Concrescence, which Amerika adopts from Whitehead's text, identifies the remix as a process of assimilating affect and repurposing it.[28]

In their responses to Chin's poetry, her readers regularly remix her words into the comments they write for her blog posts. For example, in response to "Atlanta," the commenter "Kavura" picks up on Chin's line from the poem, "Europe beckons // and Africa knows it is only a matter of time / before I visit again," and includes in the comments her own poem riffing off of that line: "i know what you speak of and africa beckons still. always did always will." Taking the line "Europe beckons" and replacing Europe with Africa, Kavura amplifies Chin's longing with her own, using Chin's own strategy of the remix, reusing and recontextualizing. The resonance between Chin and her commenters transforms Chin's initial poem; their mutual inscription of Africa connects them through shared diasporic affinities. In this vein, Chin comments about her expectations for how she and her commenters will interact on the blog: "The space also provides feedback, people email questions and comments which help me to flesh out the issues in a multi-directional process. The entries do not exist as simply entries, it is as if the comments are additional 'verses' of the 'poem'" (personal communication). Chin understands her readers to be in the process of coconstructing the blog with her when they respond to her poems. It is such exchanges that link the dynamics of the blogosphere to those of a dance circle: the blogger's reflections become a call for other poetic contributions, blurring the lines between readers and participants just as Philip describes Carnival's mas' as a site in which looking/dancing are inseparable activities.

As Chin articulates it, full personhood requires complete autonomy over her body—an autonomy that hinges on interpersonal relations and the sense of community. To recall how Marissa Chibas enacts personhood, Chin warns against a conception of the self that is isolated in its independence. In figuratively locating her chosen family under her tongue in "Atlanta," Chin negotiates the tension between the self as autonomous and as one that is bound up with the people who inhabit her. This contextual, inclusive definition of personhood is most evident in samples of speeches and poetry as she remixes them in her own poetic production. In the poem she performed at the opening ceremonies of the Gay Games VII in Chicago on July 15, 2006, she ends with a remixed version of Martin Niemöller's famous articulation of how fascist regimes take power.[29] On its own, Niemöller's reflection on Nazism speaks to the interdependence of identities:

Transcription of Martin Niemöller's speech

First they came for the communists,
and I didn't speak out because I wasn't a communist.

Then they came for the trade unionists,
and I didn't speak out because I wasn't a trade unionist.
Then they came for the Jews,
and I didn't speak out because I wasn't a Jew.
Then they came for me
and there was no one left to speak out for me.

In Chin's hands, the affective power of the citation remains, but she enacts two important shifts to speak to the present context: she moves from the temporality of past narrative to a premonitory warning, and she changes the subjects from Niemöller's dyadic "they" and "I" to a triangulated relation between "they," "we," and "you":

Last stanza of Chin's Gay Games poem

the powers that have always been
have already come for the Jew
the communist
and the trade unionist
the time to act is now![30]
Now! while there are still ways we can fight
Now! because the rights we have are still so very few
Now! because it is the right thing to do
Now! before you open the door to find
they have finally come
for you.

Chin remixes Niemöller's reflections on interpersonal connection and reliance, transforming it into a call for action.

In this last stanza, Chin asks her audience members, the "you" of her address, to bear Niemöller's reflections in mind when constructing the present fight for political liberation. The first structural change Chin makes is to flip Niemöller's historical order of events that moved from the eradication of political opponents to ethnic genocide: Chin situates us unmistakably in the referential context of the Holocaust and the emotions that charge that historical memory. In her second modification, she reorganizes the rhyme from Niemöller's couplets, using "Jew/you" to frame the stanza. She therefore changes the relationship between identities from an emphasis on the difference between the speaker and communists, trade unionists, and Jews, to a resonance between Jews and the listener. Chin links together historical with present oppressions through sound and by opening up the subjects of address from the isolated "I" of

Niemöller's lament to a communal "we" whose task is to wrestle with how to define itself. This question of self-definition is the central question of Chin's poem: Will the gay community define itself narrowly or will it include economic and racial oppressions as part of its struggle? In this question, Chin reasserts the centrality of radical oppositional politics to her experience of sexile.

Without making excuses for Caribbean homophobia, Chin also refuses to ignore the turn toward normativization that the gay rights movement has taken in the United States and the exclusions that accompany this process. José Esteban Muñoz and Jasbir Puar have written about how what Muñoz terms "homonormative gay pragmatism" (*Cruising* 21) has moved away from the idealist premises of the queer movements of the 1970s and early 1980s and instead positions itself as asking for recognition from the state.[31] In this address to the attendants of the Gay Games Opening ceremonies, a piece she alternately terms as a "speech/rant" and a "speech/rant/poem," Chin calls attention to these lacunae in the articulation of goals in the gay rights movement. In this work, Chin denounces the tendency of gay liberation movements in the United States to refuse issues of class and race on a global scale as imbricated with their political concerns. She offers the dream of nonexclusionary unity: "our community is happily expanding beyond the scope of the dream stonewall sparked within us." Her speech marks how the community fails to achieve this happy expansion to its fullest extent by citing the intersections between homosexuality and citizenship, class, and race that have been ignored by what she identifies as an increasingly corporate-driven identity politics.

Chin begins the poem by citing multiple conversations that have infuriated her—both because of their content and because, in the moment they took place, she felt silenced. In the first instance, she censors her anger, but in the second, she cites a feeling of shame as impeding her speech:

> *why can't you people just say you date other people?*
> Again I say nothing
> tongue tied with fear
> I am at once livid
> ashamed and paralyzed
> by the neo-conservatism
> breeding malicious amongst us

In linking the act of "say[ing] nothing" with shame, Chin shows how she reexperiences fear and shame, emotions that assert themselves in unexpected moments. The fear and the shame that result from it have politically quieting consequences. Unlike "Up and Down" and "Atlanta," this poem was not first written for the blog, but for the specific audience of the Gay Games and for public performance. I include it in my analyses of Chin's blog production because it demonstrates the extent to which the strategies of amplificatory remixing suited to digital writing are also part of her general poetic practice; her discussion of shame points to the urgent need for a space of protected permission, one that she and her readers cocreate in their exchanges on the blog. Such spaces are essential for exorcizing the normalizing shame to which Chin and, as we will see, Valdés are subjected.

Shame is deployed to reshape behavior.[32] For an instant, Chin makes space for the external voice that seeks to shame her into making rhetorical choices that conform to heteropatriarchal conventions. To follow Sartre's famous aphorism on shame as recognition, "Shame is by nature recognition. I recognize that I am as the Other sees me" (302). When an individual external to the self turns her gaze onto our persons, we adopt the perspective of that disapproving gaze and internalize its interdictions; shame quiets the subject because external opinions and judgments enter our consciences and override what was formerly there. Located at the intersection of public and private spaces, shame embeds social constrictions within individual psyches. In this sense, shame is an affect that spreads ideology, or breeds it, to adopt Chin's language. In addition to its ideological impacts, the affect of shame has a sensorial counterpart, as Sara Ahmed indicates: "The very physicality of shame—how it works on and through bodies—means that shame also involves the de-forming and re-forming of bodily and social spaces, as bodies 'turn away' from the others who witness the shame" (103). Chin describes the deforming choreography that Ahmed evokes by writing about how her silence impacts her body as well as the queer community.

Chin describes the impact of shame on her body through the corporeality of silence:

> even in friendly conversation
> I get the bell hooks-ian urge
> to kill mother-fuckers who say stupid shit to me
> all day
> bitter branches of things I cannot say out loud
> sprout deviant from my neck

The speech/rant/poem asks us to witness her moment of inaction and the ways her body responds when speech is deferred. After this stanza, she will shout out her responses. But for the time being, preceding her verbal retorts, silence is accompanied not only by the desire for physical violence against others but also by her consciousness of how inaction wreaks violence against her own body. Chin locates her explanation for the urges toward violence and the internal struggles to keep silent in corporeal metaphors. As in Chamoiseau's description of the storyteller's death and the "égorgette" that kills him, the words that have no audience strangle their speaker. Chin likewise imagines utterances that have no audience as stopping at the neck. But in the moment of articulation, Chin couples the muting shame that she has previously experienced with the anger that propels her current speech. When she delivers out loud the lines that describe her former silence, she uses equally timed pauses between the three descriptors—livid, ashamed, paralyzed. During that beat of silence after "ashamed" in which we wait for what Chin will say next, the interpretation that she has been shamed by the judgment of others remains possible. By the end of the phrase, it is clear that "neo-conservatism" is the passive voice subject of all three emotions. She is no longer silently ashamed of herself, but rather she is ashamed of the quieting dominant politics of a movement with which she affiliates herself. Revisiting this moment of her censure and shame provides Chin with the opportunity to critically assess the grounds on which she is judged as deviant.

Four days after its live performance, Chin cross-posted the "speech/rant/poem" on *Cyberjournal* and her MySpace page, and she sent it out to her e-mail list with a small introduction contextualizing the poem.[33] In this introduction to the text of the work she had performed, she blends her audience of regular readers with her Gay Games live audience. The phrase "there you were at the end of my delivery" implies the presence of all of her readers. Not everyone who received the e-mail or read her blog was present in Chicago, but by recirculating the speech/rant/poem, Chin used the participatory quality of blogs and social media to continue the dynamic she experienced at the opening ceremony. She amplified the poem and boosted its signal by merging the oral delivery with the delivery of an e-mail to an inbox. While most of the comments on her MySpace page and on *Cyberjournal* either expressed regret that the commenter was not present in Chicago or confirmed that he or she was in fact in the audience and reaffirmed support for Chin, several offered accounts of the audience's response to her speech. On MySpace, "lala" presented a view of the audience as divided along the same lines of relative privilege that Chin cites in the poem: "my love, you made us feel so good in that sea of pretty groomed white boys. when they realized you weren't singing about flowers and rainbows they didn't know how to fix their faces." "Jed Dulanas" commented on her blog, "Thank you for posting your words I don't think Logo will air your entire speech." The responses to Chin's speech, from cheers to resentful silence, as transcribed by her audience members on her blog and social media spaces, now become part of the speech/rant/poem. As a result of its digital circulation, Chin's refusal to be silent and to have her body deformed by the choreography of shame as articulated in the poem now includes as one of its contexts the Gay Games ceremonies, the site of the poem's performance itself. The digital environment allows her to draw on the energy from the live performance and to request of her readers that they "stand up for social justice" both corporeally and through discourse, and "continue to ask ourselves those questions that are hardest for us to hear." In the recirculation of the poem, Chin uses her digital network to amplify the physical response she experienced at the Gay Games.

In her e-mailed and blogged introduction to the poem, Chin writes: "It was good to have the opportunity to say the words with which I have been struggling." The poem made public her own private moments of humiliation as an object lesson in how the gay activist community must transform itself. In posting and forwarding the poem after its first iteration, Chin amplifies her audience and the poem's contextual resonances. The importance of commenting and forwarding the poem to new audiences and spaces is evident in the quick exchange that Chin conducts with one of her responsive readers. The only commenter to whom Chin responds directly is "the_inevitable" on MySpace, who inquires if she could repost Chin's speech on her own page. The rapidity and tenor of Chin's answer indicates how important the diffusion and continuing echoes of the poem are to her: "post it wherever you please, love. These words were meant to address the pages of all the books that need them."[34] This quick response shows how Chin shifts between live performance spaces and print publication and the role of the digital environment in facilitating that fluid movement between media. Chin's use of multiple media—the live, the print, the digital—are all part of what I identify as a strategy of amplification: in each medium, Chin's critiques take on different valences as they reach different audiences. The blog in particular allows her the immediacy of her audience's responsive presence as they together construct a virtual supranational space in which Chin's poetry prompts the exploration of the intersections between queer, Caribbean, and radical.

Zoé Valdés's Porno-Political Memory Work

Valdés's use of the blog does not rely on the amplificatory openness that characterizes Chin's online presence. Rather, what her website communicates is that the reader is a guest in her space, and as such, must hew to Valdés's tight political parameters for acceptable speech. This blog is meant to provide a personal touch to Zoé Valdés's professional persona, as evidenced by the layout of the 2010 iteration of zoevaldes.net: along the right side of the page is a picture of Valdés as a young woman sitting at a typewriter, quotes from her writing and Borges's, the logos of causes she supports, and images of her book covers hyperlinked to online booksellers. The images in the header, labeled "imagenes aleatorias," fleeting images, changed every time the page was refreshed: Valdés as a young girl in front of a decrepit building in Cuba, Valdés at a book signing with one of her heroes, Guillermo Cabrera Infante, Valdés gazing thoughtfully into the distance. Valdés's website references her personal experience as a politically invested writer as well as her professional successes, and it sets the tone for her blogging production. Valdés posts prolifically, and approximately half of these posts are links, functional as roundups to topics both political and artistic; her category cloud provides a sense of the posts' cumulative content with the tags "Castrismo" and "Cuba" applied the most frequently, followed by "Literatura," "Política," and "Zoé Valdés."[35] The blog is also a site where she keeps tabs on her writing progress, posts her already published writing by inter-cutting selected poems with photos of herself in various contexts or YouTube clips, and works through memories in essay form. In reading Valdés's blogging literary production, I analyze the temporal conflicts that emerge in Valdés's use of blog media's presentist quality to do community memory work. This last section's focus on temporality and memory work on the blog aims to illuminate the wide range of poetic and political purposes to which Chin and Valdés put their digital writing and more broadly contemplate the potential for literary experimentation within blog media.

Drawing on blogs as a site for the daily publication of incremental moments as they happen, Andrew Sullivan, political writer and blogger of *The Dish*,[36] champions blogs as providing a site for exact record-keeping—a self-serving claim to objectivity within journalism. In "Why I Blog," published in *Atlantic* magazine, Sullivan reviews the platonic ideal of a blog by meditating on its origins: a weblog was meant to be comparable to a ship's log. A daily recording of facts aims for accountability and accuracy—two characteristics that the form of the novel or even the newspaper article can gloss over in the effort to create a narrative arc: "In the middle of an expanse of blue and gray and green and in long journeys, memories always blur and facts disperse. A log provided as accurate an account as could be gleaned in real time." Thanks to its formal organization, Sullivan makes the argument that blog media is a "form of human self-correction" that counters memory work. If, as Michael Rothberg states, memory "brings together now and then, here and there" (5), the blog keeps the now and then separate into discrete posts, all of which speak in their own "now." Blog media block attempts to smooth out the past's inconsistencies into a story in which all the pieces fit an ideology perfectly.

In her September 18, 2009, post, "Memoria, libertad, supervivencia," Valdés diverges from the ethics of daily accurate accountability that Sullivan ascribes to blog media. This post is one of several where she relates her memories of Cuba. And because these memories are scattered among her daily reflections on contemporary politics, they take on the quality of present accounting implied in the reverse chronological organization of the blog media, for one of the defining elements of a blog is that what is newest is always placed at the top of the page to be read first. For readers, this "real time" effect is reinforced by one standard feature of all blogs: the reverse chronological order, which lends the genre an insistent presentism. In this post, Valdés articulates the role of memory in creating reality: after describing in the first part of the essay how she found liberty in the refuge of her imagination and writing, Valdés shifts to the story of her traumatic memory loss at the age of thirty. She compares this to her experience of exile, an equally traumatic event that entails "el cambio, brutal, [que] me permitió reiniciar mi cerebro" (The change, brutal, [that] allowed me to reboot my brain). Due to what Valdés calls her brain's rebooting, comparing her mind and memory to that of a computer's, memories are amplified or distorted in order to soften the ever-present pain of exile's loss.

> La memoria afectiva del exiliado alivia muchas de sus pérdidas concretas. No he conocido a un solo exiliado cubano que no rememore la casa confiscada y perdida, a través de los olores, de los sabores, de las presencias, de los fantasmas, de los muertos de la familia. . . . Tal vez, incluso, nada de eso ocurrió de esa manera, pero el exiliado, a través de la evocación afectiva, conseguirá reinventar su vida, y se sentirá en armonía con su verdad imaginada. ¿Constituye eso una mentira, es una trampa? ¿Qué importancia tiene?

> The exile's affective memory alleviates many of his concrete losses. I have never met a Cuban exile who does not remember the confiscated and lost home, through the smells, the flavors, the presence, the ghosts, the family's dead. . . . Perhaps, even, none of this took place in this way, but the exile, through the affective evocation, will seek to reinvent his or her life, and will feel that it is in harmony with his imagined truth. Is this a lie, a trick? What does it matter?

This passage encapsulates Valdés's view of how memory enables emotional survival. If, in order to provide this emotional support, memories must be reinvented such that an event that never occurred is nevertheless remembered as having occurred, Valdés's response is: What does it matter?

With regards to the historiography and testimony, the relationship between traumatic memory and historical research is a complex one that scholars have had to address. As Dominick LaCapra states in the context of the Holocaust, testimonial accounts can identify social significance of events even when they do not verify the "accurate empirical reconstruction of events" (88). Therefore, when I focus on Valdés's phrases "reinventar su vida" and "su verdad imaginada," I do not do so in order to invalidate the value of testimony in the historical record or the necessity of memory work. What interests me is her active memory work on her blog—media that propose the blog's contents as "accurate present-day record-keeping," to return to Sullivan's etymology. While blog media have a wide variety of uses, the most conventional is to broadcast instant responses in a confessional mode—and, for the most part, Valdés's posts follow this convention: the majority of the blog's entries agitate for regime change in Cuba on the basis of present-day human rights abuses reported in the international news as well as the loss of property and national belonging suffered by dissidents and exiles.[37] So on the relatively rare occasions when her posts perform memory work that is narrated with verb tenses that fluctuate in and out of the present, those narratives benefit from the sense of immediacy that their placement on a blog lends them.

Due to their interspersal with present-day writing, these posts based on memory read more like instantaneous responses to current events than memories that have undergone time's transformations. Valdés uses the sensation of spontaneity associated with the blogging form to create slippage between present happenings and affective memories. On Valdés's blog, reinvented memories of loss are presented with the same claim to accuracy as the log of present injustices. Though Valdés's intertwining of memory and imagination as both a political approach to the dynamics of Cuban identity and a survival strategy for exiles is not controversial, its location on the blog bears important ethical ramifications. Valdés uses the blog to mine its particular temporality in creating an intimate sense of home for those who take part in her ideological community and share her approach to Cubanness.

While Valdés frequently includes links in her posts, she has also developed a style of blog entry that mimics the hyperlink. Instead of including links to other sites within the post as an invitation to readers to follow up on her suggestions as Chin does, Valdés walks her readers through a series of memories as if her memories were the Internet's infinite number of sites and she were jumping from website to website. In "Recuerdos," posted on October 13, 2008, Valdés names this particular style of organizing posts "un juego de enlaces," literally, a game of links. This post is divided into seven sections, each with a photograph and explanatory paragraph about an event in Valdés's life. The interruptions Valdés stages in this post model how interrupted reading on the Internet can function: by expanding her attention, the reader can bring conversations and ideas that she assimilates from various different sites into one reading session. However, this blog post is itself free of actual hyperlinks even as the structure of the post is reminiscent of the reading experience of falling down an Internet rabbit hole of links. That is, the synaptic connections are not entirely fired subconsciously from within her internal bank of memories. Rather, this constellation of memories is constructed as part of a writing process that relies upon external triggers to create the game of links presented in a digital environment. Whereas Chin uses hyperlinks within her personal writing to invite readers to choose their own experience of interruption, in this type of post, Valdés controls the nature of the interruption. We experience Valdés's game of links as she experienced it.

The game of links stages an engagement between the self and her memories. Save for the last section's photo, taken at one of her first meetings with Cabrera Infante in 1995, all temporal markers that might fix the stories in a chronological relationship to one another are omitted. Valdés positions herself as being carried along by a mental activity that is beyond her control in which she, like her readers, is discovering with surprise the memories that her mind dredges up. Moreover, linking to a new memory does not mean discarding the memory that triggered the jump. Instead it requires being able to keep the first one in mind and to build a relation between two or more temporalities, two or more locations, two or more ideas. Her concluding remarks summarizing the game of links reinforce the critical need for an expansive mode of reading in order to play the game: "Estos fueron mis recuerdos de fin de semana, de toda la vida" (These were the memories from this weekend, from my whole life). She uses the form of the blog as a model for how to simultaneously condense and expand time. The equation of the weekend's memories with the experiences of her whole life in this post reflects the elastic sense of temporality that Valdés derives from the structure of the blog and uses throughout her blog writing.

As she writes in the introduction to the post, even as she moves through stories that are only tangentially related, the act of juxtaposing them solidifies the connections between them: "From one memory I make a link with another, to all appearances one has nothing to do with the next, but nevertheless, they approach one another in intensity." Valdés's conception of the game of links maps onto Landow's definition of the hyperlink: these memories come closer to one another because she links them together, and through that linkage, the initially tangential relationship between them becomes more evident. Some of the leaps are chronological; others are more affective, as when she connects her memory of seeing a Pollock for the first time at MOMA in New York City to her memory of visiting Serge Gainsbourg's grave in Paris because she was inspired with the same feeling on both occasions, "plena de vida y de arte," or full of life and art. The game of links begins and ends with connections to Cuban exiles and is centrally punctuated by the memory of evacuation.[38] The third event features a photograph of her with one friend's dog and the accompanying text briefly mentions many friends' terrible adventures in trying to leave Cuba with their pets: as the many different stories accumulate, a trade-off between traveling the world and access to Cuba emerges. At the core of Valdés's game of links is the anguish of exilic loss and the pain inflicted upon her by the Cuban state.

"Recuerdos" demonstrates Valdés's mode of Cubanness—one that she invests with artistic freedom and living outside of the island. Like her mentor Guillermo Cabrera Infante, Valdés's view is that the island of Cuba has been dying since the advent of communism and that no authentic Cuban identity can find its full expression when complicit with a repressive government. Her characterization of Cubanness is in many ways indistinguishable from the viewpoint articulated by Andrea O'Reilly Herrera in her summary of interviews with members of the Cuban exile community living in Miami: "[Many of the first-generation exiles whom I interviewed] insist that those who remained on the island following the revolution have ceased altogether to be Cuban. 'Then what are they?' I ask. 'I don't know,' one woman told me, 'but they're not Cuban. They're something else'" (182). This definition of Cuba relies on the separation of cultural identity from the geography of the nation-state. The distinction between geography and culture is expressed in two forms of Cubanness that Alma DeRojas, reading Gustavo Pérez Firmat and Fernando Ortiz, terms *la cubanía*, or the Cuban spirit, and *la cubanidad*, a civil status (181). For Cubans residing outside of Cuba, this distinction is necessary for claiming Cubanness in the absence of citizenship or physical residence. On her blog, Valdés turns to freedom of sexual expression and unconventional gender as her main claim to the Cubanness that she constructs with her readers.

Valdés's use of memory on the blog orients her online community toward a way of experiencing Cuba outside of the island; her commenters, in turn, encourage her to continue constructing community this way. In exploring how Valdés and her readers coconstruct a particular form of Cuban sexile, I focus on a series of posts from October 2008 where Valdés's community develops a political platform that begins with a demand for sexual freedom. Here, Valdés equates her self-proclaimed sexual deviance with unconventional gender and an anticommunist political position. Glossing over the differences between her relationship with the state's official artists' organizations and the criminalization of homosexuality—differences that are so great in degree that they are different in kind—she appropriates for herself the human rights discourse surrounding the treatment of gays and lesbians in Cuba.[39] In her exchanges with readers on establishing a political platform along the lines she has offered, they become "produsers" along with her. The series of posts begins with a remark Valdés reads about herself on another blog, *Habanemia*, where the Cuban blogger Lía Villares addresses Valdés to let her know that at a literary round table in Havana, the well-known Cuban art critic Eduardo Heras León had publicly insulted Valdés's writing as "pornopolítica."[40] This coinage rightly pinpoints Valdés's methodology of melding sexuality with political ideology.

Rather than respond to Villares on *Habanemia* and direct her readers to that site, Valdés follows blog etiquette by linking to her source, and then imports the salient quote into a post of her own, publishing her response to Villares on zoevaldes.net. In "Lía Villares en *Habanemia*" (October 22, 2008), Valdés notes that, like the Cuban Communist Party representatives, the Miami anti-Castristas also attempt to dismiss her for her sexual politics, calling her "soez," or vulgar.[41] Connecting the rhetorical tactics used by the dominant exile leadership to those articulated by the Cuba intelligentsia, she demonstrates the need for an alternative form of anti-Castrismo. Here she begins the work of redefining the porno-prefix, stating, "prefiero ser pornopolítica que un 'policía de la cultura'" (I prefer to be pornopolitical than to be a "cultural policeman"). By opposing porn and police, vulgarity as a practice of unconventional gender is opposed to the state apparatus of political oppression. While Heras León articulates the term disparagingly, Valdés adopts the term with glee and flips its connotation by further commenting that she finds the supposed insult to be an accurate aspect of the persona in which she takes pride. Rather than renounce the sexual overtness of her writing, she places it at the center of her politics: "Actually, Eduardo Heras León has given me an idea; when Cuba is a democracy, that is, in *Blade Runner 3000*, I'm going to run for president under the Popular Pornographic Party, the PPP, the Party for Penises" (Partido para Pingúos). With the reference to the postapocalyptic movie *Blade Runner* and the year 3000, we enter the dimension of futuristic fantasy that allows Valdés to elaborate a political platform with her readers in a playful and imaginative way.

The running joke that began as an offhand comment posted on another blog becomes a regular point of reference in Valdés's blog thereafter because her readers jump on the term and amplify her idea in their comments. Their play with the porno-prefix gives her the impetus to keep the idea going in a series of posts: the pornographic political party joke is at the center of three consecutive posts. Between October 22 and 26, 2008, Valdés uploaded fifteen posts, four of which continue riffing off of the "pornopolítica" joke, the rest of which feature her usual mix of poetry, self-promotion, and politics.[42] The four posts that directly address Lía Villares's initial note vary greatly in their composition: in "Partido Porno Poético," posted later that same day, Valdés lays out her party platform, which consists of poems excised from her chapbook *Cuerdas para el lince* paired with photos from when she was pregnant. The following day's "Historia de una foto 'pornopolítica'" is, in contrast, a long narrative of Valdés's experience as a first-time author in Cuba. The last post, "Sergio Lastres y el logo de PPPP," offers two reader-submitted drawings as possible logos for the nascent fantasy political party and puts them up for a vote. Although tied together in content, these four posts exploit blog media's different possible formal organizations for posts: a link to another blog, a montage of past work culled from various sources, a personal essay, and a set of images. Beyond their content, what connects the posts is the audience contributions as "produsers" to the posts themselves, fueling the continuation of the series.

In "Lía Villares en *Habanemia*," Valdés's readers pick up on her attempt to shift the meaning of "porno." Commenter "Santiago Martin" begins the meme of making "porno-" a complimentary prefix, calling her "pornobrillante y pornoenvidiada." Commenter "Cesár Reynal Aguilera" adds the idea of creating variations of the party name with the initials: his suggestion of "Partido Papaya" prompts Valdés's next post, "Partido Porno Poético." At the outset of the post, Valdés names all the iterations of PPP and further opens up the project by suggesting, "As you can see, the initials can be used for whatever interpretation you might like." This open inclusiveness is not only articulated, but also put into practice as Valdés updates the post to add reader comments into the main body of the post, literally integrating their voices into her own as they brainstorm ideas for the evolution of the PPP project. It is therefore largely due to the impetus of her readers' enthusiastic and imaginative comments that Valdés amplifies PPP well beyond her initial offhand joke.

Once Valdés launches herself into the elaboration of the party platform, the post becomes entirely personal as she leaves aside both her readers' suggestions and their shared explicit play with the porno-prefix. Nevertheless, rethinking the relationship between sexuality and politics is at the heart of "el programa" proposed in this post. As mentioned above, the platform does not resemble traditional political manifestos, instead consisting of poems selected from *Cuerdas para el lince*, written in the 1980s in both Havana and Paris, paired with photographs of her while pregnant in 1992. All three photos come from her personal collection, credited to her then husband Ricardo Vega. In the first photograph, the image of Valdés is a close-up of her head; in the second, we see two-thirds of Valdés's body covered by a sheet she has draped strategically around herself; in the last, the camera has panned out so that we see almost a full-body shot where a translucent sheet no longer conceals but highlights the contours of her pregnant body. In the context of the accusation that Valdés's work is nothing but "pornopolítica," posting photos of herself almost nude can serve as evidence of her defiant acceptance of the term. However, Valdés chooses photos of herself that, while technically meeting the "porno" designation, are also part of the genre of pregnancy photos, where swelling breasts and belly are coded as more maternal than sexual. Just as her commenters take the sting out of the porno-prefix by affixing it to the most laudatory of adjectives, she also articulates a refusal to be shamed for her sexual frankness—but with photographic evidence that shifts the meaning of the porno-prefix. The conversion of a private moment between husband and wife into present public circulation is an essential part of the performance of openness by which Valdés reconfigures the porno-prefix in her political program.

The progress of the photographs has its own logic, as does the progression of the pairing of poems and photographs. The first photo is a very literal illustration of the poem that it accompanies: the image of Valdés and a Yorkshire dog gazing at each other with playful seriousness is placed after the poem entitled "Venus Yorkshire," loosely about the relationship between a woman and her Yorkie. The three photographs and poems follow a similar trajectory: just as the photographs become increasingly revelatory, the poems move from opaque to obvious. But if the visual element of "el programa" softens the porno-prefix, the verbal component embraces the explicit definition of porno. "De reticente salud" (Of reticent health), the last poem in the post, is anatomically direct in its welding of graphic sex and ideology. The poem is a jeremiad against a bloated bureaucracy and all those who contribute to the social control it exerts over the general population—including the general population. Valdés's criticism is most incendiary at the poem's outset, where she attacks those who lead the system: "Yo me apiado de los dirigentes / ellos nunca sabrán lo que es virar un refajo al revés / después de la imperiosa necesidad de un pene y una vagina/ haciendo eje en un barrio residencial" (I pity the leaders / they will never know what it's like to twist around your slip / after the imperious necessity of a penis and a vagina / working it out in a residential neighborhood).[43] In this stanza, an example of the explicit writing for which Valdés is famous, she places sexual desire and fulfillment as antagonistic to the regime's goals. In selecting this poem for "el programa," she again takes ownership of the "pornopolítica" accusation, implying that the opposite of "pornopolítica" is a system dominated by sanctimony, prudishness, and sexual censorship.

The poem is organized by the refrain, "yo me apiado de . . . ," or "I pity," as it lists everyone the speaker condemns. Beginning with those most obviously in control, "los dirigentes," she goes down the line of more oblique supporters, ending with a complicit we, "nosotros," for living under the system and becoming transformed by it. The nature of that transformation, according to the last lines in Valdés's poem, "Yo me apiado de nosotros / templando como procesos judiciales bajo estos signos," is "templar," to get in tune with, or in the context of this poem, to soften and moderate one's critique and challenge. With no empathetic moderation of tone throughout the poem, the speaker holds herself at a distance from the "nosotros" with whom she associates herself by word choice. Indeed, the existence of the poem itself is evidence of her discordant refusal to harmonize with the system. The choice of personal photographs and poems in this post offers a microcosm of the way that Valdés uses the equation between unconventional gender and freedom as a central element in her anti-Castrista politics: to point to a visceral absence of freedom in communist Cuba. For unlike the complicit "we" of the poem, the exiles who meet on her blog retain the sexual freedom that Valdés posits as central to her definition of Cubanness.

Once more, Valdés uses the immediacy of blog media to give the ideologically laden claims of memory a presentist urgency. Here, she begins a discussion in which she interacts conversationally with her readers in almost real-time in October 2008 while the manifesto is composed of a collage of writings produced throughout the 1980s in Paris and Havana as well as images taken in 1992. That is, while the post is written from the diaspora, its content was created when she was navigating the beginning of her exile, perhaps a minor difference since her ideological position has remained consistent. However, in so doing, she succeeds in blurring the distinctions between the subject positions of exile and internal dissident. It is because she uses unconventional gender to integrate exile, dissidence, and diaspora that I suggest that Valdés presents her experience as that of a "sexile"—not because homophobia prompted her departure from Cuba, but because censorship of her sexually frank writing is central to her narrative of expulsion from the community of Cuban artists.

Valdés's narrative of sexile is mapped out explicitly in "Historia de una foto 'pornopolítica,'" posted on October 23, 2008. Here, she insists on the causal relationship between sex and her exile. She tells the story of how she broke with the ICAIC while attempting to publish her first novel, *Sangre azul*, by using the coinciding birth narratives of her daughter's birth and the novel's publication. The post's subtext offers a third birth narrative: that of her persona of "pornopolítica" and Cuban writer in exile. Except for herself, she tells us, only Reinaldo Arenas had attempted to negotiate a contract with a foreign editor without the explicit permission of the state, and it was only because of Arenas's defection that she was allowed to proceed without a criminal trial. However, when her novel was published by the Cuban press Letras Cubanas, she was not invited to La Feria del Libro, the book festival in Havana where her book would be launched. Only days after the birth of her daughter, she sneaked into the fair, showed up at the book presentation, and asked to sit among the front row of authors only to find that Eduardo Heras León—the same Heras León who would, fifteen years later, disparage her literary talent and coin the neologism that inspired this set of posts—had presented her book without giving her a chance to speak. This story wrenches us away from the porno-prefix that dominates her futuristic political imaginary and instead focuses on past politics and the absence of personal freedom that she consistently links to the Cuban state.

"Historia de una foto 'pornopolítica'" is an uncharacteristically long post of 1,774 words that also features three images from Valdés's archive—photos that do not focus our attention on her body as in the previous post, but rather call attention to the political context in which Valdés's body was constrained. Two of the images are documents that she has scanned and posted to prove the veracity of her story; the first is the cover art of *Sangre azul*, the second a copy of a rejection letter written about her novel by an Argentinian press. The eponymous "foto 'pornopolítica'" shows Valdés sitting in a row of chairs among other writers. Valdés sits third from the end in a group of seven; like the other participants, her face is turned toward López Sacha, whose hand gestures indicate he is midsentence. One arm crossed over her waist, the other propping up her chin with her fist, there is nothing combative or seemingly out of place in the photo itself. Only the caption she provides for the photo gives a sense of its backstory and the future that would unfold from that moment: "Les dejo con esta foto que me hicieron esa noche en la Feria del Libro, fíjense, cuando todavía no era considerada una 'pornopolítica,' pero ya evitaban que me desbocara en público" (I leave you with this photograph that was taken of me that night at the Festival of the Book, if you'll notice, when I wasn't yet considered "pornopolitical" but when they already were shutting me up in public). Ending the post in the temporal domain of the "todavía no," the not yet, Valdés again uses the form of the blog to blend Herás León's political and sexual censure to equate her anticommunist stance with the unconventional gender.

In "Sergio Lastres y el logo de PPPP," posted on October 26, 2008, and the last post of the "pornopolítica" series, Valdés returns to "produser"-generated content. This post is perhaps the most interactive of the series and is one of the most visited posts on her entire blog, in part because it overtly solicits reader participation. The post features two images donated by commenter "Sergio Lastres" as possible logos for the "partido pornopolítico." The name itself was debated in the previous post's comment section; in this post, Valdés adopts in parentheses the name suggested by "Sergio Lastres"—"Partido Porno-Poético Pingúo-Papayúo," which he argues as being inclusive by referencing both female and male sex organs—but refers to it as "PPPP." Continuing to refer to the party by its initials allows each commenter to fill those initials with the terms that best suits him or her, whether emphasizing poetry or Cuban slang. The point that Valdés overtly states throughout her blog and acts on here is that, in explicit contrast to the current Cuban government, this space is one of "la democracia participativa"—although, as goes without saying, it is a participative democracy with a limited ideological scope.

After the two large images, both drawn with pencil or graphite on sepia-colored paper, there is a plug-in poll for reader votes. Introducing the images is Valdés's quick comment presenting the credentials of "Sergio Lastres" and noting that another commenter has created a hymn for the PPPP. The first image is an almost anatomically correct drawing of a vagina; the second features a papaya, a less obvious, but still suggestive, depiction. Because the images are the same size and shape, the contrast that emerges most prominently is the artistic choice between the literal and the metaphorical. The pro-papaya faction argues for the metaphor on the basis that it best represents the "pornopoético" aspect of the party and that it allows for multiple levels of interpretation. This reasoning is in keeping with earlier conversations about creating a political party that would be as open as possible, with only one unspoken ideological requirement. Although the poll was virtually tied throughout the day, the comments eventually skewed in favor of the vagina as logo, which emerged as the winner of the poll. As Valdés phrases it in the comments: "Recuerden que el Partido es Pornoduro, no pornoblando, y que el segundo logo es una cosa más propia de la insinuación que de la chose faite. Yo elegí el 1, pero ya saben que soy la escritora más cochina, vulgar, y pornopolítica, que haya existido jamás" (Remember that party is porno-hard, not porno-soft, and that the second logo is more of an insinuation than the "done deed." I chose the first one, but you already know that I am the dirtiest, most vulgar, and pornopolitical writer who has ever existed [fourth comment]).

While keeping her rhetoric open, "yo elegí" as one vote among many, Valdés defines a concrete meaning of "pornopolítica" by linking it to the literal image and places the "pornoduro" definition of "pornopolítica" at the core of the party instead of the "pornopoético" definition. Because this set of exchanges takes place among individuals who have no face-to-face contact, Valdés invests the potentially abstract idea of a new political party with a corporeal dimension. Valdés and her commenters establish the parameters of the party by referring back to a sexual body: What kinds of politics ensue from sexual frankness? The textual practices that emerge are grounded in representations of the body—in Valdés's performance of openness, in her sexual poetry, in anatomical drawings, and in conversations that privilege play with double entendres. In the online conversation supported by the blog platform, Valdés and her commenters push one another to articulate their ideas with ever-greater precision and confidence, to continue elaborating the fantastic joke further, and to delineate what a culture of noncensorship might look like. And yet, the construction of a new form of politics remains, at its core, a politics of opposition. Valdés's blog circle demonstrates the playful, corporeal inventiveness that she claims is only possible outside of censorship. On Valdés's blog, the audience-writer dynamics are permitted and protected so long as they conform to the anti-Castrismo litmus test. In her very construction of an online space that is meant to counter the wrongs of Castrismo, Valdés also replicates the sentiment Fidel Castro articulated in "Palabras a los intelectuales" (1961): "Dentro de la Revolución: todo; contra la Revolución: ningún derecho" (Within the Revolution: everything; against the Revolution: no rights.) Within the ideological parameters set by the community's leader—Castro in Cuba, Valdés on her blog—everything is permitted and protected. Speaking outside those parameters results in rejection from the community.

The Internet is routinely heralded as a form of unfettered global connectivity. Indeed, the capacity to create spaces of belonging is premised on inclusiveness and access, and these blogs function as a site for both literary experimentation and the textual staging of the dynamics of performance spaces. Yet, mirroring the contingent ephemerality of the dance circle, Chin and Valdés find that their blogging must respond to the complexities and contradictions of a virtual space that is at times too open, at others, not open enough: Valdés must place ideological parameters around an otherwise open form to limit the debate on her site; Chin faces questions of the instability and impermanence of media built for the Internet. In these compromised spaces, the form of the blog creates conditions of difficulty that Chin and Valdés confront by developing an interruptive style that privileges the otherwise-absent body. Together with their supportive readerships, they reconstruct a sense of Caribbean relation beyond the borders of the nation.

5 "Dansez et Revivez!"

Reviving Personhood in Rosario Ferré's "Maquinolandera" and Jacques Stephen Alexis's *Les Arbres musiciens*

In Jacques Stephen Alexis's *Les Arbres musiciens* (1957), the patriarch of a Haitian peasant community, Papa Bois-d'Orme, voices a question that continues to plague Caribbean nations at the outset of the twenty-first century: "Pourquoi alors nos ancêtres ont-ils combattu? Pourquoi Dessalines a-t-il existé, si les Blancs devaient venir reprendre les terres?" (Alexis 351; So why did our ancestors fight? Why did Dessalines exist, if the whites were going to take back the land?" [my translation]). While Bois-d'Orme mournfully takes as a given the twentieth-century collusions between the nation's leaders and multinational corporations that seek a pliable work force, Alexis uses the imperfect past tense, which grammatically sets up an *unlikely* conditional statement to describe the contemporary repossession of Haitian territory. Although seemingly confronting a hopeless situation, he sets up Bois-d'Orme's question as counterfactual and insists on the possibility of future resistance to the dominant narrative of imperialism's inevitable conquest.

Contrasting temporalities mark *Arbres*: the present is dominated by exploitation, but in energizing bursts, individual persons act out the possibility for future liberation. How the representation of performance events permits the coexistence of these conflicting realities is the subject of this chapter through the analysis of Alexis's *Les Arbres musiciens* and Rosario Ferré's short story "Maquinolandera" (1977).[1] In both texts, the protagonists struggle to assert their right to self-possession as a consequence of the national loss—or absence—of sovereignty. The contexts of national status from which these texts emerge appear to be at extreme ends of the sovereignty spectrum in the Caribbean:[2] Puerto Rico's "Estado Libre Asociado" (ELA) status since 1952 is a de facto colonial status,[3] whereas Haiti's early independence remains exceptional in the Americas. Rather than view Puerto Rico and Haiti as extreme opposites, the plotlines of *Arbres* and "Maquinolandera" indicate a similar political context in both islands, a condition that Hilbourne Watson calls "limited sovereignty," in that "all interventions, invasions, and occupations of Latin American and Caribbean countries by the US since the nineteenth century have reinforced the assertion that Caribbean sovereignty has implied ' . . . asking US permission before making changes in . . . foreign policy'" (254). For the texts' protagonists, limited sovereignty is experienced as incarceration and the destruction of community.

A cognitive dissonance radiates throughout *Arbres*, where Haiti's history as the first Black republic is set against the post-Occupation influence of the United States on Haiti's internal domestic policy. At issue is the uprooting of a community so that its members will shift their livelihoods from subsistence farming or sharecropping to working for a U.S.-based company and becoming part of the proletariat. Throughout the novel, this series of events is compared to a return to slavery because it is made clear to the members of this small, vulnerable community that where they live and for whom they work is not their decision to make. While Ferré does not align her short story with as clear a political context, the frame narrative of "Maquinolandera" is that the protagonist, the iconic 1960s Puerto Rican singer Ismael Rivera, is in solitary confinement in federal prison on drug charges, and the story can serve as an allegory of the colonial constraints that the United States imposes on Puerto Rico. In both texts, the central drama is the existential threat posed to the protagonists' personhood through the virtual subjection to forced labor in *Arbres*, and the experience of the civil death of imprisonment in "Maquinolandera."

These texts propose that the dance circle nourishes acts of political resistance. In direct contestation to the status to which the state relegates them, the protagonists use music and dance to recognize one another's full personhood. The use of "Maquinolandera" as a structural device and the presence of dance as part of Vodou rites in *Arbres* mark the moments when Ferré's and Alexis's protagonists can corporeally rehearse the possible futures that otherwise exist only in their imaginations. As such, the ekphrases of performance interrupt both the social order represented in the text and the plot of the text itself. The work that Ferré and Alexis do to elicit the bond between the valorization of cultural production and the possibilities for political liberation resonates strongly with Merle Hodge's inspirational essay from the first international conference of Caribbean women writers in 1988, "Challenges of the Struggle for Sovereignty: Changing the World versus Writing Stories." Hodge uses this platform to make a case for fiction that represents the Caribbean world in all of its complexity in order to combat the region's general preference for metropolitan languages, cultural production, and goods over the local. Her own writing, she states, is a protest against what she was taught in school and in the cultural sphere of Trinidad and Tobago: "that I and my world were nothing" (202). In contrast to this miseducation, the people after whom she models herself are the women and men who are, in her view, "self-possessed." To be self-possessed is to reject the obligation to norms set forth by the metropole, as she describes it and as I use it. The practice of self-possession, or the refusal to believe yourself to be nothing, is the aim of the Fanonian circles in *Arbres* and "Maquinolandera."

In using Hodge's term "self-possession," I draw on two aspects of the term to think through the activity in these dance circles: most evidently, self-possession counteracts the state's possession. "Possession" also refers to the practice of *sevís*, in which, to return to Dayan's explication as discussed in chapter 1, a person freely invites another being to take her place in one's own person. In this chapter, I trace the development of a sense of self-possession that is neither atomistic nor objectifying but that fiercely rejects exploitation by others and that also defines the self as open to *ekstasis*. I therefore begin by analyzing in Ferré, then in Alexis, the historical contexts of both texts, as well as the linguistic workarounds and references to popular songs that they use to invoke the dance circle. In the last section, I analyze the ways that Ferré and Alexis use the ekphrasis of performance to interrupt the grim present that otherwise dominates the texts. The safety of the circle permits a full-throated demand to the right of self-possession and a demonstration of specific individuality that is tantamount to an enactment of personhood for individuals who are relegated to the status of nonpersons. In the endings of both texts, I argue that Ferré and Alexis use the qualities of performance events to break with teleology to offer utopic futures.

"Maquinolandera": Creating an Audience in Isolation

Born in Ponce in 1938, Ferré began to publish her writing in the 1970s in *Zona de carga y descarga* (Loading and unloading zone; published 1972–75), a literary journal she helped found to create a place for young, unestablished writers to articulate a Puerto Rican aesthetic. The short story I examine here, "Maquinolandera" (1977), takes part in that project by presenting a vision of Puerto Rican cultural and political sovereignty through Ferré's aesthetic experimentation. While Ferré would later famously change her political views, during the 1970s she was seen as publicly opposing her father, Luis Ferré, governor of Puerto Rico from 1968 to 1972, by demonstrating more sympathy with the *independentista* position on Puerto Rico's national status than with his prostatehood politics.[4] And indeed, in the early 1970s, fighting for independence seemed perhaps more viable than it had before or has since. In 1972, the Partido Popular Democrático (PPD) took political power, and over the course of the next few years, Puerto Rico fought for international recognition of its status as a colony that had the right to self-determination.[5] Although the hopes for an autonomous Puerto Rico would stagnate in a series of statehood referenda conducted throughout the 1990s, at the time of Ferré's writing "Maquinolandera" in the 1970s, Puerto Rico's continued colonial status was by no means a foregone conclusion.[6]

Ferré's first book, *Papeles de Pandora* (1977), which collected many of her writings previously published in *Zona*, reflects her political convictions, most visibly her feminism. To a lesser extent, *Papeles* also attests to her support for some form of Puerto Rican independence. Her approach to the relationship between politics and literature at that time in her career is articulated in a letter she and Olga Nolla, her cousin and *Zona* colleague, wrote in 1973 in response to a questionnaire sent to them by the German magazine editor Maria Bamberg.

> The writers of *Zona* are *independistas* and our cultural battle is necessarily also a political battle. We favor establishing connections with Latin America, to which we are joined by language, mentality, and human goals. We do not do party propaganda, but we do seek to raise the public's consciousness so that people will reflect on our problems. Sometimes these are political problems, or they touch on politics, but they are not of an informative nature, but an analytical approach, so to speak.[7]

Having suggested their interest in cultural if not national independence for Puerto Rico, Nolla and Ferré establish *Zona* as a site for overtly binding politics to art. While their first priority is developing cultural production that is specific to Puerto Rico, politics are part of that project. In *Papeles*, Ferré yokes cultural production to political sovereignty by questioning the colonial and patriarchal oppression in Puerto Rico.

"Maquinolandera" is a somewhat anomalous piece in Ferré's work: it is one of the only works in *Papeles* that she never translated into English, and it marks the furthest extreme of her experimentation with lending to her prose the oral qualities of Puerto Rican speech and music. As she writes in a reflective essay on her authorial trajectory, the stories in

Papeles appear in the order in which they were written. In the middle of her writing process, she observed that "in each new story the story line became more and more tenuous and the language more complicated. In writing 'Maquinolandera,' the language reigned supreme over an almost nonexistent anecdote, the linguistic 'I' had cancelled out the historical 'I.' I understood that that path was closed to me" ("Ira" 166, my translation).[8] Instead of plot or anecdote, Ferré derives loose inspiration from the song "Maquinolandera," written by Doña Margot Rivera and performed by Ismael Rivera and Rafael Cortijo y su Combo (Aparicio 59). Frances Aparicio, one of the only critics to undertake a serious analysis of this text, reads the story as having a tripartite interpretive structure:

> The first consists of the description and canonical indication of great salsa figures: Willie Colón, Eddie Palmieri, Roberto Rohena, and among the women, Iris Chacón, Ruth Fernández, and Lucecita Benítez. The second level is a pilgrimage of sorts, a traveling movement that seems to end in a concert stage, and at times is transformed into a religious procession. At the third discursive level one listens to the voice of Ismael Rivera, the *sonero mayor*, who is imprisoned. (59)

A short story of fifteen pages, "Maquinolandera" has two story lines that alternate virtually every paragraph and finally join together in the last paragraph. The first strand follows Ismael, who, in prison, reflects on his present incarceration. The second focuses on his band members, who revolt violently against the police and who perform for their audience ("nosotros," or we). When the last band member standing, Yris, meets Ismael in prison to liberate him, it becomes unclear if the second story line has been a part of Ismael's imagination all along or if the story takes a fantastic turn at the very end.

Ferré's story maps onto Ismael Rivera's personal biography in that, after his conviction on drug-smuggling charges in 1962, he spent four years in a federal penitentiary in Lexington, Kentucky, where he formed a band and wrote many of the songs on *Bienvenido Cortijo y Rivera*, recorded upon his release. As Juan Carlos Quintero Herencia writes about Rivera's imprisonment, "What stands out on the record are Maelo's constant declarations that music allowed him to 'evade' the regulations and evidence of incarceration, the nostalgia for the beloved body or the neighborhood left behind on the other side of the sea" (303, my translation). Critics have considered "Maquinolandera" as part of Ferré's feminist writing, given its insistent reminders of women's contributions to the development of salsa (Chaves 70). Others, by highlighting its fight against racism, have underlined the foundational role of the Afro-Caribbean community in Puerto Rican culture (Aparicio 46).[9] My reading addresses Ferré's use of performance as a way of practicing full personhood. "Maquinolandera" is grounded in the specificity of Puerto Rico's musical and dance form, *bomba*, in part because the interaction between the three sets of characters creates the call-and-response effect of *bomba* within the text. Dating back to the seventeenth century and invented by African slaves, *bomba* does not typically have narrative lyrics, and its signature element is that dancers and drummers improvise off one another while the singers follow a call-and-response structure between the chorus and the lead singer (Barton 189–90). As I will show, Ismael's struggle to retain his personhood while in a state of civil death in prison relies on his capacity to access a dance circle from within himself, even in isolation. The dance circle is figured within the text as a project that joins communal sovereignty with self-possession, where the self is defined in its most expansive form.

In "Maquinolandera," self-possession is both a cultural and physical battle, entailing an armed struggle on the part of the musicians: throughout the story, they are in constant physical battle against "los agentes de la ley," those who enforce the law.[10] Instruments hide weapons, and the musicians try to persuade their audience to join them in a rebellion, the aims of which go unstated. Each of the musicians takes her or his turn leading the group down to the beach. There, the crowd is already dancing as they wait for them to arrive, and off to the side, the agents in military formation watch both performers and mass audience threateningly. Ferré writes: "Eddi galvaniza las bombas de la batería, Roberto blande feliz el lanzallamas de la flauta, Ray levanta la trompeta al nivel de sus ojos listo para disparar" (214; Eddi galvanizes the bombs of the drums, Roberto happily brandishes the flame-thrower of the flute, Ray lifts his trumpet up to his eyes and takes aim). Of the three instruments, the drums lend themselves most easily to the doubling: "bomba" is both a bomb and the name of the drum that sets the rhythm for the Puerto Rican *bomba* dance and musical form. With only slight linguistic and choreographic shifts—moving the trumpet up by inches or holding the flute aloft before bringing it to the lips—musical expression can become armed revolt. But even in the only obvious example of revolt in the musicians' battle, Ferré names neither the political parties with which the musicians might be affiliated nor the musicians' enemies.

The musicians who each step up for a solo is one of the ways that Ferré attempts to imitate the structure and sounds of the song. Rather than create a story line, the song's lyrics and structure insist on bringing together a chaotic group of people who throw themselves together into the enjoyment they can create. The story begins in the "we" voice, then, following that first paragraph, shifts between Ismael's first-person-singular reflections and an omniscient third-person-singular narration of visions of his band members. In the song, after each stanza, there is an instrumental riff where the horns and saxophones play the melody for about fifteen seconds. But in the middle of the song, the horns switch into an ending cadence instead. Before resolving the cadence, they pause: for three long seconds it seems possible that the song is over, then Ismael calls out "le toca Martín" (it's Martín's turn to play) to urge the band onward and rev the musical machine back up. Likewise, in the middle of the story, Ferré brings the various protagonists to a halt and returns to the story's beginning by repeating the first few lines of the story; only now "nosotros" instead of the audience represents the musicians' collective voice. The story departs radically from the song when two of the musicians are murdered by the ever-present enforcers of the law, and the narrative returns to Ismael in his cell. At this juncture, Ismael begins to sing in solidarity with his band, fusing the three sets of protagonists into a shared desire for self-possession. Ferré's story gestures to the social conditions—and what might bring them about—that would permit this unrestrained communal joy.

Using the song as her primary source material creates a situation in which Ferré is pushed to consistently privilege sonority and the incorporation of the song's rhythms over narrative cohesion. The song's lyrics provide no identifiable story line. Instead, the song is rich with neologisms, syncopations, and spaces for Rivera's vocal improvisation. The lyrics consist primarily of variations on the phrases "se formo la choricera," "me lleva la gozadera"[11] and two onomatopoeic neologisms: "maquinolandera" and "chumalacatera." The chorus sings "maquinolandera" steadily throughout the song to provide a stable background against which the *sonero* Ismael Rivera can improvise.[12] The communal voice is present from the outset, with the "nosotros"-figure that introduces the story's protagonists. Here, Ferré develops a form of oral prosody that takes as its point of departure the neologism Ferré adopts from Rivera's lexicon, "maquinolandera," and then modifies it. This term signifies only on tonal and rhythmic registers in both the story and the song, and never acquires a clear semantic sense.[13] "Nosotros, los maquinolanderos, somos los que somos, señores, venimos, los maquinolanderos, en nuestra maquiná" (204; We, the machinelandists, we are the ones who are, ladies and gentlemen, we have come, the machinelandists, in our machine-huh). Ferré plays with Rivera's term in two ways: first, she adds the –os suffix to masculinize and pluralize the noun; second, she reduces it to the preexisting noun, la máquina, or machine, and adds the accent on the last syllable to change its pronunciation.[14] In adopting Rivera's term, Ferré also places herself in the Caribbean poetic tradition of using *jitanjáforas*, "syllables created by the poet who, in using them, does not think about their meaning; they are fresh words, fragrant and mysterious, that go to our senses."[15] Ferré speaks about this type of linguistic play, which she discovered to be a phenomenon particular to Spanish when she began to translate her writing into English:

> The Spanish (and Latin American) literary tradition permits a much greater leeway for what may be called "play on words," which generally sound frivolous and innocuous in English. In Puerto Rico, as in Latin America, we are brought up as children on a constant juggling of words, which often has as its purpose the humorous defiance of apparent social meanings and established structures of power. In undermining the meaning of words, the Latin American child (as the Latin American writer) calls into question the social order which he is obliged to accept without sharing in its processes. ("Destiny" 157–58)

Writing in 1991, Ferré links the linguistic inventiveness of puns, simple rhymes, and the creation of supposed nonsense words to a political stance that makes a sly and roundabout case for self-possession by rejecting the imposition of oppressive forms of social order.

Ferré harnesses this now-traditional form of innovative writing to create a relationship between reader and text that stresses orality and sonority instead of the norm of reading as a still and silent act. As with Chamoiseau's transcription of the storyteller's words in the annex of *Solibo Magnifique* analyzed in chapter 2, the text becomes a guide for sounding out the combinations of phonemes that generate immense aesthetic and aural pleasure. Ferré makes us aware of the song's sonority and rhythm in her modifications to traditional orthography and use of punctuation. By transforming how readers are accustomed to encountering words on the page in terms of spacing, spelling, and punctuation, Ferré makes it easier to recognize words by sounding them out loud rather than reading them silently.[16] This practice of reading aloud has two important impacts. The first is that sound takes precedence over meaning, and the second is that the subject of the story—whether it is him-, her-, or ourselves—is reconstituted through this process.

In the opening statement of "nosotros," the reader is necessarily implicated, either by identifying him- or herself with "nosotros" by reading aloud, or by receiving the address of "nosotros" as the "señores" whom "nosotros" has set out to transform: "venimos a divinarlos, llegamos a lucimbrarlos, venimos a lunizarlos hasta hacerlos dar a luz. Maquinitamelleva, gritamos, mellevalagozadera, soneamos, seformólachoricera, bombeamos, bajo el mando de Ismael" (204; we come to assess and guess you, we arrive to illuminate you, we come to shine the light of the moon on you until you give birth/to light. Thelittlemachinetakesmeaway, we shout, ittakesmeawaythepleasureofitall, we play a *son*, thebandofthieveshascometogether, we play a *bomba*, under the command of Ismael). Throughout the story, the "nosotros" voice alternates between first-person singular and plural, marking themselves both as individuals and as a group that has chosen to act collectively. In their ecstatic response to the music, "nosotros" describes their collective action by eliminating the spaces that make individual words coherent, such as "maquinita me lleva," and turning those phrases into single, breathless units. "Nosotros" outlines the revolutionary effect they intend to have upon their interlocutors, the "señores," proclaiming, we come to assess and guess you, arrive to illuminate you, we come to shine the light of the moon on you until you give birth and or become light: "divinarlos," "lucimbrarlos, and "lunizarlos." My translation is at best an approximation because only the first of these verbs has an official dictionary definition. However, the closeness of the latter two to "luz" and "lucir" suggests that "nosotros" can in succession ascertain their audience's essence, illuminate their audience, and show them how to participate in their own consciousness-raising project.

As with *jitanjáforas* and other neologisms, Ferré at times seems to make comprehension a secondary benefit to reading "Maquinolandera" aloud: first comes the pleasure of one's own voice that must articulate the alternating alliterations and rhymes, the thrice-repeated eight-syllable verbal clauses and the sharp "i" vowels that punctuate the soft series of liquid consonants. If the reader does not read aloud, he or she becomes the subject whom "nosotros" addresses and is assimilated to the "señores." But in reading aloud, the reader adds his or her voice to that of "nosotros" and becomes part of "we" under Ismael's command. From the outset Ferré sets the tone for how "nosotros" will shift from an indeterminate voice of audience protagonists within the text to the group of musicians. The challenging poetics of the story's first paragraph ensure that who constitutes "nosotros" cannot be clearly identified. This fluid definition of "we," resulting from Ferré's oral prosody and including the possibility of readers shifting in and out of that subject, is central to the development of Ismael's concept of personhood.

In contrast with the lively fight that the musicians wage against the state, Ismael is in solitary confinement. His restriction of movement and experience of isolation are so complete that it feels like a living death, or, as Ferré writes from Ismael's perspective, "sepultado vivo en las Tumbas" (205; being buried alive in the Tombs). Here, "las Tumbas," or "the graves," is both the metaphor for the prison and a reference to a song written for Rivera by fellow songwriter Bobby Capó. The lyrics of "Las Tumbas" sets up the challenge that Ismael faces: each stanza ends with the phrase "si sigo aquí, enloqueceré. Suelta!" (If I stay here, I'll go mad. Let go!). Like the catchphrase "suelta," an exclamation in the imperative to loosen up the body, the strategy Ismael uses to counter madness and preserve his sense of self in the song "Las Tumbas" is a corporeal one: as I will explain, he senses the presence of other persons in the cell with him and develops a companionship that allows him to let his body loose as he physically shakes off his constraints. Like *Night Women*'s heroine Lilith, examined in chapter 2, who touches her face to see if she still recognizes herself in her enslavement, Ismael turns to his body as a site of preserving the integrity of his person while living in an absence of freedom.

The conjunction of intellect and corporeality in the constitution of personhood for the prisoner singing in "Las Tumbas" also marks Ismael's struggle to assert himself throughout "Maquinolandera." Colin Dayan's theorization of sensory deprivation in U.S. "super-max" prisons examines the philosophical effects of civil death, where the body is alive but constrained and no longer has any civil rights or responsibilities. I cite Dayan's description at length because she contrasts the prisoners' sensory deprivation with Descartes's theory of what becomes of the body in that environment:

> The image of persons locked down in cells, where the senses are deprived (nothing to see, no one to touch, nothing to do) sets the stage for a particularly Cartesian drama. With his "Second Meditation," Descartes supposed: "I have no senses. Body, shape, extension, movement and place are chimeras. . . . I have no senses and no body. So what remains true?" In the solitude of the special cell, inmates are left alone with their minds. But these thinking things do not have the luxury of ruminating on doubt, experimenting with the limits of thought thinking itself through. . . . [T]hese captives externalize thought, inventing themselves anew, as they make matter. (*Law* 81–82)

Rather than accept Descartes's dismissal of the body when the senses have been lost, the inmates double down on the body as a site of meaning making and as a reflection of their state of civil death and mental suffering. As I discuss throughout this book, Caribbean writers insist on contesting Cartesian philosophical legacies that separate intellect from body and locate the claim to personhood in a disembodied intellect. And in the specific case of Ismael, Ferré fully invests in the "chimeras" of the body as a means of maintaining his sense of personhood. That is, rather than enter into the Cartesian meditation that questions whether the existence of the body can be proven, Ismael places all his efforts into retaining the sensibility of his body.

In the story's second paragraph, Ferré turns away from the noisy polyphony of the crowd to the reveries that Ismael draws from the corporeal experience of civil death. These reveries, which could either be flashbacks or his dreams for the future, become more fleshed out and concretized as the story proceeds until he imagines that he is reunited with the members of his band. But at the outset, he is in complete solitude, a condition that Quintero Herencia describes as monotonous in the musical sense of "una voz sin respuesta," a voice with no answer (311). Then Ismael, narrating his experience in the first person, observes the presence of unidentifiable figures in his own exhalations. At first, he names them only with the feminine object pronoun, "las," and later on in the story, "la." It is in the bond that he forms with these bodily chimeras, the amorphous figures that he produces, that Ismael is able to preserve his sense of self:

> Me quedo inmóvil sobre el piso de mi celda y las escucho, puedo vagamente escucharlas, pongo mi oído sobre las losas y las oigo cantando, bailando, envueltas en el vaho rítmico de mi respiración, en esa humedad tibia que me crece alrededor del rostro desde el cabello a la barba haciéndome invulnerable, surgiéndome de ese tufo invisible en el calor que siempre me precede, anunciándome. . . . Cierro los ojos y las veo atravesando celda por celda las galerías de los años que he pasado aquí, sepultado vivo en las Tumbas pero siempre soñando, soneando, improvisando mi retorno al mundo en cuerpo y alma, en nota y palabra, buscando con serenidad la frase exacta, la superficie precisa que separe mi rostro del vacío. Definiéndome en la oscuridad con las yemas de los dedos para saber dónde comienza, de dónde nace ese espacio que ocupo brotándome hacia adentro, palpándome una y otra vez para reconocerme, para escucharme Ismael. (205–6)
>
> I stay here still, immobile, on the floor of my cell and I listen to them, I can hear them vaguely, I put my ear on the tiles and I can hear them singing, dancing, enveloped in the rhythmic inhalation of my breath, in that

> lukewarm dampness that grows around my face from my hair to my beard making me invulnerable, bringing out of me that invisible smell in the heat that always precedes me, announces me. . . . I close my eyes and I see them passing through cell by cell the halls of the years that I have spent here, buried alive in the Tombs but always dreaming, singing, improvising my return to the world in body and soul, in note and lyric, serenely looking for the exact phrase, the precise surface that separates my visage from the abyss. Defining myself in the darkness with my fingertips to know where it starts, from where it emerges, this space that I occupy that grows inwards into me, touching my face once and again to recognize myself.

While the sections narrated by "nosotros" are heavily punctuated, which creates syncopated pauses, Ismael's narration consists of long fluid sentences where clauses are typically not separated by commas but are instead linked with conjunctions. He conjoins his observations about his own still body and his body's interaction with others, who, in contrast to himself, are in active motion. Isolated from other people, he nevertheless thinks of himself in relationship to "las/la," these others who are both within him and remain palpable but opaque. The form of personhood that he develops over the course of the story hinges on the open attitude toward difference first signaled in this passage.

Ismael's capacity to hold on to his sense of personal identity actually depends on his relationship with "las/la," other beings that flow freely through him and are part of him while retaining their specificity. He begins to experience an open and collective form of personhood that saves him from his isolation. In his imagination, "las" will soon take the shape of his band mates, Lhuz, Rhuz, and Yris, but for the moment, he coexists comfortably with them as unnamed and unidentifiable presences who, wrapped up in the rhythmic intake of his breath, occupy space within him. The attitude of comfort Ismael adopts toward "las/la" exemplifies the ethos of nonunderstanding that Glissant places at the center of his theory of *la Relation*. The relation is a concept that "inscribes a non-hierarchical principle of unity, a relation of equality with and respect for the Other as *different* from oneself" (Murdoch 876); however, violence and domination are not excluded from its processes. The Relation does not lend itself easily to thinking about individual persons, as it is articulated about cultural encounters and not interpersonal ones, a point Glissant makes clear in *Poétique de la Relation* when he notes that *Relation* "functions somewhat like an intransitive verb, and could not correspond, for example, to the English term relation*ship*" (Wing translation 27). In his further elaborations of the Relation, however, Glissant develops a number of linked terms, such as opacity and "être en relation," or the act of being in relation, that are scalable, from the encounter of communities to that of persons.

"Being in relation" is a cultural phenomenon and also requires conscious individual effort, as Glissant suggests in a 2002 interview: "C'est par l'imaginaire que nous pouvons faire sur nous-mêmes l'effort intense et difficile de tranformation de l'être qui fasse que nous ne concevions plus l'être comme être pour soi, et que nous commencions à concevoir l'être comme être en relation" (77; It's through the imagination that we can undertake the intense and difficult effort to transform ourselves, work that would make it such that we no longer conceive of the self as "to be for oneself" and that we begin to conceive of the self as "to be in relation [my translation]). Here, the work of self-transformation would seem to take place at the scale of the individual precisely and perhaps counterintuitively for the purpose of thinking beyond the scale of the individual. Mary Gallagher's reading of Glissant's *Introduction à une poétique du divers* locates in this effort to work within the imaginary the sense that "we do not abdicate our identities when we open ourselves up to other human beings" ("Relating" 93). This conclusion brings the consequences of the Relation into conversation with the concept of personhood that undergirds the encounter of consensual possession. In this way, Ismael's sensations of "las/la" provide a literal scenario for Glissant's description of Relation as "the possibility for each person to find him or herself, simultaneously, solitary and in solidarity" (*Poetics of the Relation* 145), cognizant of the other entities that flow through him and constitute him.

Ismael's trajectory toward being able to recognize his shared condition of oppression with impoverished people around the world begins by accepting the offer of solidarity made by the possibly illusory presence of others who have joined him in his forced isolation. Ismael's body remains under the control of the federal penitentiary. This encounter with others takes place within one individual person, corresponding to the expansive definition of personhood that I examined through Marissa Chibas's demonstration of *sevís*, or possession, in chapter 1. As Ismael is already in a sense owned by the state, how is another form of possession useful for regaining self-possession? As we will see in the story's ending, imagining "las/la" to be his band mates is a form of practicing being in Relation to other persons who, like himself, exist in a state of extreme dehumanization, but with whom he has no established personal relationship. In their substitutability, "las/la" work as a fungible form of Relation. Whereas I have emphasized that the dance circle offers specificity as a means of pushing against universal Cartesian definitions of personhood, "las/la" are not, in themselves, specific or detailed in any way. Rather than specificity, "degeneralized universal," a term that Natalie Melas uses from Glissant's elaborations on Relation, perhaps best describes "las/la." As a degeneralized universal, "the universal refers not to an idea or a quality but to the 'realized quantity' of all existing particulars in relation" (145). Just as Chibas offers herself up as a radio for connecting the many other persons that pass through her to each other, Ismael permits the connection of others through him, and begins by welcoming the inchoate "las/la" to live within him.

The relationship Ismael builds with "las/la" is vital to his survival, in part because "las/la" give him the capacity to both disengage from his present environment and create the sensibility of a future that is unlike his oppressive present. For when he puts his face on the cool floor, he hears "las/la" dancing along with his breathing and he locates their presence in the warm sweat that emanates from his body, in "ese tufo invisible en el calor." Tufo, a "strong and offensive smell," connotes a suspicion that something hidden is about to take place: here, the smell testifies to an unseen presence.[17] "Las/la" are intertwined with the aspects of Ismael's body that presage incipient action, and their musical presence brings into being his tactic for surviving imprisonment: "soñando, soneando, improvisando mi retorno al mundo en cuerpo y alma, en nota y palabra" (205; dreaming, singing *son*, improvising my return to the world in body and soul, in the note and the word). Ferré equates Ismael's dream-state, "soñando," with the homonym/neologism "soneando," or singing in the style of *son*, as body and soul are made equivalent with songs and lyrics through their juxtaposition. Even in his isolation, recognizing the presence of other beings within him allows Ismael to access the sensation of performance. In so doing, he anticipates his reengagement with the outside world and exercises his self-possession.

Les Arbres musiciens: Performance and the Criticism of Limited Sovereignty

In Alexis's novel, the characters who have decided to work on behalf of U.S. interests in Haiti use a sense of inevitable national decline to justify that choice. Edgard Osmin, for example, admires the hero of the Caco revolt against the Marines Occupation, Charlemagne Péralte; however, based on his experiences in the profoundly corrupt and discriminatory

Haitian military, he claims that the patriotism that motivated the Haitian Revolution is no longer salient: "Nothing had fundamentally changed in the world, just the words, the formulas, and the forms of domination had varied. Joy, happiness, these were egotistical conquests only possible at the expense of others. . . . The world would always live off of blood, tears of blood, sweat of blood!" (20). A tension coursing through the novel is how to manage exploitation—whether to push back against power that seeks to exploit or attempt to align oneself with that power. Alexis dedicates this novel, and much of his life's work, to advocating and furthering an anticapitalist struggle for national sovereignty. Born into a wealthy Gonaïves family in 1922, Jacques-Stephen Alexis died in 1961 in an insurrection against the dictator François Duvalier. As J. Michael Dash has shown, Alexis was inspired by the political actions taken by French surrealist poets during World War II, as well as by the novelist and founder of the Haitian Communist Party, Jacques Roumain.[18] Like Roumain, Alexis's body of work calls to account Haitian political actors for abandoning their responsibilities to the people. His life, death, and writing attest to his commitment to political engagement.

Les Arbres musiciens is the second of Alexis's four literary works and, like his most-read novel, *Compère Général Soleil*, is based on a then-recent political scandal. The setting of *Arbres* is the Lescot administration's support for the Société Haitiano-Américaine pour le Développement Agricole (The Haitian-American Society for Agricultural Development, SHADA) project to cultivate rubber for the American war effort in the early 1940s; this project resulted in the appropriation of fifty thousand acres of arable land and the mass displacement of the peasantry. Ultimately, because extracting rubber from the cryptostegia vine they planted was highly inefficient, the U.S. government ended the program and offered Haiti $175,000 as total compensation for the peasants' dispossession. Matthew Smith points out that when government officials such as Minister of Agriculture Maurice Dartigue were concerned about the methods employed by SHADA, their only recourse was to plead in private with U.S.-based project leaders.[19] This example of the inability of the Haitian leadership to protect the interests of the nation's most vulnerable citizens offers Alexis a platform from which to argue for the necessity of a Marxist economic transformation in Haiti, as well as for the reassertion of Haitian sovereignty over its land and resources.

Despite the hyphen that seemingly equalizes "Haitiano" and "Américaine" in its innocuous name, SHADA represented mainly U.S. financial interests. SHADA is one of many organizations that embedded the

Haitian economy into U.S. business after the Occupation and is described by Mark Finlay in *Growing American Rubber* as "wholly owned by the Haitian government but wholly funded by the United States" (165). However, the Haitian government owned the company only by dint of a $5 million loan from the U.S.-based Export-Import Bank. What Finlay calls ownership is, in actuality, a form of indebtedness; when the venture failed in 1944, it bankrupted the Haitian government, which was forced to pay off its U.S. creditors before being able to compensate those who had lost their livelihoods to the rubber vine experiment. This relationship is a holdover from the Occupation (1915–34), when the United States controlled the Haitian treasury through the figure of the Receiver General and Financial Adviser appointed by the United States, who, after collecting all of the nation's revenues, funded his office's expenses first, foreign and public debts second, then the police and army, and finally the Haitian government's expenses (Dupuy 132). During the Lescot presidency, control over finances was returned to Haitian officials, yet, as transcripts from the U.S. Department of State reveal, the repayment of foreign loans remained the budgetary priority—despite the will of the Haitian government to direct funds otherwise. Moreover, the implementation of SHADA as described by Alexis is reminiscent of Occupation strategies of the *corvée*—the involuntary labor crews building the network of roads needed for the corporate agricultural economy to operate efficiently. In these regards, there is little difference between the financial impositions experienced by Haitians during the Occupation and after the Marines' departure.[20]

In *Arbres*, Alexis introduces SHADA early on, first through the political elite's discourse of entrepreneurship, then rearticulated through the lower class's suspicion of the project. An omniscient narrator describes the official language used to depict the plan, placing in quotes only the phrases "allies" and "the great nation and friend" (65). At the end of the speech, the phrase "his policy would henceforth be a faithful reflection of the policies of the United States" betrays the narrator's cynical view of the president's characterization of the relationship between the United States and Haiti as one of mutual friendship. In this rendering of official policy, there is no room for differentiation between Haitian and U.S. interests. One set of *Arbres*' protagonists, the Osmin brothers, works to implement SHADA's plan. Born into the lower-middle class and guided toward upward mobility by their mother, each brother represents the participation of a sector of Haitian civil society in furthering SHADA's goals. Edgard, a military man, enforces the peasants' eviction; Diogène, a Catholic priest, carries out the "anti-superstition" campaign aimed at weakening the Vodou community's capacity to resist their economic dispossession; Carles, a lawyer, ultimately becomes an ambassador to the United States. Despite their misgivings and cynicism toward the Haitian government and its U.S. partners, the Osmin brothers reflect the president's ambition to twin Haiti's interests with those of the United States.

The novel approaches the destruction of the peasantry in favor of U.S. business interests from three perspectives and three sets of protagonists whose paths converge: the three Osmin brothers; the fictional vodouisant peasant community at "Nan-Remembrance"[21] led by the Vodou priest Papa Bois-d'Orme; and the young orphan Gonaïbo, who grew up in the mountain forests, completely isolated from society. Each group has its own cast of characters and plot twists, but the novel begins with the Osmin brothers and follows their deepening complicity with SHADA. When the community of Nan-Remembrance is introduced, there are rumors that their land is due to be taken over, and they immediately begin to resist their eviction and the "anti-superstition" campaign waged against them by the Catholic Church. The last protagonist to be introduced is Gonaïbo, who is chased out of his prelapsarian paradise by the arrival of the rubber plantation, after which he joins forces with Bois-d'Orme's resistance, and finally becomes part of the proletarian laboring class. Edgard and Diogène are ultimately destroyed, but not before the vodouisant community of Nan-Remembrance is defeated, scattered to the cities or forced to take up employment with SHADA as day laborers on the land that was formerly their home. Although Alexis ends the novel on a hopeful note with Gonaïbo entering into a modern, communist consciousness, all three plotlines indicate the continuous U.S. encroachment on the goal of political and economic independence that was inaugurated with the creation of the Haitian Republic. The scenario that Alexis develops through this plot presents the future communist revolution—for which Gonaïbo still waits at the end of the novel—as a deeply nationalist project that will return Haiti to a state of full sovereignty.

Arbres is studded with representations of performance, from the stories dramatizing the past told by the elder statesmen in the rural areas and the hymns that structure Vodou to the fashionable dances played in the bourgeois salons and the biting political songs invented by the urban poor. Alexis interrupts the description of the political machinations surrounding SHADA with two versions of the Andrews Sisters' 1945 arrangement of the song "Rum and Coca-Cola."[22] Both versions modified by Port-au-Prince's crowds provide a snapshot of the general population's assessment of SHADA's program. The first version is a Coca-Cola radio jingle in French. The second version, in Kreyòl, is a fierce and unabashed accusation of the Haitian government's hypocrisy. Prior to the introduction of the song, Alexis critically assesses the Lescot administration, focusing on how its policies of colorism, which Alexis calls "la mulâtromanie lescotiaque," diverted attention from the transfer of national resources from Haiti to foreign investors. A wartime jingle naming Coca-Cola as the drink of choice among heads of state, "Roosevelt Coca-Cola! Churchill Pepsi-Cola! Acheson Soya-Cola!," is modified by the Haitian populace with the addition: "Lescot est un papa-caca" (161). This scatological insult, inspired by the assonance between "cola" and "caca," illustrates how the Haitian people compare Lescot to other heads of state.

The second version of the song departs radically from the original lyrics, replacing them with a litany of accusations of graft. This version is written in Kreyòl. Because Kreyòl rarely appears in the body of the text, the politics of its use throughout *Arbres* bear on the interpretation of this exceptional use in the transcription of the popular song lyrics. As it was for many writers of his generation, engaging Haiti's culture, language, and political life was essential to Alexis's work.[23] But like the late-twentieth-century writers Chamoiseau and James, whose use of vernacular creole languages I analyze in chapter 2, Alexis faced the problem of how to remain legible to metropolitan readers while incorporating Kreyòl. While Kreyòl words are interspersed throughout *Arbres* to reference local plants, foods, or spiritual terms,[24] the primary instances of full Kreyòl phrases are Alexis's inclusion of song lyrics, that is, the linguistic element of the performance events that mark the text.[25] Léon-François Hoffman links this mode of including Kreyòl to the familiar phenomenon in French regionalist novels where bilingualism is used to "give 'local color'" (42). For Alexis, however, the inclusion of songs in Kreyòl is an opportunity to demonstrate the political awareness and satirical savvy on the part of the urban masses he represents in the Port-au-Prince sections of the novel.

The Kreyòl lyrics indicate that the people singing their own version of "Rum and Coca-Cola" were fully conscious of the economic impact of Lescot's policies, and that their attention was not diverted by the identity politics that consumed the governing classes.

> Hé wa! Hé wa!
> Yo barré Lescot!

> Yo barré Lescot sept fois devant caisse l'État ap volè
> Yo barré Sauveur sept fois devant cimitiè l'Arcahaie!
> Yo barré Lacroix, yo barré Gontran . . .
>
> Note 1: We surprised Lescot seven times in front of the State's coffers while he was stealing! We surprised our savior seven times in front of the Arcahaie cemetery, etc. (161)

The criticism in this version of the song is precise: Lescot and his associates are named in rhythmic order. Following the repetition of the "Yo barré" accusation, the lyrics forego insults in order to denounce the specific abuses of power and position.

The appropriation of "Rum and Coca-Cola" by the Haitian masses references a broader Caribbean history of musical social commentary. The lyrics to "Rum and Coca-Cola" were originally written and performed by the Trinidadian calypsonian Lord Invader, whose version is more pointedly caustic than that of the Andrews Sisters.[26] Like the fictional Nan-Remembrance community whose land was taken over for the U.S war effort, the people who lived on the northwest peninsula of Trinidad were evicted and their homes demolished to make space for a United States air base. The circulation of this song reveals a regional critique of the United States' forcible inclusion of the Caribbean in its sphere of influence. Therefore, even in using the somewhat softened version of "Rum and Coca-Cola" performed by the Andrews Sisters, Alexis connects Haiti's Kreyòl songs with the practices of Trinidad's calypsonians, who, as Ray Funk writes, voice "a subversion of the status quo, a move from a respectful deference to colonial rule to a new postcolonial consciousness" (58). The Haitian citizens whose singing Alexis references draw on a pan-Caribbean tradition of protest songs as they voice their consciousness of how colonial dynamics reemerge, even in a country that claims the status of independent nation.

In *Arbres*, Alexis imagines the ways that the state's limited sovereignty impacts one small community. This focus brings into relief two different approaches to the state's failures, one encapsulated by the disillusioned military officer Edgard Osmin, the other by the naïve mountain man Gonaïbo.[27] Despite his fury at the current government, Edgard's opinion is that a militaristic nationalism is the only way for Haiti to recoup its sovereignty. He articulates this idea from the perspective of what Michel de Certeau calls the "totalizing eye," which possesses the power of the distanced survey (92). The macrovision and lack of concern for the fate of individual persons in favor of national aims put his approach at odds with the mode of interaction that Gonaïbo, the novel's hero, will eventually adopt when he comes into contact with other individuals. Gonaïbo's only interaction with the state has been through SHADA, the company to which the government has deferred its decision making. Therefore, rather than invest in the idea of the nation as Edgard does, Gonaïbo builds his community one individual at a time, interacting with each person on an almost cellular level, as we will see. Given Gonaïbo's status as a man born in the wild who has neither been corrupted by society nor had the opportunity to belong to a community, the sections of the novel that focus on his perspective explore how a person can be in relation.

The fundamental methodological distinction between their approaches is a difference of scale. Edgard sees the nation on a macro level, whereas Gonaïbo attends to what can be seen at the micro level. Geographers such as Neil Smith have theorized these differences in various scales and have attributed a social dimension to them: "Scale is an active progenitor of specific social processes. In a literal as much as metaphorical way, scale both *contains* social activity, and at the same time provides an already partitioned geography within which social activity *takes place.* Scale demarcates the sites of social contest, the object as well as the resolution of contest" (66). Scale, then, determines how social action takes place. What I want to elicit in contrasting the scales at which Edgard and Gonaïbo operate is how their different senses of proportion also identify what they each find worthy of their respective attention and what is within the scope of intelligibility. In shifting between macro and micro, Alexis suggests rethinking self-possession through community formation on a small scale rather than at the scale of the nation.

When Edgard Osmin is invited by his Dominican counterpart Raúl Cordero to take a plane flight to survey their shared national border, Edgard experiences the vertigo of envisioning space at various geographical scales in rapid succession: he evinces a sense of mastery over the landscape that he sees from a bird's-eye view, and he glories in the interpretations of the nation that this perspective's "totalizing eye" lends him. Three sentences in a row end in exclamation points as Edgard entertains an exultant ultranationalist fantasy of reconquering the entire island of Hispaniola; due to his elevated position, he has arrogated to himself the right of interpretation of the landscape. Alexis links Edgard's cold execution of SHADA's orders to destroy the community of Nan-Remembrance with the arrogant pleasure he derives from this large-scale perspective. Edgard's fantasy of mastery is momentarily interrupted by the recognition that his interpretation discounts the energy and movement that the landscape exercises: "With a clarity that he hadn't recognized until that moment, Edgard suddenly realized that this land was alive. He felt incredibly afraid. So, what looked like nothing but a disorganized heap of vegetable matter rumbled with a secret life? . . . Was that right? At the scale of, and from the perspective of the eyes, was immobility nothing but slowness?" (190). When Edgard shifts geographical scales from the "totalizing eye" to what Alexis calls "à l'échelle des yeux," the scale of an individual's eye, he acknowledges the possibility that what he has chosen to interpret as static and haphazardly organized is propelled by an internal logic that drives its movement. At the scale of the individual body, in contrast to the panoramic scale that can privilege only national concerns, he is forced to confront the landscape as a being that does not exist simply to be rearranged according to his will but rather as one that moves of its own volition. In the movement between macro and micro, what had been evident at one scale disappears as another set of observations becomes available.

Edgard's desire to see the world from above is opposed to Gonaïbo's instinct to interact with the world on a cellular level. To return to the treatment of visibility and opacity in chapter 3, Certeau's "totalizing eye," which I identify with Edgard's scale, corresponds to a commodifying and instrumentalizing gaze, whereas Gonaïbo's scale, as I will show, almost displaces visibility in favor of physical sensation as the mode of interaction. Gonaïbo interacts with others not from a lofty height that erases individual concerns in favor of broader geopolitical goals but from the most minor scale available to the naked eye. It is this scale that Gonaïbo insists on employing to challenge the U.S. economic invasion of his territory. Shortly after he is introduced in the novel, he comes upon an injured stranger, and as he heals the man who will later be revealed to be the third Osmin brother, Carles, Gonaïbo imagines himself gliding through the unknown injured body. The way he moves through the body of another person echoes Marissa Chibas's onstage method of portraying personhood as fluid and open, as theorized in chapter 1. Whereas Chibas and Ismael in "Maquinolandera" take other beings into their bodies, Gonaïbo reverses this process and fits himself into the body of the stranger, tracing the path of Carles's traveling neurons.

As Gonaïbo observes Carles's lightly rustling body, he thinks: "Chaque homme est revêtu d'une cotte de mailles, d'une tunique qui le gante des pieds à la tête, n'est-ce pas?" (55; Each man is dressed in chainmail, a tunic that gloves him from head to feet, is that not the case?).

The premise that skin is a piece of clothing, necessary but penetrable protective armor for one's interior, permits Gonaïbo to imagine Carles's insides. Using the methodology he employs to analyze and interpret the structure of plants and animals in his area, Gonaïbo begins to move through Carles's body, investigating it at a cellular scale:

> Gonaïbo se fit petit, il s'insinua par les seules fissures qu'il trouvât, les yeux, la bouche, les narines. Par la pensée il s'allongea dans le blessé couché sur son lit d'herbes fraîches. Oui, puisqu'il le voulait, il pouvait pénétrer dans cet inconnu. Idéalement, il mit ses jambes dans les siennes, son thorax dans le sien, il enfila ses bras dans ceux du gisant et se laissa aller. Il avait l'impression de ressentir toutes les perceptions internes de l'homme. Il éprouva toutes ses sensations physiques, le poids d'une cuisse sur un autre, la plaque moite que faisait le gras du bras contre le pectoral, toute la cénesthésie des organes endormis et du sang fusant. Il s'emplit de tout ce lourd sommeil, profond et dolent qui engourdissait le blessé. Il éprouva tous ses neurones dont un bouquet électrisé descendait du cerveau à travers la moelle jusqu'à cette cheville épouvantablement blessée. Aïe! cette conscience! (55–56)

> Gonaïbo made himself very small, he insinuated himself into the only fissures he found, the eyes, the mouth, the nostrils. With his thought he laid down inside the wounded man who was lying down on a bed of fresh herbs. Yes, because he wanted to do so, he could penetrate into this unknown. Through the imagination, he put his legs inside his, his thorax inside his, he slipped his arms inside those of the immobile man and let himself relax. He thought he felt all of the man's internal perceptions. He experienced all his physical sensations, the weight of a thigh of another, the moist plank formed by the thick arm against the chest, all of the malaise of the sleeping organs and the sliding blood. He was filled with all the heavy sleep, heavy and suffering that paralyzed the injured man. He felt all his neurons in an electrified grouping descending from the brain through the marrow all the way to the horribly injured ankle. Aie! that conscience!

The body he describes is, despite its unconscious, injured condition, a body whose intellect and physicality are inseparable. Alexis echoes Gonaïbo's conception of the skin as the body's clothing: he describes Gonaïbo settling his chest into Carles's as if nestling the palm of a hand into that glove. Once in place, Gonaïbo experiences the functioning of the body on an ever-more-minute scale, first with the shape and weight of the body, then its internal organs; then he accompanies the flow of blood and the cells it carries with it as it circulates throughout the body.

In conjoining the body's neurological functions with Carles's consciousness and his limbs, Alexis fuses physicality and psyche.

In his description of Gonaïbo's approach to interacting with another person, Alexis weaves together mind and body, incorporating the diction of his medical training to present a view of the body that is both physiologically precise and poetically imaginative.[28] Gonaïbo treats each limb and organ as a source of knowledge that, particularly in the description of sleeping organs, seems to possess its own anthropomorphic qualities. For Alexis, the workings of the conscience and those of the body's parts are indistinguishable in that both are powered by the brain's neurons. In this regard, he describes what Elizabeth Grosz calls "embodied subjectivity, or psychical corporeality" (22) in her theorization of a feminist philosophy of the body, which she defines as "avoid[ing] the impasse posed by dichotomous accounts of the person which divide the subject into the mutually exclusive categories of mind and body" (21). I have argued that the refusal to separate knowledge production from corporeality that Grosz ascribes to feminist philosophy is also the project that Caribbean writers take up in their representation of performing bodies and their kinesthetic intelligence. Linking scale to the analysis of performance events highlights a mode of attending to bodies that will be crucial to the meanings Alexis and Ferré allot to dancing bodies in the endings of both texts. Being privy to how the communities of Nan-Remembrance and Ismael Rivera's band members insist that they are persons and not laboring things requires a willingness to adjust one's scale, recalibrating it so as to include those whose exclusion makes their claims to personhood unintelligible to the state.

Dance as Momentum: Final Interruptions

In the phrase "nada se interrumpe, nada comienza, nada termina" ("Maquinolandera" 207; nothing gets interrupted, nothing begins, nothing ends), Ismael identifies the absence of change in the temporality that permeates both texts: time simply is. For the Osmin brothers, people from Nan-Remembrance, and Ismael and his band members, social transformation seems impossible. And yet, at the ends of both texts, Ferré's and Alexis's ekphrases of performance stage interruptions to the status quo of exploitation. In "Maquinolandera," the narrative ceases to alternate between Ismael's reveries and the reality of his prison cell, instead diving deep into a possibly fantasy world where Yris dances through the bars of his prison cell, breaking them down and freeing him; in *Arbres*, Alexis counteracts the sounds of chainsaws destroying natural and human habitats with scenes of Diogène Osmin wandering the forest and taking note of its eternal presence, the community of Nan-Remembrance dancing to continue its traditions, and Gonaïbo forming family. At the close of both texts, Ferré and Alexis use these final performance events to create a momentum that can push beyond the protective confines of the circle. To recall Fanon's disappointment that the dance circle seems to function as an outlet for repressed energies rather than an opportunity to choreograph armed revolt, in these texts, what begins as small communal exchanges around dance spills out of the dance circle and into a more general sense of the political. In *Arbres*, the dance circle cements the community's resistance despite their continued oppression, and in "Maquinolandera," the dance circle is the impetus for self-possession. Here, they do not write about the oppressive impacts of limited sovereignty at the national scale, but instead focus on the details and meanings of the dancers' movements at the scale of the human eye. The representation of performance allows the protagonists to generate the momentum with which, against all realistic expectations, they mount a challenge to their dispossession and assert their full personhood.

As the narrative strands of "Maquinolandera" come together at the end of the story, they all participate in the project of Ismael's reclamation of personhood while incarcerated: "las/la" are now fully physicalized as his band members whom the audience accompanies into the cell and form a dance circle around him. But after all the musicians have perished in their fight against the law's agents, only Yris, the dancer, remains. She takes command of the *tarima*, the stage, and in her dance, she fends off the agents and encourages her audience to do the same. By incarnating constant movement, her gyrations create a visually unfixable subject that keeps "las/la" opaque and indefinable, even when its presence is filled with the specter of one of Ismael's band members. Indeed, the most specific definition that Ferré will provide for "las/la" is their association with the "the implacable rhythm of her voice fomenting the revolution." The story's last incarnation of "las/la" is Yris, but Lhuz and Ruz, the singers who preceded Yris in battle and were subsequently killed, also embodied "las/la" by inciting their listeners to revolution. Therefore, "las/la" do not refer to one messianic individual, but to the momentum-building corporeal rhythms and vocalizations that the musicians each take their turn performing.

In the story's last three paragraphs, Ferré's characters overcome their losses as "nosotros," Ismael, and "las/la" are finally able to join each another in an exuberant reunion. When the singer Lhuz dies and the dancer Yris takes her place, "nosotros" once again use the rhythmic neologisms that invite the reader to read out loud: "Traigounabomba, coreamos, comounatromba, quinteamos, suenasabroso, tumbeamos, bajo el mando de Ismael" (220; I'mbringinga*bomba,* wechant, I'meatingatrombone, we quintet, itsoundsdelicious, we drum, under the command of Ismael).[29] As in the first paragraph where Ferré introduces this technique, the communal first-person-plural "we" sing lyrics that articulate the voice of a first-person-singular *sonero*, the "I" voice that throughout the story is associated with Ismael. After reminding the reader of her investment in the "nosotros" voice, the perspective shifts back to omniscient third person to describe Yris's assumption of the responsibility for galvanizing the audience with "un movimiento poderoso que arrastrara a las masas" (221; a powerful movement that would drag the masses along with it). The paragraph ends with the description of her body in the moment before she begins to dance; as she does, she enters into Ismael's consciousness, bringing "nosotros" along with her.

Ferré represents the dancer's body in motion by describing not only her movements but also the ways in which her audience members are impacted by the performance, a strategy we've also seen employed by Chamoiseau and Cabrera Infante. Yris has two different kinds of audience members, each of whom requires a different relationship: "nosotros" and "señores." The former refers to those who have come to participate in Ismael's performance; the latter references the law's agents, those who have come to shut the show down. To the latter, she shouts "Nometoques" (donttouchme) as the agents rush at her with dogs. Despite the violence of these attacks, each of the law's six assaults is countered with the phrase "nadie se atreve a tocarla" (222; no one dares to touch her). Yris's corporeal actions bring into being her imperative demands. Her dance is a call to arms echoed in her command: "yo soy la checha, señores, sacúdanse, al son de su último elepé" (221; I am the boss [feminized neologism of *el cheche*], gentlemen, shake yourselves, to the sound of his latest LP); under her guidance, the audience takes up the rifles, flame-throwers, and machine guns abandoned by the fleeing agents of the state. Because of the reaction she prompts in her audience, Yris's presence brings armed rebellion into Ismael's cell at the end of the story:

> Por fin ha entrado por las puertas de mi celda como quien pasa por las puertas de la gloria. El cuerpo helado erguido ante mí, destellando ira hasta enceguecerme, la observo, supurándola gota a gota por los ojos como un veneno mortal, destilándola lentamente por los surcos de mis mejillas en las lágrimas

> cristalinas de la yuca, cuajándola en el llanto de los siglos, en los sollozos de todos los descastados y de todos los oprimidos, de los destituidos y de los ajusticiados, de los abandonados para siempre por la esperanza, supurada de sangre por todas la heridas, empantanada de pus, encenegada de semen y enlodada de heces, parida con terror por entre feces et urinae saca la cara al sol y escucho su grito: Chúmalacateramaquinólandera! (222)
>
> Finally, she has come in through the doors of my cell like she's passing through heaven's gates. The freezing body standing straight in front of me, emitting rays of anger until I'm blinded, I watch her, watching her fester through the eyes drop by drop as though she's a mortal poison, distilling her slowly through the hollows of my cheeks in the crystal tears of the yucca, coagulating her in the tearful cries of the centuries, in the sobs of all the outcasts and of all the oppressed people, of the destitute and of the condemned, of those abandoned forever by hope, pus festering through the blood of all her wounds, submerged in pus, mired in semen and soiled with shit, birthed with terror in between feces and urine thrusts her face up to the sun and I hear her shout: Chúmalacateramaquinólandera!

The writing practice that Ferré has developed throughout the story of pushing words together to imitate their spoken rhythm and pushing together clause after clause pays off in the story's final paragraphs: this section produces the sensation of an unstoppable train and, in its aesthetics, matches the content of Ferré's description of Yris's dance. With only four sentences dividing a paragraph of thirty lines, the reader is carried through the scene with few grammatically authorized stopping points. These sentences are, by and large, fragment sentences, composed of parallel nominal clauses anchored in present participles that describe Yris's movements. This series of seemingly unending fragments forms a linguistic trace of the awed audience members' sensorial overload; the overwhelming excess they experience is then communicated to the reader through a syntactical overload. Using the present progressive tense to represent Ismael's response to Yris's energized and dancing body, Ferré creates a sense of continuous action that builds momentum into the future. The linguistic momentum Ferré generates in her ekphrastic writing represents the multiple sources of energy that Yris controls in her dance: explosions and lightning originate from hips and breasts respectively, while her whirling hair acts as a fisherman's net.[30] Locating energy and movement in multiple sites of the body simultaneously is a performance principle that Brenda Dixon Gottschild identifies as rooted in the African movement tradition of polycentrism. As Dixon Gottschild explains, "From the Africanist standpoint, movement may emanate from any part of the body, and two or more centers may operate simultaneously."[31] Yris's capacity to address multiple audiences and to interact with them differently results from the dance technique in which each segment of the body is allotted its own activity and differentiated effect, functioning as a "democracy of parts" (Dixon Gottschild 14). In the movement's multiple directions, Yris mirrors how Ismael has come to allow a multiplicity of voices to reside within his own consciousness.

After the announcement of her arrival, the rest of the paragraph is one long sentence of nested clauses that moves the reader through Ismael's neural pathways as one realization leads to the next. We begin with Yris's body and the first main clause: "I observe her." Looking at her, what he sees first is his own interactive interpretations of this body: *supurándola, destilándola, cuajándola.* Then, he reflects on what he is coagulating her into: the tears and shouts of those Fanon calls *les damnés.* With the historical sweep of centuries and the absence of descriptors identifying the specific populations that have been dehumanized in their exploitation, Ferré deliberately moves away from the precise case of Puerto Rico and U.S. imperialism in the twentieth century. Similarly, in this moment of global consciousness, Ismael concentrates neither on his own individual welfare nor on the question of political independence. Instead, his attention is focused on the most open, most inclusive set of connections possible: self-possession at the scale of his own body and all of the connections that bind him to his audience members and fellow performers. This string of clauses naming the dispossessed, placed as it is within the description of Yris's body, demonstrates that Ismael has refocused his vision of "las/la" from just Yris to Yris and the voices inhabiting her body. This moment of recognition is magnified in the last words of the story when he hears what Yris shouts. Her cry, which articulates the cry of the masses he sees within her, is his own song lyric. Here, temporalities converge: "las/la," incarnated by Yris, arrive in his present prison cell to help him reclaim his personhood. The dance through which they enact that defiant self-defense, the "nometoques," is fueled by Ismael's previous performances of the song "Maquinolandera." By singing the *son* that brought Yris and the audience together, Ismael galvanizes them into action and transforms them into an oppositional force, both anticipating and making possible his own experience of self-possession.

Throughout "Maquinolandera," Ferré drives "nosotros" and the group of musicians toward the same beach, while Ismael is separated from them, yearning and alone. In the very last moments of the story, she brings them all together when Yris bursts through the prison. The anxiety and searching that have motivated "Maquinolandera" seem to have reached a resolution: "Por fin," it begins, "at last!" Despite the reference to marching through heaven's gates, the arrival is not a specific destination nor does it signal the successful conclusion of an event. In one sense, the prison break and Ismael's physical freedom are nothing more than fantasy. But in another, this moment of exultant liberation is his present reality, brought into being by Ismael's capacity to articulate his relationship with "las/la," who have kept him company during his imprisonment. In Yris's arrival, Ismael recognizes the transformation that has been taking place in his consciousness. His willingness to give "las/la" the space to be unknown and opaque to him and then to be replaced with different persons now prepares him to recognize the fluidity of "las/la," who have been expanded to include the world's most vulnerable and damaged populations. Unknown to him as individuals, they are nevertheless as much a part of him as his own breath. Through Yris, whose presence is both generated by his imagination and, in turn, fuels his imagination, Ismael is filled with a sense of solidarity that takes him far beyond his prison cell. The spatial reach of solidarity enables him to "recognize myself [as] Ismael" (206).

Ismael's response to the depersonalization of imprisonment is to delve deeply into his interiority. He draws on his memories of a corporeality that is denied to him in isolation, and, in spite of that isolation, creates an experience of solidarity. To access this experience and refashion his present, he uses memories of performance events. In immersing Ismael and the reader in the feeling of solidarity, Ferré pushes aside the reality of the future in prison that lies before him. Her use of performance within the text maps onto what Jill Dolan terms the "utopian performative," discussed in chapter 1, where utopia is defined as politics and ideas of which we are not yet conscious (Muñoz 3).[32] The means of making these daydreams a present reality may not be evident—and in the political framework of these two texts, may seem impossible—but their presence is palpable. As "a performative that 'does' utopia in its utterance" (173), the utopian performative's strength is in the affect it elicits from its audience: "The utopian performative, by its very nature, can't translate into a program for social action, because it's most effective as *feeling*. Perhaps that feeling of hope, or that feeling of desire, embodied by that suddenly hollow space in the pit of my stomach that drops me into an erotics of connection and commonality—perhaps such intensity of *feeling* is politics enough for utopian performatives" (19–20). Yris's presence in the jail cell and Ismael's physical liberation cannot be accounted for in the world of the text. The relations built through these ephemeral performances, the "las/la" that live in Ismael's breath, cannot last. In spite of their impossibility, these communities bring themselves into being in the dance circle. Through their dance, they interrupt a political context that would deny them personhood.

In the penultimate chapter of *Arbres*, many of the novel's major characters are removed from the action: Bois-d'Orme dies and is buried by Gonaïbo; Edgard Osmin is shot and killed by one of the peasants of Nan-Remembrance, who then commits suicide; Carles Osmin has left for Washington, D.C., as a diplomatic liaison, and Diogène Osmin suffers a mental breakdown; the bulldozers finally arrive at Nan-Remembrance and finish the complete destruction of the community's homes that had begun with Diogène's "anti-superstition" campaign. Despite this destruction, the novel ends on a hopeful note. While *Arbres* does not veer so far from the realism of its context and in fact does propose a Marxist revolution, Alexis's evocations of performance toward the end of the novel, like Ferré's, rely on the feeling of connection that Dolan names the utopian performative. Alexis calls on two elements to justify that hope, the eternal musicality of the eponymous *arbres musiciens* and the corporeal practice of resistance embodied in the Vodou dance performed by the members of the community of Nan-Remembrance at the outset of their exodus.

The last chapter of *Arbres* continues this interweaving of endings and endurance, this time focusing on the interactions between the remaining characters and the forest, which is itself being cut down to make way for the rubber plantations. Diogène, his senses heightened by his madness, is aware of the forest's activity on a very small scale and interprets this activity as the force of the Haitian people and source of the spiritual strength that he had so recently sought to crush (398). As his brother Edgard had suspected, at the scale of the eye, the forest reveals its vital movement: Diogène observes the bustling lives of mushrooms and reads into the forest's ecosystem of predators and prey the brutal human struggles for power. Telescoping out from the drama of insects and mushrooms, we see that the forest as a whole also functions cohesively: "The entire forest is an enormous pipe organ that articulates its melody with a polyphonous voice. . . . Each one of the colossal tree trunks . . . makes music with its own sonority, each pine tree is a tube of the extraordinary instrument. The great centenarian trees act in concert with hundreds of voices and chromatic resources that are unceasingly renewed" (395). Alexis builds a poetic metaphor out of a literal description of Haiti's *filao* trees, in English called "whispering pines" because of their sounds. In this description, Alexis stresses the quantity and variety of different participants in the musical form as well as the capacity for each participant to have a unique sound and yet create a unified and musically complex whole. If the forest represents the Haitian people for Diogène, then by analogy, this description offers an example of belonging and social contribution with no mention of socioeconomic or racial hierarchy. Equally as important, because Alexis endows the forest with constancy, the Haitian forest signals continuity through its hundred-year-old trees that are ceaselessly renewing their voices. Despite the fact that this very forest was being felled to plant cryptostegia at the moment that Diogène wandered through it and observed its eternal qualities, Alexis depicts the forest as engaged in a continuous act of musical performance in which the Haitian people can always find recourse.[33]

Just as the example of the forest's eternal continuity in the midst of its present decimation seems rife with internal contradiction, the Vodou dance of the community of Nan-Remembrance defiantly practices the continuity of ritual even as this group is about to be destroyed. While awaiting dispossession, the peasant community of Nan-Remembrance continues its business of harvesting crops and, for the last time, performs important rituals such as cleaning the cemetery to pay respect to the dead. Alexis presents as both surprising and essential that in the midst of this activity, an unnamed drummer starts up the beat of the traditional Haitian *mahi* rhythm, and the community gathers around him to dance.[34] After a brief description of the dancers, Alexis begins to write a Fanonian circle, by broadening his description from the dancers' engagement with the music and tying the very act of dancing to what he calls "l'invariable optimisme du paysan haïtien" (386; the unwavering optimism of the Haitian peasant). The invariability of their attitude acts as a corrective to the sociopolitical upheaval, and this constancy finds its corporeal expression and physical renewal in the dance:

> À l'ouest, le vieux soleil se roule dans un lit de nuages multicolores et de l'est accourt une nuit bleue sur la campagne ragaillardie par le tam de joie. Dansez, frères! Foulez aux pieds l'amer, l'incolore, le stupide et blême découragement! Recréez la joie au cœur même de la douleur, faites jaillir la faim et le désir de vos corps abandonnés! Manger et aimer sont les deux mamelles de la vie, mais l'homme peut de lui-même relancer son cœur grâce aux fontaines-joies

qu'il a inventées. . . . L'entrelacs de sons et de rythmes s'enchevêtre, la forte poésie des corps qui ondulent ébranle les colonnes du malheur, la féerie des couleurs, la magie des mots-souvenirs et la toute-puissante imagerie des merveilles resculpte l'homme. . . . Dansez, frères! Secouez vos hanches, faites tomber les frimas qui s'accrochent à l'âme, dansez et revivez! (387)

To the west, the old sun rolls in a bed of multicolor clouds and from the east, a blue night rushes up on the countryside that is once again lively with the joyful drum. Dance, brothers! Push down at your feet the bitter, colorless, stupid and bland discouragement. Re-create joy in the very heart of pain, thrust hunger and desire out of your abandoned bodies! Eating and loving are the two breasts of life, but man can from his own self relaunch his heart thanks to the joy-founts that he has invented. . . . The interlacing of sound and rhythm tangle themselves up, the strong poetry of bodies who undulate weaken and shake the columns of misery, the magic of colors, the magic of memory-words and the all-powerful imagery of marvels re-sculpts man. . . . Dance, brothers! Shake your hips, let the thick fog hanging onto your soul fall away, dance and be reborn!

On the one hand, the *mahi* stands in for human creativity, Alexis's chosen example of the "fountains of joy" that people invent. But on the other hand, the pushing down, thrusting, and undulating to which Alexis makes reference is not metaphorical: it is a literal description of the *mahi* dance.[35] In *The Drums of Vodou,* Lois Wilcken and Frisner Augustin describe the *mahi* as concentrating the movement in the shoulders and back, while also requiring intricate foot movement: the shoulder and back movement is produced when "the chest is thrown backwards by a forward movement of the shoulders on each medium binary pulse," and the footwork choreography requires the dancer to "support herself on the left leg; the dancer raises the right to outline an arc no higher than knee level in the space behind her. Her right foot touches the ground on the first slow pulse and is followed by a left step, then a right step in place" (105). The *mahi* is a fast tempo dance, and the feet stay close to the ground, as Katherine Dunham mentions, sliding and scraping against it in rough and almost constant contact. When dancing the *mahi*, the feet push down against the ground, while the shoulders shake. The community of Nan-Remembrance will be scattered from its grounded location, and its former members will lose the objects and places that held them together. However, the performance tradition of Vodou rituals will also allow them to carry the physical movements that hold memory within them: "remembrance" is built into the discipline of heels that alternately touch and scuff against the ground 240 times per minute and shoulders that thrust raised palms out in a gesture of openness. This moment is a rehearsal, cementing the muscle memory of a community so that after the dispersal, the communal body can be revived every time one of its members brings it into being with the *mahi.*

Drawing on Delores Cayou's identification of "functionalism—becoming what you dance" as the way that identity can be constructed through African diasporic performance, Thomas DeFrantz argues further that "a hallmark of social dance practice in the African diaspora is the communal valuation of the dancer's ability to speak *in the imperative* through dance movement" ("Black Beat" 69–70, my emphasis). More so than personal identity, the repetition of this traditional movement at this particular moment reaffirms a sense of communal identity; it also expresses optimism that this shared identity will be retained despite the dispersal. The narrator interprets the meaning of the dance as a set of imperative commands: dance, shake your hips, and live once more. According to the last command of the series, by dancing the *mahi*, the dancers shake off their metaphysical angst as they shake their hips.

As with Ismael's imprisonment, the community of Nan-Remembrance has undergone the absolute devaluation of their livelihoods, as well as the spiritual practices around which they organize their lives. Their nation's leaders, ashamed of their Vodou practices lest Haiti be judged as primitive, have reduced these persons to a dispensable remainder whose only use is determined according to the needs of U.S. industry. But in this moment, the dancers contest their transformation into pure labor-value. "Dansez et revivez": by dancing, they revive themselves and use what Grosz calls their "embodied subjectivity" to defend their full personhood. With these commands—*foulez*, *faites jaillir*, *secouez*, *faites tomber*, or push down, thrust out, shake off, topple—Alexis describes the *mahi* as an act of defiant refusal to internalize misery and calls upon it to act as "la forte poésie des corps qui ondulent ébranle les colonnes du malheur" (387), or the strong poetry of bodies-who-undulate that shakes the columns of misery and sorrow. Locating the assertion of personhood in the corporeal movement of the *mahi* dancers and Yris, Alexis and Ferré present performance as a mode of interrupting the civil death of incarceration and the instrumentalization of racist capitalism. By canalizing the collective force of the shared dance, they revive devalued persons and restore community.

As Muñoz writes about performance and queer futurity at the beginning of *Cruising Utopia*, when "the here and now is a prison house, we must strive, in the face of the here and now's totalizing rendering of reality, to think and feel a *then and there*" (1). For Alexis and Ferré the "*then*" is a moment in the future that will activate the past, and the role of performance is to create a "*there*" where people can keep the muscle memory of revolt in shape. Like Fanon's description of the dance circle, Alexis demonstrates the poetic value of the corporeal work of the dancers, and in so doing, opens up the possibility of making a case for corporeal performance practices as part of a Caribbean intellectual tradition of making meaning. In the majority of the texts analyzed in *Performance and Personhood in Caribbean Literature*, the acts that take place in the circle are limited to the circle's temporal and spatial confines. I end with "Maquinolandera" and *Arbres* because in these texts it seems as if, instead of the energies in the circle either dissipating, having to be hidden, or being captured by intruders, the circle opens midperformance, and the performers and audience members are propelled out into the world. In bringing the circle's energies with them even once the circle is broken, they perform how to make the here and now accountable to the then and there of their desire.

Coda

Performance and Personhood in Caribbean Literature is about Fanon's *damnés* and how social performance can function as a site for rehearsing self-possession. The texts examined here underscore the socioeconomic conditions and philosophical grounds that have led to their protagonists' exclusion from the body politic. They also highlight the interruptions to those conditions in the moments to which I have turned our attention, the ekphrastic descriptions of performance events that break from the plots of the texts in order to inform them. In the breaks, they depict the spaces where the distended time of performance both ruptures and extends the present moment so that the circle's participants can enact alternative social realities. By stressing the temporarily transformed time and space that characterize performances, these writers explore the conditions under which their otherwise deeply exploited and dehumanized protagonists are able to redefine personhood by shifting from a traditionally Eurocentric view of self-contained individualism to open relationality drawn from African diasporic thought and spiritual practice. In Marissa Chibas, Solibo in *Solibo Magnifique*, Jean-Paul in *L'Envers*, and Ismael in "Maquinolandera," we have characters who expand their conceptions of "self" to include the copresence of others within them as well as to place themselves in the bodies of others. Such an open approach can also be seen in Valdés and Chin, whose definitions of authorship in the blogosphere include their commenters. Using the theatrical tradition of substitutability, these writers look to social performance practices to articulate a change in how personhood is conceived.

The Fanonian circle of depicting and explicating corporeal movement creates textual space for how bodies make meaning. In order to create this conceptual space, Caribbean writers fashion words and bend syntax to create the syllabic intelligence that corresponds to local experiences.

These workarounds, intended to address the problem of standard orthography not matching the sounds of oral performance, challenge readers' expectations of how writing should look on a page. Beyond this literal act of representing the sound of spoken language on the page, the writers considered here must contend with the problem that Glissant identifies: how to bring the sensibility of corporeal movement into writing when writing bodies are stilled bodies. In some cases, writers such as Santos-Febres, Chamoiseau, and Chin build their reflections on this problem into the text itself; in so doing, they bring writing closer to live performance while they simultaneously mark the gap between the two genres. In the workarounds they invent to circumvent the impossibility of fully and completely representing performances in the text, Caribbean writers systematically draw on the function of temporality, the possibility of alternative community formations, and most of all, the kinesthetic intelligence from performance practices in order to insist on the ways that the moving body makes meaning.

In focusing on the representation of performance in a group of texts by late-twentieth-century and early-twenty-first-century Caribbean writers, I have sought to outline a regional aesthetic practice that is based on translating between artistic genres. Because I locate this aesthetic practice in Fanon's evocations of spiritual renewal, I claim a connection between this aesthetic and anticolonial politics. In that regard, my thinking about the stakes of what happens when writing performance as a Fanonian circle has been shaped by two sets of political theorists: Jacques Rancière and his rearticulation of politics as a dissenting interruption, and the work done by the #blacklivesmatter movement, particularly Alicia Garza, Patrisse Cullors, and Opal Tometi, who coined the phrase in 2013, and @nettaaaaaaaa, Johnetta Elzie, and @deray, Deray McKesson, whose twitter feeds amplify, synthesize, and theorize the political praxis of people demanding that attention be paid to the specific ways in which they have been dispossessed of what Rancière calls a "part" in the body politic. Reading their work alongside Caribbean literature primed me to pose the questions that fuel the close readings throughout this book: how knowledge is produced, who can produce it, and what interpretive methods one uses to engage that knowledge. I have argued that the regional practice of representing performances and explicating their potential meanings is a way of modeling for readers how to recognize corporeal movement as epistemology. This is the core of the work done within the Fanonian circle, which has as its task to textually explicate corporeal performance: the identification of emotional meaning and intelligibility of performance practices as a form of political expression.

Identifying corporeal movement as a site of intelligible knowledge production places value on moving bodies and contests philosophies that consign bodies to pure labor value. These writers commit themselves to attending to people who are treated as disposable, to demonstrating how they refuse such categorizations, and to exploring the approaches to personhood that they create in the circle. To recall Bois-d'Orme's lament to Carméleau Melon with which I began the last chapter, Why did we fight the Revolution if the whites were going to take back our land? Carméleau's answer shows how, within his current state, he nevertheless acts as a "man-o-words" (Abrahams) to activate the past and prepare for a future revolution:

> Moi, je sais qu'un jour Dessalines reviendra sur la terre d'Haïti, il reviendra pour mettre fin aux gémissements, aux plaintes et pour combattre à la tête de ses enfants. Il ne peut pas ne pas revenir! Il sortira des entrailles de la terre! Alors ce sera le jour de la vengeance, le jour de la justice, le jour des nègres-sales, le jour des nègres-orteils, le jour des nègres-mornes, des nègres-feuilles, des nègres-nègres. . . . En attendant le peuple souverain, Carméleau Melon gagne sa vie, il coupe des arbres, il scie du bois, des planches, il se fait insulter. Il travaille pour les autres, mais partout où il va, il donne la parole de Dessalines au peuple. À voix basse, à voix haute, partout il dit aux enfants de Dessalines de s'unir en silence, de préparer le *lambis* et les torches, pour qu'un jour éclate de nouveau le cri de 1804 devant un peuple debout et ressemblé. (353)
>
> Me, I know that one day Dessalines will return to the Haitian land, he will return to put an end to the tearful sobs, to the complaints and to lead his children in battle. He cannot not return! He will emerge from the earth's innards! And that will be the day of vengeance, the day of justice, the day of the dirty-blacks, the day of the toes-blacks, the day of the blacks-of-the-hills, of the blacks-of-the-leaves, of the blacks-blacks. . . . And while he waits for the sovereign people, Carméleau Melon makes a living, he cuts trees, he saws wood, planks, he receives insults. He works for others, but everywhere he goes, he passes along the word of Dessalines to the people. Quietly, shouting, everywhere he tells Dessalines's children to unite themselves silently, and to prepare the conch-shell and the torches, so that one day the cry of 1804 will burst forth anew before an upright and united people.

Presenting himself as an everyman of the Haitian underclass by describing his actions in the third-person singular, Carméleau prepares for the revolution for his own sake, for that of the nation to come, and, most importantly, for those who will be vindicated by Dessalines's return: "les nègres-sales, nègres-orteils, nègres-mornes, nègres-feuilles, des nègres-nègres," all people whose social degradation is signaled either by their physicality or their naturalization. Like them, Carméleau endures a present of humiliation and oppression under the command of others. Nevertheless, he retains his sense of self-possession and uses his speech as a link between his community's present devastation, the past of Dessalinian revolt, and that revolt's future embodiment when it will burst forth from the earth's viscera. Like the hum of the forest and the embodied subjectivity of the Nan-Remembrance community, the momentum created by the ecstatic movement in Fanon's dance circles, and Lilith's growing sense of corporeal knowledge, Carméleau's proselytizing creates a baseline of anticipation for revolution to be reactivated by bodies that are standing together, prepared to act. "He cannot not return!," Carméleau shouts, his double negative underscoring the current reality of Dessalines's absence and all that that implies.[1] Where a future of unstinting misery seems inevitable, the performance events depicted by this constellation of writers create a physical space where their protagonists imagine, rehearse, enact—that is, perform—their personhood.

Notes

Introduction

1. Britton here attends specifically to the areas of the Caribbean that are under French administration. However, what she articulates about the quandaries created at "the subjective level of collective identity" is, to varying degrees and in different manifestations, applicable beyond the Overseas Departments as well.

2. See, for example, http://ccnmtl.columbia.edu/projects/jazzglossary/b/break.html.

3. In a discussion of the temporality of Carnival, Gerard Aching works through this distinction persuasively and argues that "our conception of carnival is weakened by a notion of it as little more than a safety valve that suspends ideologies by giving way to festive abandon" ("Carnival Time" 417). Carnival time, like the temporality of performance, is not outside of the exploration of freedom in everyday life, it is central to it.

4. We might also think here of the development of the clock as an instrument of control and labor extraction in E. P. Thompson's "Time, Work-Discipline, and Industrial Capitalism."

5. Regarding Fanon's "muscular tensions," see Neetu Khanna's "Fanon's Explosion: Time and the Visceral in the Writings of Frantz Fanon."

6. I am also inspired to call this type of translation of movement into literary practice "Fanonian" because of Fanon's own investment in the corporeality of his rhetoric. In her description of Fanon's lyrical style, Jane Gordon mentions that Fanon's spouse Josie would type as Fanon would speak and walk about the room and that, in the act of writing, "he wanted 'to sink beneath the stupefying lava of words that have the color of quivering flesh' (quoted in Macey, 2002, 159)" (82). The various ways in which Fanon connected the thinking body and its textualization resonates with his use of the dance circle in this passage.

7. Torres-Saillant laments a now "prevailing climate that seems to favor a concern for expressive forms over proposals for social transformation" (49) and argues that the relationship between cultural production and political reflection

and an emphasis on cultural studies has actually resulted in a lessened interest in political activism or mobilizations for socioeconomic change.

8. It is telling that, within Patrick Chamoiseau's oeuvre, the novel that explicitly centers on a performance, *Solibo Magnifique*, is a lament for the loss of specific Martinican cultural forms in the face of globalization, whereas in *Texaco*, which tells the story of how to create a resistance movement and sustain it despite multiple setbacks, performance practices do not hold the same central importance.

9. The *Oxford English Dictionary* locates its first citation in 1944, but as Best shows, corporate personhood became legal doctrine with *Santa Clara County v. Southern Pacific Railroad* (1886)—a particularly poignant observation given that the basis for the railroad's rights were located in the Fourteenth Amendment.

10. All my thanks go to Haun Saussy for bringing my attention to this moment in Kant's thinking as part of his keynote presentation, "Communications and Constitutions: Transparency, Irony, and the Avatars of the Enlightenment Subject," where Saussy elaborates: "The antithesis between God and the criminal, which like antitheses, includes a parallel. . . . Neither God nor the criminal is a genuine Enlightenment subject, but both are related to one."

11. The continued impact of this legacy is visible in the rates of incarceration for Black and Latino men and women in the United States.

12. Scholars of the seventeenth century argue against the use of "Cartesianism" to refer to the mind/body split and its legacies: Christian Braider makes the case that classical dualism was hotly contested in its own time and that French classical thought is, in fact, thoroughly embodied; Erec Koch identifies Descartes's interest in the *sens commun* as a hinge by which body and mind could move each other (407); Timothy Reiss presents the fact that Descartes's figure of the slave is not racialized and that Descartes did not "exclude any humans from this rational ability to willfully control senses" (18) to protest the use that scholars of decolonization make of Descartes's legacy. Nevertheless, the term "Cartesianism" continues to have staying power as a keyword that links subjects to minds and objects to bodies in the work of scholars such as Colin Dayan if only in part due to the fact that *De Homine* and *The Meditations* provide an important point of reference for nineteenth- and twentieth-century justifications of racial superiority. Moreover, as Stephan Palmié makes clear, Descartes's ideas are primarily important because they were "a symptom of a new economic order dawning on the horizon of societies in which transactions in commodified objects were beginning to reshape the contours of selfhood and legal subjectivity" (3).

13. In using this term, I bear in mind Peter Hallward's work separating the specific from the singular: "While the singular presumes that the only valid criteria for Creation are immanent to creation itself, the specific recognises that the essential criteria for action are always external to the particular action itself—and thus a

matter of conflict, deliberation, and decision" (253). While such distinctions are valuable to my thinking, I do not adopt the strictness of his definitions, as when, for example, he argues that Glissant's work after *Poétique de la Relation* is characterized by nonrelational singularity, a position that Guillermina De Ferrari has usefully reconsidered ("The Ship" 192–96). I also bear in mind examples such as Agamben's writing about the "singularity" of politics that are not organized around identity: the relation that binds the subjects Agamben describes in "Tiananmen" concords with Hallward's definition of the specific, despite their difference in terminology.

14. In "The State of Research on Performance in Africa," Drewal draws on the work of anti-Cartesian scholars who contest the mind-body divide and furthermore links up the disembodiment of knowledge and the strong historical association between dancing, the most corporeal of the performing arts, and Africans, women, and gay men (25).

15. Siglind Bruhn's argument in "A Concert of Paintings" that the parameters of ekphrasis should be expanded from solely the visual to include the musical arts as well is a model for me in expanding the term further to consider performance events as possible subject matters for the genre of ekphrasis.

16. I owe this line of thought to Norma Alarcón's article "Traddutora, Traditora," where she traces how the figure of Malintzin/Marina/Malinche/la Chingada has been historicized as having facilitated Mexico's colonization and what impact, if any, the recuperation of this figure by late-twentieth-century Chicana writers can have on indigenous women.

17. Rose Réjouis's reading of what she has termed "dark horse poetics" in Benítez-Rojo's introduction aligns this "certain kind of way" more broadly with "defining Caribbean ways of knowing, . . . an alternative space out of the reach of the authoritarian monotheism of the Western episteme" (109). I likewise argue that ekphrases of performance also aim to create spaces for articulating anti-Cartesian epistemology.

18. In the essay "Contra lo universal," the title of which is softened to "Lo universal y lo global" in the 2009 edition of *Sobre piel y papel*, Santos-Febres considers the historical roots of equating universalism with Eurocentrism. In the essay's opening gambit, she hints at the effect it can have on non-European writers, possibly such as herself: "En muchos lugares de América, soñar con 'lo universal' es acceder a una corriente de pensamiento que niega lo particular, desprecia lo local y crea inseguridad acerca del 'tono' y la visión con que una ve el mundo" (194; In many places throughout the Americas, dreaming with "the universal" is to accede to a line of thought that denies the particular, devalues the local, and creates a sense of insecurity surrounding the 'tone' and vision with which one sees the world). Balancing accessibility with specificity is particularly difficult when accessibility the former prioritizes the access of North American and European readers.

19. See, for example, Velma Pollard's use of a similar phrase, "Creole flavor," in her analysis of Earl Lovelace's *Salt* where she pinpoints how Lovelace will use

only one Creole feature in a large section of the text and how this sole feature "giv[es] a Creole flavor to the whole" ("Mixing" 96).

20. "But, in order to soothe the song, it is worth noting that the British ex-colonies have the same problem, the French Overseas Departments, the still young African nations, and African American writers. Not to mention of the Filipinos who write in Tagalog. The same as the Curaçaoans and their Papiamento and the Haitian poets and their Creole" (191).

21. I am sensitive to this distinction in great part due to my conversations with the dance and theater scholars Susan Foster, Sue-Ellen Case, Harmony Bench, Cindy García, and Hannah Kosstrin who have evoked the discomfort that Jane Desmond discussed in 1997: "The humanities disciplines' emphasis on words is exemplified in the histories of the disciplines. . . . Until recently, dance has remained the most ephemeral of the arts, its 'texts' existing primarily in the moment of viewing and leaving little in the way of material residue. The field remains predominantly a 'corporeal' tradition, passed on from person to person in both formal and informal settings" (60). My aim here is to highlight the value and respect that writers pay to corporeal meaning making, not to subsume embodied practice into textual practice.

22. This definition of performance is hotly debated: Schechner's "restoration of behavior" uses performance's repeatability which "differs markedly from that of Peggy Phelan, who argues for performance as fundamentally non-repeatable, as a reiteration whose chief feature is its non-reproducibility" (Jackson 14).

23. In her discussion of W. E. B. Du Bois's *The Souls of Black Folk*, Adelaide Holton nuances Derrida's notion of iteration as repetition with a difference with her suggestion that iteration produces cyclical repetition whereas increments connote cumulative growth (40). It is this distinction that I use to guide my own taxonomy here.

1. Performance and the Expansion of Personhood in Marissa Chibas's *Daughter of a Cuban Revolutionary*

1. I base my analyses of Marissa Chibas's one-woman show *Daughter of a Cuban Revolutionary* on notes taken at the January 19, 2007, performance at REDCAT, Los Angeles, with additional detail from the recording of the performance with the permission of Marissa Chibas. Special thanks to Jessie Delgado for coordinating the DVD viewing.

2. In order to avoid the confusion of referring to the performer and the character as both "Marissa Chibas," I will refer to the character of the narrator as Marissa and the performer/creator of the piece as Chibas. Following their most common spellings, I also use Chibas to refer to Marissa, Dalia, and Raúl, but Chibás for Eddie and Arturín.

3. Chibas refers to the medal and the color she is wearing—the medal of Ochún around her neck, her shirt the color of Ochún's yellow flowers, both of

which she had chosen before knowing Ochún was synchretized with La Virgen de la Caridad del Cobre.

4. In *Haiti, History, and the Gods,* Dayan explains how *sevís* engages with—and turns possession on its head—by returning to slavery's terminology of constraint: "To be ridden by the *mèt tèt* [master of the head], to be seized by the god, is thus to destroy the cunning imperial dichotomy of master and slave, or colonizer and colonized. Submission to the god thrives on the enhancement of ambiguity, which could be described as follows: you let yourself be taken over by something outside of you, a force you want and don't want, control and don't control, and you get a sense of yourself that you did not have before" (72).

5. Julia Cresswell's etymological definition of the Greek *ekstasis*, cited in "ecstasy" (*Oxford Dictionary of Word Origins*).

6. As Guérin Montilus explains, every person has two shadows: the principle of material life, *ye gli* or *ti bon anj* (little good angel) in the Adja Fon and Haitian Creole terms respectively, and the principle of consciousness and metaphysical life, *ye gaga* or *gwo bon anj* (big good angel). Because the former sustains the body, it is connected to a person's physical body until death. But the *gwo bon anj* can separate itself from the physical body through dreams, or depart to make space for other spirits to temporarily occupy a person's spiritual life (2).

7. Roach's neologism "surrogation" is based on Richard Schechner's theorization of performance as "restored behavior" whose reinvention will always be imperfect (3).

8. Translated as "whatever" by Michael Hardt throughout *The Coming Community*, I use the term "whateverbeing" to identify this position.

9. See Pettman on "Ease" (151); and del Rosario Acosta López on "Outside" (103).

10. De la Durantaye argues that the impetus motivating Agamben's theorization of whateverbeing is the need to change the relation of the singular to the universal. Rather than following the Hegelian dialectic in which singularity is subsumed into a larger unity, Agamben proposes "an idea of singularity not of indifferent importance but, on the contrary, conceived of in all its rich difference from other singularities—whatever they may be" (160–62).

11. As Ian Baucom remarks, the use of the radio to represent diasporic communities is a common trope in narratives of postcolonial nationhood. He cites Salman Rushdie's *Midnight's Children* and James Joyce's *Finnegans Wake* among examples where "the radio, as instrument or figure, has been put to the service of anticolonial nationalists, postcolonial antinationalists, and those, like Julien, seeking to elaborate the contours of a diasporic community that transcends the categories of the nation" (19).

12. The "Special Period" officially began in 1991, when the Soviet Union collapsed, leaving Cuba without the economic subsidies and military security to which it had been privy since 1962. See Richard Gott, "Cuba Stands Alone, 1985–2003" (273–320).

13. In a previous broadcast, Eddie Chibás had accused the minister of education of graft. When his informant disappeared and he was thus unable to prove his accusations, he faced legal and political repercussions. Chibás was famous for the passionate radio addresses he delivered every Sunday evening on CQM radio. "Dalia" alludes to this in an offhand comment that on Sundays at 8:00 p.m., "you could walk down any street in Cuba and hear his voice because we were all tuned in." Eddie's power was grounded in this show, which he hosted from 1944 until his death. Abel Maestre, one of the co-owners of CQM during Chibás's era, comments in an interview: "While [Cuban citizens] admired his attacks against corrupt politicians, they also felt uncomfortable in seeing people's reputations destroyed" (qtd. in Salwen). Moreover, Maestre insinuates that, in shooting himself in the stomach instead of the heart or mouth, Eddie Chibás sought the restoration of his political credibility based on his personal courage without expecting to die. I thank Raúl Fernández for bringing this to my attention.

14. In 1946, Eddie Chibás broke off from Ramon Grau San Martin's political party, Los Autenticos, in order to form the "Ortodoxos" political party, which was similar to the Autenticos in terms of policies and platforms, but campaigned on governmental transparency in response to the charges of corruption marring Grau's administration.

2. Creole's Thinking Body

1. See Sam Vásquez's article "Violent Liaisons: Historical Crossings and the Negotiation of Sex, Sexuality, and Race in *The Book of Night Women* and *The True History of Paradise*" for her discussion of the complexities of Lilith's relationship with her overseer. This relationship is represented from Lilith's perspective as a compulsory, domestic, and romantic one through which she could "creat[e] a fantasy, albeit a disturbing facsimile of domestic bliss and protect herself from other men's sexual assaults. These representations help readers understand that such dalliances were not zero-sum equations" (51).

2. On the choice of Fielding as his intertextual reference, James comments: "It's important to remember that even though these books were instruments in the night women gaining a sort of independence, they were there originally for the enjoyment of men. I like the proto-feminist subversion of that" (James, interview by Newton). Henry Fielding's bildungsroman of a young servant who undergoes many cruel and unfair trials resonates with Lilith's situation, but the fact that he always narrowly escapes complete disaster, and that his love interest Fanny often narrowly escapes being raped, differs radically from Lilith's experience in which the protections she receives nevertheless leave her open to immense physical and sexual abuse.

3. Coulibre is owned by the Roget family originally from Saint-Domingue, who are, by clear implication in the text, much more barbaric in their treatment of enslaved persons than the British plantation owners at Montpelier.

4. As Guillermina De Ferrari explains, there is no single and exact translation for "writer" in Creole (*Vulnerable* 48). The phrase Chamoiseau uses to describe writing, "le marqueur de paroles," or word-scratcher, evokes both the physical inscription of symbols on paper and also resonates with one phrase for "drummer" in Creole, le *tambouyé* (le marqueur de tambour), as Gladys Francis points out (188).

5. Mervyn Alleyne identifies five separate categories describing the place of Creole in various nations, ranging from multilingual to monolingual, wherein Haiti and the French West Indies have a diglossia and Jamaica has a "continuum" defined as "different graded levels of language beginning with a polar variety commonly called 'creole' or 'patois' and moving through intermediate levels to a standard norm of English at the other pole" (166). I use the less precise term of diglossia for Jamaica's linguistic context because, as Carolyn Cooper and Hubert Devonish point out, the term references the language politics that relegate Creole's low social status in Jamaica (62).

6. All translations cited are from Patrick Chamoiseau, *Solibo Magnificent*, trans. Rose-Myriam Réjouis and Val Vinokurov.

7. See De Ferrari for a compelling analysis comparing Pilon to Solibo (*Vulnerable* 60).

8. See Statement of Purpose at www.mona.uwi.edu/dllp/jlu.

9. Doris Sommer argues that the presence of strange or foreign words within a dominant-language text produces the experience of estrangement, a "roughness [that] can irritate the senses pleasantly enough to notice both the artist at work and a refreshed world that may have grayed from inattention" (30).

10. The Cassidy system of Jamaican orthography was first published in 1961 and is based on phonetic spelling.

11. James, interview by Chris Lydon.

12. While Marie-José N'Zengou-Tayo's analysis specifically addresses *Texaco*, the techniques and strategies she outlines are also applicable to *Solibo*.

13. In *Solibo*, various characters are distinguished by their particular forms of expression, such that a spectrum of creole idiolects develops over the course of the novel. Charlot the saxophone player, for example, is described as speaking "créole de ville" (80), or city Creole. His speech patterns differ markedly from Standard French only in occasional onomatopoeias and when he cites spoken exchanges.

14. As N'Zengou-Tayo states, Chamoiseau's version of Creole poses difficulties for speakers of Creole as well. In playing with the reader's recognition of vocabulary across both languages, "he creates a language that is both strange and familiar for Creolophones and non-Creolophones" (163, my translation). This equal absence of accommodation for Creolophones is perhaps particular to Chamoiseau, as Velma Pollard points out that in the work of Olive Senior and Lorna Goodison, "both local and foreign readers are accommodated by these two artists, although admittedly, one group, for whom this complexity

of codes is mothertongue, responds to each text on more levels than the other" ("Mothertongue" 231).

15. Here, I am inspired by Erna Brodber's *Louisiana* and how memory and recording orality intersect with literary production.

16. "By combining oraliture and literature, the creator addresses him- or herself neither to illiterate practitioners of orality nor literary readers but rather to a cross-section of the two: he is himself is the first figure of this cross-section because the text, in its creation, produces its reader" (51, my translation).

17. The reader is directed to the "Dits de Solibo" from the footnote on page 33, which reads "See in the annex an attempt at restoring Solibo's words during that fatal night" (13).

18. Schechner points out that almost all elements of a performance "if broken down finely enough and analyzed—are revealed as restored behaviors" and repetitions. This constitutive aspect of performance is framed by Heraclitus's doctrine of flux and the "onceness" of performance, which "is a function of context, reception, and the countless ways bits of behavior can be organized, performed, and displayed" (29).

19. In "'I Was Born': Slave Narratives, Their Status as Autobiography and as Literature," James Olney asserts that the iconic event in the slave narrative is the observation of a whipping, not the experience of a whipping.

20. Douglass's description of the whipping itself is limited to the sentence, "He commenced to lay on the heavy cowskin, and soon warm, red blood (amid heart-rending shrieks from her, and horrid oaths from him) came dripping to the floor" (26). James amplifies the details of the whipping itself, expanding Douglass's single sentence to three full paragraphs.

21. The narrator's description insists upon how she "pick herself up" (164) after each whipping and how she "raise her chin," both physical signifiers of pride or resolution, but does not allude to Lilith's interior state at this juncture of the narrative.

22. Because her body was never found and she was never confirmed dead, the possibility remains that she and "the struggle" with which she is equated are still alive. Additional evidence of Homer's survival is offered in this chapter, where it is suggested that one of the narrator's informants, "the blind nigger-woman in the bush," is Homer because they share similar traits—short white hair, the smell of mint.

23. Chamoiseau draws on Glissant's idea that writing requires bodily stillness and adds to it. As Solibo instructs "Chamoiseau": "Stop scribbling scritch-scratch, and listen: to stiffen, to break the rhythm, is to call on death . . . Ti-Zibié, your pen will make you die, you poor bastard" (44; see Chamoiseau 76 for the French). Of the many critical assessments that Solibo issues about the uselessness of trying to write down his words, this pronouncement speaks beyond writing Creole, but to writing generally: the stillness that writing requires, Solibo argues, is a murderous stillness because it impedes self-expression as he conceives of it—as generated by rhythm of the moving body.

24. My reading is influenced by this approach, exemplified in Francis Higginson's "Patrick Chamoiseau et le Gwo-Ka du chanté-parlé," which focuses on music and drumming specifically to disrupt the opposition between writing and speaking. Given the attention my analysis pays to corporeality in oral performance, however, I disagree that Chamoiseau can "duplicate the same performance he ascribes to his main character" (420).

25. Chamoiseau weaves this mission into the novel, whereas it appears primarily in the last pages of *Night Women.* James corroborates this purpose in an interview with Warner by recalling "an African proverb that goes, 'Until lions tell their stories, tales of the hunt will always glorify the hunter.'"

26. A broad definition of "kinesthetic intelligence" as the potential to use the whole body to address and "solve problems" is offered in Howard Gardner's *Frames of Mind*, in which he attempts to categorize multiple forms of intelligence.

27. These two sentences begin the first paragraphs of chapters 3, 11, 18, 25 and 31, located on pages 32, 118, 218, 304, and 411 respectively.

28. Ernest Boreman, in *The Roots of Jazz*, will identify circumlocution as an inheritance of African aesthetic practices: "In language, the African tradition aims at circumlocution rather than at exact definition. The direct statement is considered crude and unimaginative; the veiling of all contents in ever-changing paraphrases is considered the criterion of intelligence and personality" (qtd. in Mackey 38).

3. From Spectator to Participant

1. Howes gives the example of the early-nineteenth-century natural historian Lorenz Oken, cited in Classen, who "went so far as to invent a racial hierarchy of the senses. In his scheme the European 'eye-man' was at the top of the scale, followed by the Asian 'ear-man,' the Native American 'nose-man,' the Australian 'tongue-man,' and, at the bottom, the African 'skin-man' (Classen 1997: 405)" (Howes 5).

2. Such challenges to these associations are now long-standing, and addressed well in such works as Constance Classen's *Worlds of Sense* and the essay collection *Thinking Through the Body*, edited by Yannis Hamilakis, Mark Pluciennik, and Sarah Tarlow.

3. Leslie-Ann Jordan explains this marginalization in her article about tourism in twin-island Caribbean states: "Tobagonians have often complained of a legacy of neglect, domination and inequitable budgetary locations on the part of the Trinidad-based central government. Several factors have helped to reinforce Tobago's peripheral condition, including the need for Tobagonians to travel to Trinidad to access many essential services, the absence for many years of Tobagonian representation in Parliament, and the lack of equitable treatment in terms of financial expenditures" (101). See also Ralph Premdas, *Trinidad and Tobago: Ethnic Conflict, Inequality, and Public Sector Governance.* The

majority of the study concentrates on Trinidad, but early on, he compares the two islands: "Trinidad is the larger of the two islands in terms of both population (1,220,000) and geographical size (4,820 square kilometres), and has a more variegated population of six ethnic communities, while Tobago—with only 15,000 people and 303 square kilometres—is almost entirely ethnically homogeneously Afro-Creole" (25).

4. Glossing Glissant's etymological work with the verb "comprendre," Britton explains the grounds for his rejection of understanding, "'In order to "understand" and therefore accept you, I must reduce your density to this scale of conceptual measurement which gives me a basis of comparisons and perhaps for judgments (*Poétique* 204).' In other words, understanding appears as an act of aggression because it constructs the Other as an *object* of knowledge" (*Glissant* 20).

5. My thanks go to Curdella Forbes for this observation that the scopic as the dominant tourist affect is being displaced in favor of "feeling" in the marketing of the Caribbean. The Jamaica Board of Tourism Campaign that uses Bob Marley's song "One Love" and changes the lyrics from "Let's get together and feel alright" to "Come to Jamaica and feel alright" is a particularly salient example of this use of the sense of tactility. This repurposing of the Marley song assumes that the uneven tourist dynamic implicit in "coming to Jamaica" can supplant the mutual relationality of "let's get together."

6. In her analysis of the role of music in *Tide Running*, Jennifer Rahim cites the machismo of Buju Banton's song "Champion," arguing that "the music weaves its own brand of fantasy with regard to love and sexual enjoyment that are unconnected to class and monetary realities, not to mention moral responsibility" in the context of the AIDS epidemic (30).

7. This theme recurs in each of the songs' stanzas, most explicitly when Buju Banton sings of his own desire to reach Shashamane, the land outside of Addis Ababa that Haile Selassie set aside for the Jamaican Rastafari community's relocation to Ethiopia.

8. See Rachel Roth Chiguluri's "The Politics of Discourse and Discourse of Politics in *Tres tristes tigres*" for further discussion of the biographical aspects surrounding the creation of the novel.

9. See William Luis's "Exhuming *Lunes de Revolución*" on the relationship between *Lunes* and *P.M.*

10. Although the title *Tres tristes tigres* is a tongue-twister that literally translates to "three sad tigers," Suzanne Jill Levine and Cabrera Infante decided to title the English-language version *Three Trapped Tigers* to preserve as much as possible the machine gun–like rat-tat-tat of the alliterative effect in Spanish as well as the abbreviation *TTT*. Hereafter I will use *TTT* to refer to the 1999 edition of the Spanish-language *Tres tristes tigres*.

11. Because the popularization of photography accompanied the rise of global tourism throughout the twentieth century, vision takes on outsized importance

in the tourist experience. Moreover, the link between photography and tourism is a global phenomenon extending far beyond the Caribbean region, as Mimi Sheller's insight that "the sites/sights of ancient Egypt were photographically organized" demonstrates (*Consuming* 66).

12. My thanks go to Joseph Bauerkemper for pointing out the historical weight of settler colonialism in the verb "to capture."

13. Oliva dancing the rumba is particularly notable in this regard: as Nathaniel Hamilton Crowell Jr. explores in "What Is Congolese in Caribbean Dance," the rumba is a social dance whose connection to African dance forms is evident. When the dance is performed in pairs, "much of the object of the rumba, *guaguancó*, is for the man to catch his partner in a compromising position, although she doesn't want him to and does all she can to avoid him. . . . She in turns keeps him dancing and keeps him attracted and interested. But, she does it on her own terms: that is to say, without letting him catch her when she doesn't want to be caught" (12). While Oliva's dance is a solo, given Códac's insistence on wanting to capture her movement, we might extrapolate that Códac is Oliva's partner in this narrative.

14. The tourism industry's vertical integration usually consolidates receipts, from airfare to meals, into the hands of multinational corporations based outside of the Caribbean. Analyzing data available in the 1990s, Polly Pattullo comments that the Caribbean tourism industry has an unusually high rate of "leakage." As she explains the tourism industry term, a 70 percent leakage rate "means that for every dollar earned in foreign exchange 70 cents is lost in imports" (38).

15. Strachan explicitly draws on Gordon Lewis's observation in 1968 that "what sugar once was to the West Indies tourism is today to Nassau" (93).

16. BUMIDOM (Office for the Development of Migration in the Overseas States) was a domestic policy that resulted in massive migration from the overseas departments in order to supply France with its workforce between 1963 and 1982.

17. By mentioning the Value Added Tax, Anadine also cites the urgent problem of incommensurately high prices for consumer goods, an important factor in triggering the 2009 general strikes. In her work on the early 2000s labor movement in Guadeloupe and the "Lyannaj Kont Pwofitasyon" (Alliance against Profiteering), Yarimar Bonilla shows that Guadeloupe "has one of the highest per capita incomes in the region, and the minimum wage is the same as in France (almost $1,200 per month when the strike began). However, these high salaries are accompanied by even higher prices on most consumer goods and services—ranging anywhere from 20 to 170 per cent more expensive than in mainland France. Merchants argue that high transportation costs, taxes and tariffs oblige them to charge more for imported goods. Local political activists contend that the high prices are also the product of a larger racial and economic history" (120). See also D. E. Ager's chapter "Economic Dependence," where he

outlines the workings of what he terms the "special VAT regime" characterized as "public money flows out [of the overseas departments] and private money flows back [from France]" (78).

18. In *An Eye for the Tropics*, Krista Thompson describes this cycle of expectations as beginning with tourism advertisements of various illustrated kinds (5), followed by the confirmation of these expectations through the snapshots that visitors would themselves take of their travels (8–9).

19. Choucoune's name refers us to the eponymous character from Oswald Durand's 1883 poem in which a beautiful Haitian woman leaves the Haitian poet for a French sailor who will ultimately desert her (Lang, "Primer" 132). The love triangle is heavily racialized as the woman is a "marabou," or a creole woman with dark skin and long straight hair, the poet a black man, and the French sailor white. Because it is Jean-Paul who seeks to integrate himself into Choucoune's cultural sphere, Pépin reverses stereotypical plots and offers a new version of interracial relationships.

20. The origin stories of the Haitian *compas* and the Dominican *merengue* are wound together, as Paul Austerlitz explains in the *Bloomsbury Encyclopedia of Popular Music of the World*: "*konpa* emerged from the direct influence of *merengue*, the national music of the Dominican Republic . . . (a potentially controversial provenience due to the fact that many Haitians consider Dominican *merengue* to be an offshoot of Haitian *mereng*)" (414). Nemours Jean Baptiste, who created and popularized the form of the Haitian *compas*, is credited with the metaphor that the *compas* is like a top in that no matter how you throw it, it will ultimately turn on its head—that is, return to the main musical sentence.

21. For a concise summary of *gwoka*'s cultural and political significance, see Camal (221–23).

4. Staceyann Chin and Zoé Valdés

1. Manuel Guzmán defines sexile as "the exile of those who have had to leave their nations of origin on account of their sexual orientation" (227). Lawrence La Fountain-Stokes elaborates the term to include a broad spectrum of experiences: "Sexile can be the result of implicit family rejection that leads to personal anxiety and unhappiness, or individual and collective (family, church, government) aggressions that entail outright physical and emotional abuse, censorship, punishment, public harassment, job discrimination, and violence. Some sexiled people leave because of their personal perceptions and intuitions, while others are quite literally expelled from their communities of origin" (296).

2. Richard Gott estimates that between April and October 1980, 125,000 Cubans left Cuba for the United States; prompted initially by political dissidents, the Cuban government opened the border specifically for individuals considered "undesired," identifying them in an editorial in *Granma* as "criminals, lumpen, and anti-social elements, loafers, and parasites" (266–67). See also Julio Capó Jr., "Queering Mariel."

3. In *Thiefing Sugar*, Tinsley demonstrates the many ways in which Caribbean resistant sexualities manifest differently from the politics of recognition that dominate U.S.-based LGBTQI rights organizations and furthermore demonstrates that the comparison between the two discourses often generates an "imperialist rhetoric that sees Caribbean lesbians as passive victims of the Global South's 'underdevelopment' of sexual identity who need assistance from more advanced northern sisters" (8).

4. Sexile's ur-narrative is the Cuban writer Reinaldo Arenas's *Before Night Falls*. As Yolanda Martinez–San Miguel has demonstrated, Arenas's narrative of sexual identity is twinned with exile: "Arenas literally resignifies 'coming out' as 'coming out of Cuba' and not as 'coming out of the closet.' The act of stating publicly that he is gay did not transform him into a public political subject—the traditional meaning of this practice as conceived in the U.S.—but it became a strategy which enabled him to emigrate from the island" (34).

5. When the arc of the plot ends shortly after migration, narratives of sexile can have the effect of positioning the location to which the subject has migrated as a beacon of sexual liberation in comparison, if only because the forms of repression are reconfigured.

6. Chin primarily posted long-form poetry on *Cyberjournal*, and, like Valdés, uses Facebook status updates to post short political commentary. The "notes" section of Facebook corresponds best to what used to be reserved for *Cyberjournal*, however, on Facebook, Chin is part of a larger matrix of interaction. Although the comments are very similar, while dramatically increased in number, I treat Facebook and MySpace as categorically different from the blog because, on her blog, Chin's writing is central, rather than one of many updates and notes that scroll by the reader's eyes on the sidebar.

7. See Martin Manalansan IV's exploration of this multivalent aspect of queer diasporic identity, focused on how "self-identified [Filipino] gay men realign the closet in light of other experiences as immigrants in America" (434).

8. Valdés consistently compares her experiences to that of Reinaldo Arenas's, basing that comparison on the fact that both had to smuggle their writing out of Cuba, but glossing over the fact that Arenas was imprisoned for three years while she was not. La Fountain-Stokes's suggestion that Arenas's queerness and public platform together led to his political persecution bolsters Valdés's case: "Sexuality always operates in tandem with other realities. . . . It is not simply that Arenas was a homosexual and openly and militantly engaged in sex with other men; it is that he was gay and a writer and an outspoken dissident, a fearless critic of the regime" (296).

9. Similarly to the breadth of King's "unconventional gender," Guillermina De Ferrari groups together sexual transgressions, including queerness, under the heading of "perversions" that "highlight the unsettling character of unorthodox sexuality in the social fabric" of post-Soviet Cuba (*Community* 138).

10. While bloggers will often mention having worked on a post for a few days, or will refer back to previous posts, the understanding between bloggers and their readers is that the blog is built post by post, not written offline in its entirety and then uploaded. The self-sufficiency of each entry is rooted in the blog's technology: each blog entry has its own permanent web address. These permanent links, or "permalinks," assign an individuated URL to every blog entry. This allows readers to access specifically referenced blog entries instead of having to scroll through the blog in its entirety to find a singular entry.

11. For example, the Jamaican writer Geoffrey Philp, who now resides in Miami, posted about his experience blogging, "Coming from a place with people who love to decide who should have a voice and who shouldn't, then you can only imagine the level of independence that I feel every time I post. It's a way of whispering in the dark: I am here. I am alive. Is anyone out there?" (June 24, 2009).

12. This type of exchange ceases to function when blogs become too highly trafficked and bloggers can no longer moderate or participate in their comment sections. Smallness is essential to the performance dynamic on the blog because bloggers such as Yoani Sánchez, who averages about 1,500 comments on any given post, cannot logistically sustain the relationships with her readers that Chin and Valdés do. Larger sites not only lose the sense of intimate responsiveness but also cannot set the tone for the conversation among commenters. As Nick Denton, founder of the megalith Gawker Media, commented at SXSW 2012 in an interview with Doug Gross: "I don't like going into the comments. . . . For every two comments that are interesting—even if they're critical, you want to engage with them—there will be eight that are off-topic or just toxic. . . . And as sites get more popular, it's harder to control the comments, which inevitably get nastier."

13. Chin and Valdés both maintain a social media presence including blogs as an offshoot of their already-extant performing and publishing careers. Blogs, along with other social media, are seen as an important marketing strategy for authors.

14. As part of Web 2.0 Internet production, blogs, along with Wikipedia, YouTube, Flickr, Facebook, Twitter, and Pinterest, among others, only function if they are used by readers. Rettberg summarizes Tim O'Reilly's distinction between first- and second-generation websites along the lines of interactivity: "The first wave of Web developers focused largely on publishing content. Web 2.0, on the other hand, develops services that allow users to share their own content and to use the Web as a platform. [Services such as blogs] become valuable because they are being used" (9).

15. For example: "1. Thoughts are combined and points are made in ways that are additive rather than supportive; differently put, people string syntactic elements together with 'and' rather than with subordinate clauses. 2. The elements of thoughts and ideas are aggregative rather than analytical (a contemporary

example might be the slogans, clichés, and memes that catch on and stand-in for ideas and feelings that remain unexplored)" (48).

16. The periodic wipes of old sites, such as the much-publicized erasure of Geocities by Yahoo in 2009, comes into conflict with the supposedly endless storage capacities of the Internet and the privacy experts' warning that "the Internet is forever" as a caution against people posting to Facebook and Twitter without consideration for who will be able to access those posts and for how long.

17. The much-commented-upon "digital divide" has several referents: first, access to the necessary equipment of a computer and an Internet connection; second, that the age and cultural capital of users might prevent them from acquiring familiarity with navigating the Internet; third, the increasingly important gap between institutions and individuals who can move behind subscription- and pay-walls with ease. Above and beyond these differences of access, efforts to infringe on Net Neutrality, such as the 2011 SOPA/PIPA legislation supported by cable/Internet providers that would have linked the loading speed of pages to payment by the pages' owners, will make each of these points moot by limiting the Internet's access and usability even more stringently than the aforementioned current obstacles, a threat that remains relevant despite the 2015 FCC ruling (published 13 April 2015) that classified broadband access as a telecommunications service, thus protecting Net Neutrality.

18. All translations of Valdés's blog are my own.

19. This is not true of her MySpace page or her guest posts on sites like the Huffington Post, where she occasionally has contentious interactions with commenters.

20. On the main page, there were four modes that visitors could use to make their presence known: a link to a "contact" page, the possibility of signing up for an e-mail list, a "shoutbox" where readers could post general comments, and a guestbook where visitors could post their reflections and register their presence.

21. Audio recordings and images were available under the category "Poetry" on the main site.

22. As Nicolas Burbules explains, hyperlinks create one-to-one static pairs determined by the writer of the post: "The same link will always take users to the same URL unless the author changes the underlying HTML code" (77). With increasing frequency, hyperlinks are coded so that, rather than have the new post replace the old one, a link will open in a separate window or tab, permitting the reader to toggle between the original and suggested posts, rather than click away from the first post, never to return. The reader can also choose this form of display by holding down the control key while clicking on the hyperlink, thereby overriding the page's coding. Early on in website design, "breaking the back button" was considered a cardinal error (see "The Top Ten Web Design Mistakes of 1999" at useit.com) because forcibly opening up a new

tab severs any connection between the links, thereby effacing any metaphorical or historical relationship between the two sites.

23. The death of reading as we know it at the hands of texting, Tumblr, Twitter, etc. has replaced initial arguments that blogs offered nothing that was not feasible in print form. As Ta-Nehisi Coates, a blogger and feature writer for the *Atlantic*, points out in a post entitled "How We Read," blogging is often intertwined with long-form reading. He observes of his own site, "The posts that do the best, in terms of traffic and comments, aren't quick hit, off the cuff, witty observations . . . but the dense, long-ish stuff that usually comes from reading books. . . . This is probably particular to me, but nothing has encouraged me to read more books than blogging here. It provides content for the site but it also makes book-reading more enjoyable." Likewise, in the post "Warm Rain," Staceyann Chin provides references to www.democracynow.org as well as June Jordan, whose name is not hotlinked because Chin reads Jordan as print matter.

24. Louis Pagenante, for example, highlights the ways in which both Sterne and Cabrera Infante "are quite fond of interrupting their conversation to make an anticipatory response to some hypothetical objection of ours" (137). Pagenante proposes that such interruptions mark the importance of the audience as built into the novel's construction.

25. No longer extant, Jouvay.com was a website dedicated to Caribbean entertainment in the United States.

26. Timothy Chin identifies a similar tension in the work of the Jamaican novelist Patricia Powell, who reveals that her capacity to write about gay themes relies on her being "in foreign": "Powell's comments illustrate how distance—the distance associated with her diasporic positioning, for example—can sometimes enable the writer to say what she otherwise perceives to be 'unspeakable' in another 'local' context" (535).

27. From her speech at the Opening Ceremonies of Gay Games VII.

28. Definition from the *Oxford English Dictionary* online: "a) growth by assimilation (obs); b) *Biol.* Coalescence or growing together of cells, organs, etc.; the coalescence of two individual organisms of low type in generation; c) *Embryol.* The growing together of two parts during the development of the vertebrate embryo."

29. In this regard, Chin follows in a long tradition of "remixing" Niemöller's speech to fit different audiences and contexts. As described on the United States Holocaust Memorial Museum website, "Much controversy surrounds the content of the poem as it has been printed in varying forms, referring to diverse groups such as Catholics, Jehovah's Witnesses, Jews, Trade Unionists, or Communists depending upon the version." The date of first publication is also uncertain, but it was likely articulated in the late 1940s.

30. This choice of verbs echoes Chin's reference to the political activist group Act Up in a previous verse: "HIV/AIDS was once a reason for gay white men to act up."

31. In *Terrorist Assemblages*, Jasbir Puar places the legislative battles for gay marriage in the international context of a post-9/11 global war on terror, arguing that gay marriage provides European nations with a veneer of "tolerance" that is used to contrast with "perversely sexualized and racialized Muslim populations (pedophilic, sexually lascivious and excessive, yet perversely repressed) who refuse to properly assimilate, in contrast to the upright homosexuals engaged in sanctioned kinship norms" (20).

32. I follow Liz Constable's assessment that "shame is about monitoring propriety, appropriate behavior" (5).

33. This performance is not publicly available on the Internet, and it is not included in the spliced-together video montages of the opening ceremonies. A video of Chin's performance of a modified version of this poem does exist, on YouTube, provided by The Culture Project.

34. This inquiry was posted by "the_inevitable" on Wednesday, 19 July 2006 at 8:18 a.m. on Chin's MySpace page. Chin's response is time-stamped at 8:35 a.m. that same day.

35. Valdés writes up to 142 posts per month (as in July and November 2009) and regularly calls attention to political events in Cuba, frequently dedicating multiple posts to these events. For example, when the Columbian musician Juanes announced that he would perform a concert in Havana in August 2009, Valdés posted 29 individual entries protesting what she argued was his support of a dictatorial government. Additionally, while his concert was taking place on September 19, Valdés created her own concert of sorts by posting embedded YouTube clips of Cuban musicians in a series of 47 posts that she labeled "Concierto por la libertad de Cuba."

36. A high-profile early-adopter of blogs, Sullivan was among the first to convert his blogging into a combined staff position, first at the *Atlantic*, then at *Time*, finally returning to individual blogging with a subscription model. He retired in February 2015 after twenty years of virtually daily blogging.

37. Muñoz defines much of Cuban American politics of memory as "a politics of nostalgic reconstruction where pre-revolutionary Cuba is figured as a utopic lost homeland. This memory is meant to undermine the Cuban revolution. It is meant to posit an imaginary ideal that was 'lost' with the advent of socialism" ("No es fácil" 76).

38. The aesthetics of the blog hyperlink are also characteristic of her novelistic production. My thanks go to the manuscript's anonymous reviewer for this observation. *Café Nostalgia* (1997) is a good example, as we see in Alvarez Borland's description: "In *Café Nostalgia*, Paris and Havana establish a counterpoint that allows the reader an understanding of two spaces and simultaneous time frames. The present in Paris closely resembles Valdés's own story of exile, whereas the past narrates Marcela's childhood and adolescence in Havana. Sensorial memory evokes Marcela's remembrances as she jumps in a Proustian manner, from present to past and from Paris to Havana using as bridges familiar sounds, sensations, tastes, and smells" (345).

39. Valdés considers the recent efforts on the part of Mariela Castro to end discriminatory practices within Cuba as nothing more than a public relations campaign.

40. The last paragraph of a Lía Villares post issues a specific plea to Valdés to become a part of her readership: "Y ya que estamos en la bobería y en la graciecita, Zoé, si me lees, y aunque no venga mucho al caso, tengo el gusto de hacerte conocer el termino usado para referirse a ti por Eduardo Heras León en un pasado festivalito en plena conferencia acerca de las tendencia actuales, el escritor y los medios y los géneros y subgéneros en la narrativa latinoamericana, a cargo de Luis Britto García, Liliana Heker et Sergio Gómez . . . ahí te va porque realmente no tiene desperdicio: eres una 'pornopolítica.'" (And since we're already talking about nonsense and niceties, Zoé, if you read me, and even though it doesn't have much to do with the topic at hand, I have the pleasure of letting you know the term that Eduardo Heras León used to refer to you at a little festival at the round table about current trends in authorship and media and the genres of Latin American narrative, organized by Luis Britto García, Liliana Heker et Sergio Gómez . . . here you go because it really cannot go to waste: you are a "pornopolítica.")

41. In his discussion of Reinaldo Arenas, Ricardo Ortiz corroborates this equivalence and comments that the Castro government and Miami exile community discriminate equally against queer writers (50).

42. Although all political discussions are filtered through Valdés's ideology of anti-Castrismo, they often broaden to include global events. Interspersed throughout the "pornopolítica" posts are other posts propounding conspiracy theories about then-presidential candidate Barack Obama and deriding other prodemocracy figures like Columbian Ingrid Betancourt and Cuban blogger Yoani Sánchez. Some of the posts that are seemingly unrelated make reference to her "Partido," such as "Nacho Vidal, el rey del porno español, trabajó en Cuba," a post pointing out the hypocrisy of the Cuban government's official policy on prostitution.

43. The literal translation of "haciendo eje" is "making it central," but it can also mean "exercising" or "working it out."

5. "Dansez et Revivez!"

1. All translations of "Maquinolandera" and *Arbres* are my own.

2. For a recent approach to this debate, see the essays collected in *Caribbean Sovereignty, Development and Democracy in an Age of Globalization*, in particular, Yarimar Bonilla's "Nonsovereign Futures? French Caribbean Politics in the Wake of Disenchantment."

3. As Cesar Ayala and Rafael Bernabe put it, Luis Muñoz Marín had hoped to transform Puerto Rico into a self-governing entity by using the process of negotiating Public Law 600 with President Truman and Congress as leverage. But by installing the ELA status ("Commonwealth of Puerto Rico," literally

translated as "Free Associated State"), "Muñoz Marín had betrayed not independence but any meaningful—that is to say, non-colonial—concept of autonomy" (167).

4. In a New York Times Op-Ed piece, "Puerto Rico, U.S.A.," published on 19 March 1998, Ferré argued that the United States could incorporate Puerto Rico as a state without the island needing to abandon its linguistic and cultural specificity. Furthermore, in an interview by Frances Negrón-Muntaner in 2002, Ferré denies ever having held an *independista* position: "If I had been in favor of statehood earlier in my career, I would not have been given a chance. The kind of reputation that people created for me, because I did not create it, would never have been what it was. People read me and interpreted me in a certain way, and I believe that is why those books were so successful" (170).

5. The culmination of these efforts can be traced back to the Grito de Lares in 1868. The PPD was not a nationalist or pro-independence party: under Muñoz Marín's leadership, it advocated a form of affiliated autonomy. Between 1973 and 1975, the United Nations and the Non-Aligned Nations approved Puerto Rico's right to independence. However, in 1976, the pro-statehood PNP regained the governorship and the United States was able to postpone any discussion of Puerto Rico's colonial status until 1978 (Zavala 8–9).

6. As of the November 2012 election, public opinion has shifted toward prostatehood among the majority of voters who desire a change in Puerto Rico's status. Referenda regarding Puerto Rico's relationship with the United States were held in 1991, 1993, and 1998, with voters electing to retain its status as U.S. territory. In November 2012, however, when asked to choose a new status, "statehood won with 61 percent. 'Sovereign free association,' which would have allowed for more autonomy, received 33 percent, and independence garnered 5 percent" (Fox).

7. "Los escritores de Zona somos independentistas y nuestra batalla cultural es necesarimente [*sic*] también una batalla política. Favorecemos establecer nexos con la América Latina, a la cual nos unen idioma, mentalidad y objetivos humanos. No hacemos propaganda partidista, pero sí buscamos conscientizar [*sic*] un público para que reflexione sobre nuestros problemas. Aveces [*sic*] son problemas políticos, o que rozan la política, pero no son de índole noticiosa o informativa sino de índole analítica, en términos más amplios." While the letter (27 August 1973) is signed only by Nolla in the archival materials, the letter is attached to the envelope in which Ferré kept her copy, on which she has written "Carta a Olga y la revista y respuesta de Olga y mía" (Letter to Olga and the magazine, and Olga's and my response).

8. In a later version of this essay, translated with Lizabeth Paravisini-Gebert and published in *Callaloo* in 1994, Ferré distances herself even further from this story, stating that "wordplay reigned supreme over an almost non-existent anecdote—and I had distanced myself almost completely from what I was trying to say" (902).

9. Aparicio highlights Ferré's introduction of Afro-Caribbean discourse and music into literature to strengthen her reading of the story as focused on the political need for a realignment of social hierarchies to reflect the cultural contributions and demographic importance of the marginalized and disparaged Afro-Puerto Rican population.

10. Whether these are local police forces who must abide by the Puerto Rican Constitution or U.S. federal agents who are not bound by this document is not clear.

11. "Se formo la choricera" can be loosely translated as "the ragtag group gets together" (literally, "choricera" means "disorder") and "me lleva la gozadera" as "I get carried away by the fun/pleasure."

12. This is generally the role of *soneros*, singers who improvise against the backdrop of the band. Ismael Rivera's signature punctuating phrase in this song is "E-cua-huey!" For a detailed analysis of Ismael Rivera's improvisation style, see Ángel Quintero Rivera's "!*Saoco*! o el swing del soneo del Sonero Mayor" (275–324).

13. The word is absent from dictionaries, and the only definitions I have found are: Aparicio's explanation of the neologism; an anonymous YouTube commenter who suggested that "Maquinolandera, es la lavandera del barrio, en portorro, y chumalacatela, hace mencion a que saque la cartera antes del lavado"; a series of answers in response to the question "What do the Spanish words 'chuvelacandela' and 'maquinolandera' mean?" posted on answers.yahoo.com, where one answer states that "maquinolandera" is the shortened version of "máquina holandera" for a type of Dutch stove imported in Puerto Rico during the 1930s and 1940s.

14. Ferré changes the spelling of words like "máquina" and "fidelidad" to "maquiná" and "fidelidá" to emphasize, in the first case, the rhythmic shift in pronunciation from the first syllable to the last, and in the second case, to remind us of the Caribbean Hispanophone speech pattern that does not generally stress the pronunciation of ending consonants.

15. This definition of the *jitanjáfora*—"words created by the poet who, in using them, does not think about their meaning; they are fresh, fragrant, mysterious words that hit our senses"—was articulated by the literary critic Alberto Reyes in 1942 when he selected the Cuban symbolist poet Mariano Brull's (1891–1956) playful coinage and used it to describe Brull's style of using neologisms to emphasize a sensorial rather than semantic experience of poetry (qtd. in Cruz 44, my translation). *Negrista* poets such as Luis Palés Matos (Puerto Rico, 1898–1959) and Nicolás Guillén (Cuba, 1902–1989) relied on sound's denotations—its resonances with popular speech or popular musical forms—to create an alternative to linguistic interpretive codes. Both Guillén's and Palés Matos's early writing, which brought into print the linguistic practices of Afro-Caribbeans and the rhythms of Afro-Caribbean music, radicalized the production of poetry.

16. In light of the emphasis on the sonority of spoken Puerto Rican Spanish in the text, Aparicio suggests that "'Maquinolandera' resists being read traditionally as a story; instead it proposes itself as a performance, an act of utterance and listening, a process of signifying more than denotative text" (60). While I am deeply sympathetic to and influenced by Aparicio's reading, my methodological approach retains distinctions of genre between textual depictions of performances and performance events.

17. Definitions sourced from *Velázquez Spanish-English Dictionary* and *Real Academia*, respectively.

18. Pierre Roumel is an invented character who appears in several of Alexis's novels and is loosely based on the life of the Haitian novelist and political activist Jacques Roumain.

19. Matthew Smith summarizes the correspondence between Maurice Dartigue and the project leader Thomas Fennell in February 1943: "[Dartigue] implored Fennell to recognize that if SHADA was to succeed in its venture it had to understand 'the mentality and legitimate interests of the Haitian peasant and city dwellers'; failure to do so would foster greater hostility toward the company. The government, he argued, was willing to do what was necessary to guarantee the success of the project, 'but only after all methods of persuasion had been exhausted'" (45–46).

20. The U.S. Department of State, publishes the correspondence between Secretary of State Cordell Hull and "Chargé in Haiti" Selden Chapin concerning "efforts to reduce the adverse effects of the termination of a cryptostegia program in Haiti sponsored by the United States" from April to September 1944 (U.S. Dept. of State, *The American Republics, 1944,* 1169–80). What emerges throughout this correspondence is how every request from President Lescot and his ministers of finance and agriculture to cushion the devastating effects of the termination of the program on the Haitian economy is rebuffed by the U.S. secretary of state. Notably, in the discussion of repayment, the secretary of state writes to Ambassador Orme Wilson (25 August 1944) that, while the Haitian government had hoped to "pay $800,000 for amortization of the notes held by the Bank and $350,000 for amortization of the six percent bonds" (1177), a more onerous payment plan had been decided upon by the secretary of state. He continues: "This matter has been considered carefully in the Department and the conclusion has been reached that the Department can not support an approach to the Foreign Bondholders Protective Council on a basis of less than $700,000 for amortization on the Haitian 6s' during 1944–45," that is, twice as much as the Haitian government thought itself capable of paying down. The rhetoric here indicates that the U.S. secretary of state is not a partner entering into negotiations but the decision-maker in Haitian affairs. The letters begin with a dismissive assessment of the involvement of the Haitian peasantry: "As [the peasants] understanding of external affairs is limited and their knowledge of war issues restricted, it may be assumed that, if their lands are returned to

them to cultivate in food crops, they would be as contented as in cultivating the hitherto unknown Cryptostegia" (1170)—an assessment that Alexis contests in his representation of the peasants' awareness of foreign influence on their lives.

21. While the community of Nan-Remembrance is fictional, Alexis provides geographical reference that would place it in Fonds-Parisien, located on the edge of Saumâtre Lake, at the southern border with the Dominican Republic.

22. Given the dates during which the song as sung by the Andrews Sisters hit the *Billboard* charts, these accusatory lyrics would have circulated in the streets from a hum under the breath to a roar after SHADA's failure in 1945—rather than at the outset in 1943, when the novel takes place. Alexis, then, likely misremembers the timing, or chooses to highlight the clever disjunction between the jaunty quality of the melody and its bitingly sarcastic lyrics.

23. Particularly influential to Alexis's formation in terms of aesthetic practices and ideological commitments was the 1928 publication of Jean Price-Mars's *Ainsi parla l'oncle*, which argued against looking solely to France for artistic inspiration and inspired the writers who followed Price-Mars to draw from Haiti's popular culture and traditions.

24. George Lang shows in *Entwisted Tongues* that the current ethno-linguistic research on the formation of creoles indicates that Haitian Kreyòl has a deep grammatical structure based on African languages with an overlay of French vocabulary. However, throughout most of the twentieth century, Kreyòl was at best considered a degraded version of French. Alexis's infrequent explanations seem to concur with this view, as when he defines "*Abonocho*: corruption de *abrenuntio*" (48), or when he shows the etymological origins of the phrase "un nègre *cansonfer*" in the footnote: "Homme à 'caleçon-de-fer', celui qui n'a peur de rien" (224). In the first case, the word "corruption" would seem to correspond to the view that Kreyòl is a lower form of other latinate languages; moreover, the fact that Alexis provides no definition for the word "abrenuntio," the first-person singular, present active of the Latin verb *abrenuntiare*, to renounce, possibly identifies who his assumed reader is. In the second case, Alexis again places French as the original language from which Kreyòl is derived.

25. Alexis's use of Kreyòl follows the example set by his model, Jacques Roumain, in the genre of the "roman paysan," or peasant novel. Léon-François Hoffman explains how Roumain manages Kreyòl within the text: when a Kreyòl word is included in the main body of the text, it is prefaced by two of its French synonyms; when the lyrics of a song in Kreyòl are introduced, their French translation is provided in the footnote (42). Alexis uses footnotes rather than rely on context or bracketing Kreyòl words with their French counterparts, but otherwise emulates Roumain's format closely.

26. Describing the changes wrought by the presence of U.S. GIs stationed at Chaguaramas air base ten miles north of Port-of-Spain, the Lord Invader version opens with a clear reference to prostitution: "And when the Yankees first went to Trinidad / Some of the young girls were more than glad / They said

that the Yankees treat them nice / And they give them a better price." While the Andrews Sisters' version retains Lord Invader's chorus, "Both mother and daughter / Working for the Yankee dollar," the opening stanza of the Andrews Sisters' version softens the note of monetary exchange to offer an exotic vision of paradise in which the islanders are friendly and musical in their very nature: " If you ever go down Trinidad / They make you feel so very glad / Calypso sing and make up rhyme / Guarantee you one real good fine time."

27. See Munro on Gonaïbo as an exoticized figure in between "the myths of the wild man and the noble savage" (*Exile* 48).

28. As a student in Haiti, Alexis began his college career at the Faculté de medicine, where he declared his specialization in neurology and neuropsychiatry (see Mudimbe-Boyi 16). Aura Marina Boadas also points out that throughout his work, medical and anatomical diction is an important part of Alexis's lexicon, which otherwise features Haiti-specific vocabulary inserted into high literary French: "Las expresiones provenientes de la ciencias médicas de la anatomía abundan: invaginés, tetanie, anestésiée, occiput, névrosée" (19).

29. For "comounatromba," the definition of "la tromba" is technically waterspout and "el trombón" is trombone, but it is in keeping with Ferré's style here to sacrifice precision of diction in favor of rhyming with the sentence's first clause. "Quinteamos" is Ferré's neologism converting noun to verb form.

30. "Explotándolo todo con las calderas de sus caderas para arrasar con todo, para derribarlo todo antes de volver a empezar. Fulminando a los que tratan de detenerla con los fuetes de sus pezones, apresándolos en la tarraya de su melena roja," (182; Exploding all of it with the sugar-boilers of her hips to obliterate all of it, to decimate everything before starting over again. Emitting lightning to those who try to stop her with the whips of her nipples, seizing them in the net of her red mane).

31. To further home in on the African specificity of this aesthetic value, Dixon Gottschild contrasts polycentrism in African diaspora dance with the quintessential Western dance form of ballet: "Polycentrism runs counter to academic European aesthetics, where the idea is to initiate movement from one locus—the nobly lifted, upper center of the aligned torso, well above the pelvis" (14).

32. For further explanations of this approach to utopia, see José Muñoz's reading of Bloch and the German idealist tradition in *Cruising Utopia*.

33. The massive deforestation that Haiti has continued to experience since then thus represents a significant spiritual loss, as well as the more evident ecological and economic impacts, as Paravisini-Gebert analyzes in "Deforestation and the Yearning for Lost Landscapes in Caribbean Literatures."

34. Also spelled "maïs" (Courlander) or "mayi" (Wilcken).

35. Interpretations of the *mahi* dance vary. On the two videos featured on the Library of Congress website as part of the project to document Katherine Dunham's dance technique, two explanations are offered: Rachel Tavernier, the teacher leading the performances of the dance segments, defines the

mahi as "a plantation dance. The movements of the feet suggest making furrows in the ground and the movements of the arms suggest sowing seeds." Yvonne Daniel supports this view in her description of the *mahi* as an "agriculturally rooted dance" announcing the arrival of Azaka, the *Lwa* of farmworkers and agriculture (112). Dunham's voice-over on a video of Haitian women dancing the *mahi*, however, explains that the dance "undoubtedly represents the Mahi tribe of West Africa. I have always felt that the foot sliding backwards on earth arouses a dream world and that they could be preparations for war or they could be preparations to bring in the god that might be angry rather than just beneficent." Since Alexis provides his own contextual interpretation of the dance, my interest in describing the dance is to isolate its specific movement vocabulary.

Coda

1. See Dayan's *History, Haiti, and the Gods* for Dessalines's lasting importance in the Haitian popular imaginary (16–54).

Bibliography

Abrahams, Roger. *The Man-of-Words in the West Indies: Performance and the Emergence of Creole Culture.* Baltimore: Johns Hopkins University Press, 1983.

Aching, Gerard. "Carnival Time Versus Modern Social Life: A False Distinction." *Social Identities* 16.4 (2010): 415–25. doi:10.1080/13504630.2010.467699.

———. *Masking and Power: Carnival and Popular Culture in the Caribbean.* Minneapolis: University of Minnesota Press, 2002.

———. "The Slave's Work: Reading Slavery through Hegel's Master-Slave Dialectic." *PMLA* 127.4 (2012): 912–17.

Acosta López, María del Rosario. "A 'Tiny Displacement' of the World: On Giorgio Agamben's *Coming Community.*" *Epoché* 16.1 (2011): 92–112.

Agamben, Giorgio. *The Coming Community.* Trans. Michael Hardt. Minneapolis: University of Minnesota Press, 1993.

Ager, D. E. *"Francophonie" in the 1990's: Problems and Opportunities.* Clevedon, UK: Multilingual Matters, 1996.

Ahmed, Sara. *The Cultural Politics of Emotion.* New York: Routledge, 2004.

Alarcón, Norma. "Traddutora, Traditora: A Paradigmatic Figure of Chicana Feminism." *Cultural Critique* 13 (1989): 57–87.

Alexander, M. Jacqui. "Not Just (Any) Body Can Be a Citizen: The Politics of Law, Sexuality and Postcoloniality in Trinidad and Tobago and the Bahamas." *Feminist Review* 48 (1994): 5–23.

Alexis, Jacques Stephen. *Les Arbres musiciens.* Paris: Gallimard, 1957.

Alleyne, Mervyn. "A Linguistic Perspective on the Caribbean." *Caribbean Contours.* Ed. Sidney Mintz and Sally Price. Baltimore: Johns Hopkins University Press, 1985. 156–79.

Alvarez Borland, Isabel. "'A Reminiscent Memory': Lezama, Zoé Valdés, and Rilke's Island." *MLN* 119.2 (2004): 344–62. doi:10.1353/mln.2004.0089.

Amerika, Mark. "Becoming a Remixologist: Art, Theory and Sound Practice." *Magazine électronique du CIAC* 36 (2010): n. pag. 8 Feb. 2012.

Andrews Sisters. "Rum and Coca-Cola." *Rum and Coca-Cola.* Deca, 1945. LP.

Aparicio, Frances. *Listening to Salsa: Gender, Latin American Popular Music and Puerto Rican Cultures.* Hanover, NH: Wesleyan University Press, 1998.

Austerlitz, Paul. "Konpa." *Genres: Caribbean and Latin America.* Ed. John Shepherd and David Horn. Vol. 9 of *Bloomsbury Encyclopedia of Popular Music of the Word.* London: Bloomsbury, 2014.

Ayala, Cesar, and Rafael Bernabe. *Puerto Rico in the American Century: A History since 1898.* Chapel Hill: University of North Carolina Press, 2007.

Bailey, Amanda. *Of Bondage: Debt, Property, and Personhood in Early Modern England.* Philadelphia: University of Pennsylvania Press, 2013.

Banton, Buju (Mark Myrie). "'Til I'm Laid to Rest." By Mark Myrie and Bobby Dixon. *'Til Shiloh.* Island Def Jam Music Group, 2002. CD.

Barnes, Natasha. *Cultural Conundrums: Gender, Race, Nation and the Making of Caribbean Cultural Politics.* Ann Arbor: University of Michigan Press, 2006.

Barton, Halbert. "The Challenges of Puerto Rican Bomba." *Caribbean Dance from Abakua to Zouk: How Movement Shapes Identity.* Ed. Susanna Sloat. Gainesville: University of Florida Press, 2002. 183–98.

Baucom, Ian. "Frantz Fanon's Radio: Solidarity, Diaspora, and the Tactics of Listening." *Contemporary Literature* 42.1 (2001): 15–49.

Benítez-Rojo, Antonio. *The Repeating Island: The Caribbean and the Postmodern Perspective.* Trans. James Maraniss. Durham: Duke University Press, 1996.

Benjamin, Walter. *Reflections.* Ed. Peter Demetz. Trans. Edmund Jephcott. New York: Schocken, 1986.

Bérard, Stéphanie. "Patrick Chamoiseau, héritier du conteur? Respect ou trahison de la tradition orale dans *Manman Dlo contra la fée Carabosse.*" Ed. Marie-Christine Hazaël-Massieux and Michel Bertrand. *Langue et identité narrative dans les littératures de l'ailleurs: Antilles, Réunion, Québec.* Aix-en-Provence: Publications de l'Université de Provence, 2005. 91–105.

Berrian, Brenda. *Awakening Spaces: French Caribbean Popular Songs, Music, and Culture.* Chicago: University of Chicago Press, 2000.

Best, Stephen M. *Fugitive's Properties: Law and the Poetics of Possession.* Chicago: University of Chicago Press, 2004. ProQuest ebrary.

Birkenmaier, Anke. "Dirty Realism at the End of the Century: Latin American Apocalyptic Fictions." *Revista de Estudios Hispánicos* 40 (2006): 489–512.

Blakemore, Colin, and Sheila Jennett. "Personhood." *The Oxford Companion to the Body.* Ed. Blakemore and Jennett. Oxford: Oxford University Press, 2001. doi:10.1093/acref/9780198524038.001.0001.

Blanco Borelli, Melissa. "'¿Y Ahora Qué Vas a Hacer, Mulata?': Hip Choreographies in the Mexican *Cabaretera* Film *Mulata* (1954)." *Women and Performance* 18.3 (2008): 215–33. doi:10.1080/07407700802495951.

Boadas, Aura Marina. *Lo barroco en la obra de Jacques Stephen Alexis.* Caracas: Premio Fernando Paz Castillo Mención Ensayo, 1990.

Bogart, Anne. *And Then, You Act: Making Art in an Unpredictable World.* New York: Routledge, 2007.

Bonilla, Yarimar. "Guadeloupe Is Ours: The Prefigurative Politics of the Mass Strike in the French Antilles." *The Legacies of Caribbean Radical Politics.* Ed. Shalini Puri. New York: Routledge, 2011. 115–27.

Braider, Christopher. *The Matter of Mind: Reason and Experience in the Age of Descartes.* Toronto: University of Toronto Press, 2012.

Britton, Celia. *Edouard Glissant and Postcolonial Theory: Strategies of Language and Resistance.* Charlottesville: University of Virginia Press, 1999.

———. *The Sense of Community in French Caribbean Fiction.* Liverpool: Liverpool University Press, 2008.

Bruhn, Siglind. "A Concert of Paintings: 'Musical Ekphrasis' in the Twentieth Century." *Poetics Today* 22.3 (2001): 551–605.

Bruns, Axel, and Joanne Jacobs. Introduction to *Uses of Blogs (Digital Formations).* Ed. Bruns and Jacobs. London: Peter Lang, 2006. 1–8.

Burbules, Nicolas. "The Web as a Rhetorical Space." *Silicon Literacies: Communication, Innovation and Education in the Electronic Age.* Ed. Ilana Snyder. London: Routledge, 2002. 75–84.

Burton, Richard D. E. "Débrouya pa peché, or Il y a toujours moyen de moyenner: Patterns of Opposition in the Fiction of Patrick Chamoiseau." *Callaloo* 16.2 (1993): 466–81. www.jstor.org/stable/2931956.

Butler, Judith. *Bodies That Matter: On the Discursive Limits of "Sex."* New York: Routledge, 1993.

Cabrera Infante, Guillermo. "The Invisible Exile." *Mea Cuba.* Trans. Kenneth Hall and Cabrera Infante. New York: Farrar, Straus and Giroux, 1994. 483–88.

———. *Three Trapped Tigers.* Trans. Donald Gardner and Suzanne Jill Levine. London: Dalkey Archive Press, 1971.

———. *Tres tristes tigres.* Barcelona: Editorial Seix Barral, 2001.

Camal, Jerome. "DestiNation: The Festival Gwoka, Tourism, and Anticolonialism." *Sun, Sea, and Sound: Music and Tourism in the Circum-Caribbean.* Ed. Timothy Rommen and Daniel Neely. New York: Oxford University Press, 2014. 213–37.

Capó, Bobby. Lyrics. "Las Tumbas." *Soy Feliz.* Perf. Ismael Rivera. Vaya, 1975. CD.

Capó, Julio, Jr. "Queering Mariel: Mediating Cold War Foreign Policy and U.S. Citizenship among Cuba's Homosexual Exile Community, 1978–1994." *Journal of American Ethnic History* 29.4 (2010): 78–106.

Carr, Nicholas. "Digital Clutter: Why How We Read Matters." *Encyclopedia Britannica Blog.* Encyclopedia Britannica, Inc., 25 Jan. 2010. http://blogs.britannica.com/2010/1/digital-clutter-why-how-we-read-matters.

Castro, Fidel. "Palabras a los intelectuales." Salón de Actos de la Biblioteca Nacional, Havana. 30 June 1961. Ministerio de Cultura de la República

Cubana. 25 June 2013. www.min.cult.cu/loader.php?sec=historia&cont=palabrasalosintelectuales.

Certeau, Michel de. *L'Invention du quotidien I: Arts de faire.* Paris: Gallimard, 1990.

———. *The Practice of Everyday Life.* Trans. Steven Rendall. Berkeley: University of California Press, 1984.

Chamoiseau, Patrick. *Solibo Magnifique.* Paris: Gallimard, 1988.

———. *Solibo Magnificent.* Trans. Rose-Myriam Réjouis and Val Vinokurov. New York: Vintage, 1997.

charlessmith702210@sbcglobal.net. "What Do the Spanish Words 'Chuvelacandela' and 'Maquinolandera' Mean?" *Yahoo! Answers.* Yahoo Inc., 2009.

Chaves, María José. "La Alegoría como método en los cuentos y ensayos de Rosario Ferré." *Third Woman* 2.2 (1984): 64–76.

Chibas, Marissa, perf. *Daughter of a Cuban Revolutionary.* By Chibas. Redcat, Los Angeles. 19 Jan. 2007. Performance.

Chiguluri, Rachel. "The Politics of Discourse and the Discourse of Politics in *Tres Tristes Tigres.*" *Revista de Estudios Hispánicos* 37.2 (2003): 249–69.

Chin, Staceyann. "Atlanta." *Cyberjournal.* 7 Dec. 2004.

———. Interview by Maya Trotz. "Staceyann Chin." *Jouvay.com.* 9 Nov. 2004.

———. "Re: From Staceyann Chin." Message to the author. 10 Oct. 2006. E-mail.

———. "Speech at the Gay Games VII." *Cyberjournal.* 18 July 2006.

———. "Up and Down . . . " *Cyberjournal.* 29 Oct. 2003.

Chin, Timothy. "The Novels of Patricia Powell: Negotiation Gender and Sexuality across the Disjunctures of the Caribbean Diaspora." *Callaloo* 30.2 (2007): 533–45.

Christensson, Per. "Hyperlink." TechTerms.com, 2006.

Classen, Constance. *Worlds of Sense: Exploring the Senses in History and across Cultures.* New York: Routledge, 1993.

Coates, Ta-Nehisi. "How We Read." TheAtlantic.com: Ta-Nehisi Coates, 9 Feb. 2010

Cobham, Rhonda. "'Mwen na rien, Msieu': Jamaica Kincaid and the Problem of Creole Gnosis." *Callaloo* 25.3 (2002): 868–84.

Comaroff, Jean, and John Comaroff. *Theory from the South: Or, How Euro-America Is Evolving toward Africa.* Boulder, CO: Paradigm, 2012.

"Concrescence." *OED* online. Oxford University Press, 2013.

Confiant, Raphaël. "Un nouveau départ." *Espace Créole* 9 (1997). www.potomitan.info/travaux/espacecreole.htm#dep.

Constable, Liz. "Introduction—States of Shame." *Esprit Créateur* 39.4 (1999): 3–12.

Cooper, Carolyn. *Noises in the Blood: Orality, Gender, and the 'Vulgar' Body of Jamaican Popular Culture.* Durham: Duke University Press, 1993.

Cooper, Carolyn, and Hubert Devonish. "A Tale of Two States: Language, Lit/

orature and the Two Jamaicas." *The Pressures of the Text: Orality, Texts and the Telling of Tales*. Ed. Stewart Brown. Birmingham: Centre of West African Studies, 1997. 60–74.

Courlander, Harold. *The Drum and the Hoe: Life and Lore of the Haitian People*. Berkeley: University of California Press, 1960.

Cresswell, Julia. "Ecstasy." *Oxford Dictionary of Word Origins*. 2009. Oxford Reference Online.

Crowell, Nathaniel Hamilton, Jr. "What Is Congolese in Caribbean Dance." *Caribbean Dance from Abakuá to Zouk: How Movement Shapes Identity*. Ed. Susanna Sloat. Gainesville: University of Florida Press, 2002. 11–20.

Cruz, Rosa Valdés. "Tres poemas representativos de la poesía Afroantillana." *Hispania* 54.1 (1971): 39–45.

Culture Project. "Opening Celebration (Part 16): Staceyann Chin." *YouTube*. 19 Nov. 2007.

Dalleo, Raphael. *Caribbean Literature and the Public Sphere: From the Plantation to the Postcolonial*. Charlottesville: University of Virginia Press, 2011.

Daniel, Yvonne. *Dancing Wisdom: Embodied Knowledge in Haitian Vodou, Cuban Yoruba, and Bahian Candomblé*. Urbana: University of Illinois Press, 2005.

Dash, J. Michael. "The Generation of 1946." *Black Images* 3.4 (1975): 9–16.

Davis, Angela. Interview by George Yancy. "Angela Y Davis." *African American Philosophers: 17 Conversations*. Ed. Yancy. New York: Routledge, 1998. 13–30.

Davis, Rocio. "Oral Narrative as Short Story Cycle: Forging Community in Edwidge Danticat's 'Krik? Krak!'" *Melus* 26.2 (2001): 65–81.

Dayan, Colin (Joan). *The Law Is a White Dog: How Legal Rituals Make and Unmake Persons*. Princeton: Princeton University Press, 2011.

———. *Haiti, History, and the Gods*. Berkeley: University of California Press, 1998.

Dean, Jodi. *Blog Theory: Feedback and Capture in the Circuits of Drive*. Cambridge: Polity, 2010.

De Ferrari, Guillermina. *Community and Culture in Post-Soviet Cuba*. New York: Routledge, 2014.

———."The Ship, the Plantation, and the Polis: Reading Gilroy and Glissant as Moral Philosophy." *Comparative Literature Studies* 49.2 (2012): 186–209. http://muse.jhu.edu/journals/comparative_literature_studies/v049/49.2.deferrari.html.

———. *Vulnerable States: Bodies of Memory in Contemporary Caribbean Fiction*. Charlottesville: University of Virginia Press, 2007.

DeFrantz, Thomas. "The Black Beat Made Visible: Hip Hop Dance and Body Power." *Of the Presence of the Body: Essays on Dance and Performance Theory*. Ed. André Lepecki. Middletown, CT: Wesleyan University Press, 2004. 64–81.

———. *Dancing Revelations: Alvin Ailey's Embodiment of African American Culture.* Oxford: Oxford University Press, 2004.

de la Durantaye, Leland. *Giorgio Agamben: A Critical Introduction.* Stanford: Stanford University Press, 2009.

Deleuze, Gilles. "Bégaya-t-il . . . " *Critique et Clinique.* Paris: Éditions de Minuit, 1993. 135–43.

DeRojas, Alma. "*La Cubanía* in Exile." *Cuba Transnational.* Ed. Damian Fernández. Gainesville: University of Florida Press, 2005. 179–204.

Desmond, Jane. "Embodying Difference: Issues in Dance and Cultural Studies." *Every-Night Life: Culture and Dance in Latin/o America.* Ed. Celeste Fraser Delgado and José Esteban Muñoz. Durham: Duke University Press, 1997. 33–64.

Dixon Gottschild, Brenda. *Digging the Africanist Presence in American Performance: Dance and Other Contexts.* Westport: Praeger, 1996.

Dolan, Jill. *Utopia in Performance: Finding Hope at the Theater.* Ann Arbor: University of Michigan Press, 2005.

Douglass, Frederick. *Narrative of the Life of Frederick Douglass: An American Slave.* New York: Signet, 1968.

Drewal, Margaret Thompson. "The State of Research on Performance in Africa." *African Studies Review* 34.3 (1991): 1–64. www.jstor.org/stable/524119.

Dupuy, Alex. *Haiti in the World Economy: Class, Race and Underdevelopment since 1700.* Boulder, CO: Westview, 1989.

Duval, David Timothy, and Paul Wilkinson. "Tourism Development in the Caribbean: Meaning and Influences." *Tourism in the Caribbean: Trends, Development, Prospects.* Ed. Duval. New York: Routledge, 2004. 59–80.

Edmonsdon, Belinda. *Caribbean Middlebrow: Leisure Culture and the Middle Class.* Ithaca, NY: Cornell University Press, 2009.

Ellingston, Laura. "Embodied Knowledge." *The SAGE Encyclopedia of Qualitative Research Methods.* Ed. Lisa Given. Thousand Oaks, CA: Sage, 2008. 245–46. doi:10.4135/9781412963909.n127.

Elliott, Jane. "Suffering Agency: Imagining Neoliberal Personhood in North America and Britain." *Social Text* 31.2 (2013): 83–101. doi:10.1215/01642472-2081139.

Fanon, Frantz. *Les Damnés de la terre.* Paris: Gallimard, 1961.

———. *The Wretched of the Earth.* Trans. Constance Farrington. New York: Grove Weidenfeld, 1968.

Ferré, Rosario. "De la ira a la ironía, o sobre cómo atemperar el acero candente del discurso." *A la sombra de tu nombre.* México D.F.: Alfaguara, 2001. 163–68.

———. "From Ire to Irony." Trans. Lizabeth Paravisini-Gebert. *Callaloo* 17.3 (1994): 900–904.

———. "Maquinolandera." *Papeles de Pandora.* México D.F.: Editorial Joaquín Mortiz, 1976. 204–23.

———. "On Destiny, Language, and Translation; or, Orphelia Adrift in the C. & O. Canal." *The Youngest Doll.* By Ferré. Lincoln: University of Nebraska Press, 1991. 157–58.

———. "Puerto Rico, U.S.A." *New York Times* 19 Mar. 1998: A21.

Ferré, Rosario, and Olga Nolla. "Carta a Olga y la revista y respuesta de Olga y mía." TS. Rosario Ferré Papers, Box 2, Folder 7. Department of Rare Books and Special Collections, Princeton University Library.

Finlay, Mark. *Growing American Rubber: Strategic Plants and the Politics of National Security.* New Brunswick, NJ: Rutgers University Press, 2009.

Fischer, Jennifer. "Tangible Acts: Touch Performances." *The Senses in Performance.* Ed. André Lepecki and Sally Banes. New York: Routledge, 2006. 166–78.

Foster, Susan Leigh. "Movement's Contagion: The Kinesthetic Impact of Performance." *The Cambridge Companion to Performance Studies.* Ed. Tracy Davis. New York: Cambridge University Press, 2008. 46–59.

Fox, Ben. "Puerto Rico Vote Endorses Statehood with Asterisk." AP.org. 7 Nov. 2012.

Francis, Donette. "The Last Stitch: A Praise Song for My Mother Who Mothered Me." *Small Axe* 14.2 (2010): 160–67. doi:10.1215/07990537-2010-015.

Francis, Gladys. "Fonctions et enjeux de la danse et de la musique dans le texte francophone créole." *Nouvelles Études Francophones* 26.1 (2011): 179–94.

Frank, Henry. "Haitian Vodou Ritual Dance and Its Secularization." *Caribbean Dance from Abakuá to Zouk: How Movement Shapes Identity.* Ed. Susanna Sloat. Gainesville: University of Florida Press, 2002. 109–13.

Funk, Ray. "In the Battle for Emergent Independence: Calypsos of Decolonization." *Music, Memory, Resistance: Calypso and the Caribbean Literary Imagination.* Ed. Sandra Pouchet Paquet, Patricia Saunders, and Stephen Stuempfle. Kingston, Jamaica: Ian Randle, 2007. 57–75.

Gallagher, David. "Guillermo Cabrera Infante (Cuba 1929–)." *Guillermo Cabrera Infante.* Ed. Julián Ríos. Madrid: Fundamentos, 1974. 47–79.

Gallagher, Mary. "Relating (in Theory) in a Globalized World: Between Levinas's Ethics and Glissant's Poetics." *World Writing: Poetics, Ethics, Globalization.* Ed. Gallagher. Toronto: University of Toronto Press, 2008: 86–121.

———. *Soundings in French Caribbean Writing since 1950: The Shock of Space and Time.* Oxford: Oxford University Press, 2002.

Gardner, Howard. *Frames of Mind: The Theory of Multiple Intelligences.* 10th anniversary ed. New York: Basic, 1993.

Gilroy, Paul. *The Black Atlantic: Modernity and Double Consciousness.* Cambridge: Harvard University Press, 1993.

———." . . . To Be Real: The Dissident Forms of Black Expressive Culture." *Let's Get It On: The Politics of Black Performance.* Ed. Catherine Ugwu. London: ICA, 1995. 12–33.

Glissant, Édouard. *Caribbean Discourse: Selected Essays.* Trans. J. Michael Dash. Charlottesville: University of Virginia Press, 1999.

———. "Entretien avec Edouard Glissant: La Relation, Imprédictible et Sans Morale." *Rue Descartes* 37 (2002): 76–95. doi:10.3917/rdes.037.0076.

———. *Le Discours antillais.* Paris: Gallimard, 1997.

———. *Poetics of the Relation.* Trans. Betsy Wing. Ann Arbor: University of Michigan Press, 1997.

———. *Poétique de la Relation.* Paris: Gallimard, 1990.

Gmelch, George. *Behind the Smile: The Working Lives of Caribbean Tourism.* Bloomington: Indiana University Press, 2003.

Gopinath, Gayatri. *Impossible Desires: Queer Diaspora and South Asian Public Cultures.* Durham: Duke University Press, 2005.

Gordon, Jane Anna. *Creolizing Political Theory: Reading Rousseau through Fanon.* New York: Fordham University Press, 2014.

Gott, Richard. *Cuba: A New History.* New Haven: Yale University Press, 2004.

Grønstad, Asbjørn. "Ekphrasis Refigured: Writing Seeing in Siri Hustvedt's *What I Loved.*" *Mosaic* 45.3 (2012): 33–48. http://muse.jhu.edu/journals/mosaic/v045/45.3.gronstad.html.

Gross, Doug. "Have Online Comment Sections Become 'a Joke'?" CNN.com/Tech, 15 Mar. 2012.

Grosz, Elizabeth. *Volatile Bodies: Toward a Corporeal Feminism.* Bloomington: Indiana University Press, 1994.

Guzmán, Manuel. "Pa' la escuelita con mucho cuida'o y por la orillita': A Journey through the Contested Terrains of the Nation and Sexual Orientation." *Puerto Rican Jam: Rethinking Colonialism and Nationalism.* Ed. Frances Negrón-Muntaner and Ramón Grosfoguel. Minneapolis: University of Minnesota Press, 1997. 209–28.

Hallward, Peter. *Absolutely Postcolonial: Writing between the Singular and the Specific.* Manchester: Manchester University Press, 2001.

Harris, Wilson. "The Fabric of the Imagination." *TWQ* 12.1 (1990): 175–86.

Hartman, Saidiya. *Scenes of Subjection: Terror, Slavery and Self-Making in Nineteenth-Century America.* Oxford: Oxford University Press, 1997.

Heffernan, James A. W. *Museum of Words: The Poetics of Ekphrasis from Homer to Ashbery.* Chicago: University of Chicago Press, 1993.

Heller-Roazen, Daniel. *Caliban's Reason: Introducing Afro-Caribbean Philosophy.* New York: Routledge, 2000.

———. *The Inner Touch: Archaeology of a Sensation.* New York: Zone, 2007.

Henry, Paget. *Africana Political Philosophy and the Crisis of the Postcolony.* Spec. issue of *Socialism and Democracy* 21:3 (2007): 36–59. doi:10.1080/08854300701599809.

Higginson, Francis ("Pim"). "Patrick Chamoiseau et le Gwo-Ka du chanté-parlé." *Studies in 20th & 21st Century Literature* 28.2 (2004): 411–27.

Hodge, Merle. "Challenges of the Struggle for Sovereignty: Changing the World versus Writing Stories." *Caribbean Women Writers: Essays from the First International Conference*. Ed. Selwyn Cudjoe. Wellesley: Calaloux Publications and University of Massachusetts Press, 1988. 202–8.

Hoffman, Léon-François. *Essays on Haitian Literature*. Washington: Three Continents, 1984.

Holton, Adelaide. "To 'Tell Again in Many Ways': Iteration and Translation in *The Souls of Black Folk*." *Arizona Quarterly* 66.3 (2010): 23–43. http://muse.jhu.edu/journals/arizona_quarterly_a_journal_of_american_literature_culture_and_theory/v066/66.3.holton.html.

Howes, David. *Sensual Relations: Engaging the Senses in Culture and Social Theory*. Ann Arbor: University of Michigan Press, 2003.

Huntington, Julie Anne. *Sounding Off: Rhythm, Music, and Identity in West African and Caribbean Francophone Novels*. Philadelphia: Temple University Press, 2009.

Jackson, Shannon. *Professing Performance: Theatre in the Academy from Philology to Performativity*. New York: Cambridge University Press, 2004.

"Jamaican Language Unit." *University of the West Indies at Mona, Jamaica Online*. University of the West Indies. www.mona.uwi.edu/dllp/jlu/.

James, Marlon. *The Book of Night Women*. New York: Riverhead, 2009.

——— Interview by Nicholas Laughlin. "Talking to Jamaican Writer and Blogger Marlon James." *Global Voices Online*, 8 May 2009.

———. Interview by Chris Lydon. "You're Headless without History." Radio Open Source, 28 May 2009.

———Interview by Maud Newton. "Interview with Marlon James." MaudNewton.com, 17 Apr. 2009.

———Interview by Toby Warner. "Exclusive: Jamaican Author Marlon James Talks Storytelling." *Flavorwire*, Feb. 2009.

——— "Q&A with Marlon James, author of *The Book of Night Women*. Mon, 02/23/2009." Penguin.com. Penguin Group USA, 23 Feb. 2009.

Jones, Caroline. "The Mediated Sensorium." *Sensorium: Embodied Experience, Technology, and Contemporary Art*. Ed. Jones. Cambridge: MIT Press, 2006. 5–50.

Jordan, Leslie-Ann. "Institutional Arrangements for Tourism in Small Twin-Island States of the Caribbean." *Tourism in the Caribbean: Trends, Development, Prospects*. Ed. David Timothy Duval. New York: Routledge, 2004. 99–118.

Josephs, Kelly Baker. "Dissonant Desires: Staceyann Chin and the Queer Politics of a Jamaican Accent." *Mosaic* 42.2 (2009): 153–70.

Jütte, Robert. *History of the Senses: From Antiquity to Cyberspace*. Trans. James Lynn. London: Polity, 2005.

Kant, Immanuel. *Opus Postumum*. Trans. Eckart Förster and Michael Rosen. Cambridge: Cambridge University Press, 1994.

Kempadoo, Oonya. *Tide Running*. New York: Farrar, Straus and Giroux, 2001.

Khanna, Neetu. "Fanon's Explosion: Time and the Visceral in the Writings of Frantz Fanon." 2013. Manuscript.

King, Rosamond. *Island Bodies: Transgressive Sexualities in the Caribbean Imagination*. Gainesville: University of Florida Press, 2013.

Koch, Erec. "Cartesian Corporeality and (Aesth)Ethics." *PMLA* 121.2 (2006): 405–20.

LaCapra, Dominick. "Holocaust Testimonies: Attending to the Victim's Voice." *Writing History, Writing Trauma*. Baltimore: Johns Hopkins University Press, 2001. 86–113.

La Fountain-Stokes, Lawrence. "Queer Diasporas, Boricua Lives: A Meditation on Sexile." *Review: Literature and Arts of the Americas* 41.2 (2008): 294–301.

Landow, George. *Hyper/text/theory*. Baltimore: Johns Hopkins University Press, 1994.

Lang, George. *Entwisted Tongues: Comparative Creole Literatures*. Amsterdam: Rodopi, 2000.

———. "A Primer of Haitian Literature in 'Kreyòl.'" *Research in African Literatures* 35.2 (2004): 128–40.

Laroche, Maximilien. *La Double scène de la représentation: Oraliture et littérature dans la Caraïbe*. Québec: Université Laval (GRELCA), 1991.

Levine, Suzanne Jill. *The Subversive Scribe: Translating Latin American Fiction*. Saint Paul, MN: Graywolf, 1991.

Lewis, Linden, ed. *Caribbean Sovereignty, Development and Democracy in an Age of Globalization*. New York: Routledge, 2013.

Lindemann, Kurt. "Live(s) Online: Narrative Performance, Presence, and Community in LiveJournal.com." *Text and Performance Quarterly* 25.4 (2005): 354–72.

Lionnet, Françoise. "Continents and Archipelagoes: From *E Pluribus Unum* to Creolized Solidarities." *PMLA* 123.5 (2008): 1503–15.

Lord Invader. "Rum and Coca-Cola." *Calypso: Best of Trinidad*. Caribbean Music Group, 2004. CD.

Ludwig, Ralph. "Introduction." *Écrire la parole de nui: La nouvelle littérature antillaise*. Ed. Ludwig. Paris: Gallimard, 1994. 13–25.

Luis, William. "Exhuming *Lunes de Revolucion*." *CR: The New Centennial Review* 2.2 (2002): 253–83.

Mackey, Nathaniel. *Discrepant Engagement: Dissonance, Cross-Culturality, and Experimental Writing*. New York: Cambridge University Press, 1993.

"Mahi." N.d. *Performing Arts Encyclopedia*. Katherine Dunham Collection, Library of Congress. From *A Visit with Katherine Dunham*, 1983. Dir. Chris Hegedus and D. A. Pennebaker. MPEG (Moving Picture Expert Group). 19 Aug. 2012.

Manalansan, Martin, IV. *Global Divas: Filipino Gay Men in the Diaspora*. Durham: Duke University Press, 2003.

Martínez–San Miguel, Yolanda. "Sexiles: Towards a New Phenomenology of Caribbean Erotics." *World Affairs Review* 4 (2009): 27–43.

McCarthy Brown, Karen. *Mama Lola: A Vodou Priestess in Brooklyn.* Berkeley: University of California Press, 1991.

McClintock, Anne. *Imperial Leather: Race, Gender and Sexuality in the Colonial Contest.* New York: Routledge, 1995.

Melas, Natalie. *All the Difference in the World: Postcoloniality and the Ends of Comparison.* Stanford: Stanford University of Press, 2007.

———. "Re-Imagining the Universal." *Unpacking Europe: Towards a Critical Reading.* Ed. Salah Hassan, Iftikhar Dadi, and Leslie Adelson. Rotterdam: Museum Boijmans Van Beuningen, 2002. 134–51.

Michel, Claudine. "Vodou in Haiti: Way of Life and Mode of Survival." *Vodou in Haitian Life and Culture: Invisible Powers.* Ed. Michel and Patrick Bellegarde-Smith. New York: Palgrave, 2006. 27–38.

Mignolo, Walter. "Epistemic Disobedience, Independent Thought and Decolonial Freedom." *Theory, Culture and Society* 27.7–8 (2009): 159–81. doi:10.1177/0263276409349275.

Miles, Adrian. "Media Rich versus Rich Media (Or Why Video in a Blog Is Not the Same as a Video Blog)." *Proceedings of BlogTalk DownUnder.* Sydney, May 2005. http:// incsub.org/blogtalk/?page_id=76.

Millay, Amy Nauss. *Voices from the Fuente Viva: The Effect of Orality in Twentieth-Century Spanish American Narrative.* Lewisburg, PA: Bucknell University Press, 2005.

Montilus, Guérin. "Vodun and Social Transformation in the African Diasporic Experience: The Concept of Personhood in Haitian Vodun Religion." *Haitian Vodou: Spirit, Myth, and Reality.* Ed. Claudine Michel and Patrick Bellegarde-Smith. Bloomington: Indiana University Press, 2006. 1–6.

Moore, Robin. "Poetic, Visual, and Symphonic Interpretations of the Cuban Rumba: Toward a Model of Integrative Studies." *Lenox Avenue: A Journal of Interarts Inquiry* 4 (1998): 83–112. www.jstor.org/stable/4177070.

Morris, Mervyn. Interview by Loretta Collins. "The Role of Creole Orature, Caribbean Performance Poetry, and Across-Class Collaborations in the Development of Jamaican Literary and Popular Arts: An Interview with Mervyn Morris: Interviewed by Loretta Collins, February 25, 1997." *Journal of Commonwealth and Postcolonial Studies* 6.1 (1999): 31–65.

Morton, Timothy. *Ecology without Nature: Rethinking Environmental Aesthetics.* Cambridge: Harvard University Press, 2007.

———. *The Poetics of Spice: Romantic Consumerism and the Exotic.* New York: Cambridge University Press, 2000.

Moten, Fred. *In the Break: The Aesthetics of the Black Radical Tradition.* Minneapolis: University of Minnesota Press, 2003.

Mudimbe-Boyi, M. Elisabeth. *L'oeuvre Romanesque de Jacques-Stephen*

Alexis: Une écriture poétique, un engagement politique. Montréal: Humanitas, 1992.

Muñoz, José Esteban. *Cruising Utopia: The Then and There of Queer Futurity*. New York: NYU Press, 2009.

———. "'No es fácil': Notes on the Negotiation of Cubanidad and Exilic Memory in Carmelita Tropicana's 'Milk of Amnesia.'" *TDR* 39.3 (1995): 76–83.

Munro, Martin. *Different Drummers: Race and Rhythm in the Americas*. Berkeley: University of California Press, 2010.

———. *Exile and Post-1946 Haitian Literature: Alexis, Depestre, Ollivier, Laferrière, Danticat*. Liverpool: Liverpool University Press, 2007.

Murdoch, H. Adlai. "Edouard Glissant's Creolized World Vision: From Resistance and Relation to Opacité." *Callaloo* 36.4 (2013): 875–90.

Nair, Supriya. "Creolization, Orality, and Nation Language in the Caribbean" *A Companion to Postcolonial Studies*. Ed. Henry Schwarz and Sangeeta Ray. Oxford: Blackwell, 2000. 236–51.

Negrón-Muntaner, Frances. "*Sin pelos en la lengua:* Rosario Ferré's Last Interview." *Centro Journal* 42.1 (Spring 2012): 154–71.

Nettleford, Rex. *Caribbean Cultural Identity: The Case of Jamaica; An Essay in Cultural Dynamics*. Kingston: Institute of Jamaica; Herald Ltd., 1978.

"Niemöller, Martin." *Holocaust Encyclopedia*. United States Holocaust Memorial Museum. www.ushmm.org/wlc/en/article.php?ModuleId=10007392.

N'Zengou-Tayo, Marie-José. "Littérature et diglossie: créer une langue métisse ou la 'chamoisification' du français dans *Texaco* de Patrick Chamoiseau." *TTR: traduction, terminologie, rédaction* 9.1 (1996): 155–76.

Olney, James. "'I Was Born': Slave Narratives, Their Status as Autobiography and as Literature." *Callaloo* 20 (1984): 46–73. www.jstor.org/stable/2930678.

O'Reilly Herrera, Andrea. "The Politics of Mis-ReMembering: History, Imagination, and the Recovery of the *Lost Generation*." *Cuba: Idea of a Nation Displaced*. Ed. O'Reilly Herrera. Albany: SUNY Press, 2007. 176–93.

Ortiz, Ricardo. *Cultural Erotics in Cuban America*. Minneapolis: University of Minnesota Press, 2007.

Pagenante, Louis. "*Three Trapped Tigers* in Shandy Hall." *Lawrence Sterne in Modernism and Postmodernism*. Ed. David Pierce and Peter de Voogd. Amsterdam: Rodopi, 1996. 133–46.

Palmié, Stephan. "Thinking with Ngangas: Reflections on Embodiment and the Limits of 'Objectively Necessary Appearances.'" *Comparative Studies in Society and History* 48.4 (2006): 852–86. www.jstor.org/stable/3879367.

Paravisini-Gebert, Lizabeth. "Deforestation and the Yearning for Lost Landscapes in Caribbean Literatures." *Postcolonial Ecologies: Literatures of the Environment*. Ed. Elizabeth DeLoughrey and George Handley. New York: Oxford University Press, 2011. 99–116.

———. "Writers Playin' Mas': Carnival and the Grotesque in the Contemporary Caribbean Novel." *Cross-Cultural Studies*. Ed. A. James Arnold. Vol.

3 of *A History of Literature in the Caribbean*. Amsterdam: John Benjamins, 1997. 215–36.

Paterson, Mark. *Senses of Touch: Haptics, Affects and Technologies*. Oxford: Berg, 2007.

Pattullo, Polly. *Last Resorts: The Cost of Tourism in the Caribbean*. London: Cassell, 1996.

Pépin, Ernest. *L'Envers du décor*. Paris: Le Serpent à Plumes, 2006.

Pettman, Dominic. *Love and Other Technologies: Retrofitting Eros for the Information Age*. New York: Fordham University Press, 2006.

Phelan, Peggy. *Unmarked: The Politics of Performance*. New York: Routledge, 1993.

Philip, Marlene NourbeSe. "Race, Space and the Poetics of Moving." *Caribbean Creolization: Reflections on the Cultural Dynamics of Language, Literature, and Identity*. Ed. Kathleen Balutansky and Marie-Agnès Sourieau. Gainesville: University of Florida Press, 1998. 129–54.

Philp, Geoffrey. "Blogger and Me: A Three Year Journey." *Geoffrey Philp*, 24 June 2009.

Piedra, José. "Hip Poetics." *Everynight Life: Culture and Dance in Latin/o America*. Ed. Celeste Fraser Delgado and José Esteban Muñoz. Durham: Duke University Press, 1997. 91–140.

Plattner, Annatina. "Patrick Chamoiseau et Luis Rafael Sánchez: de l'oralité à l'écriture carnavalesque." *Parallelismen, parallélismes, paralelismos: Mélanges de literature et d'analyse culturelle offerts à Peter Fröhlich*. Ed. M. Burkhardt et al. Tübingen: Gunter Narr Verlag, 2009. 229–23. www.zora.uzh.ch/25821/2/Parallelismen_Plattner.pdf.

Premdas, Ralph. *Trinidad and Tobago: Ethnic Conflict, Inequality, and Public Sector Governance*. New York: Palgrave Macmillan, 2007.

Priam, Mylène. "Beyond 'The Drama of Consciousness' and Against the 'Drama of the Manifesto': Poetic License and the Creolist Discourse." *Research in African Literatures* 44.1 (2013): 19–35.

Prieto, Eric. "Edouard Glissant, Littérature-Monde, and Tout-Monde." *Small Axe: A Caribbean Journal of Criticism* 33 (2010): 111–20.

Pollard, Velma. "Mixing Codes and Mixing Voices—Language in Earl Lovelace's *Salt*." *Changing English* 6.1 (1999): 93–101.

———. "Mothertongue Voices in the Writing of Olive Senior and Lorna Goodison." *Caribbean Literary Discourse: Voice and Cultural Identity in the Anglophone Caribbean*. Ed. Barbara Lalla, Jean D'Costa, and Velma Pollard. Tuscaloosa: University of Alabama, 2014. 221–31.

Program Notes. *Daughter of a Cuban Revolutionary*. By Marissa Chibas. Perf. Chibas. Redcat, Los Angeles. 7 Nov. 2007.

Puar, Jasbir. "Global Circuits: Transnational Sexualities and Trinidad." *Signs* 26.4 (2001): 1039–65.

———. *Terrorist Assemblages*. Durham: Duke University Press, 2007.

Quintero Herencia, Juan Carlos. *La máquina de la salsa: Tránsitos del sabor.* San Juan: Ediciones Vértigo, 2005.

Quintero Rivera, Ángel. *Cuerpo y cultura: Las músicas "mulatas" y la subversión del baile.* Madrid: Iberoamericana, 2009.

Quiroga, José. *Cuban Palimpsests.* Minneapolis: University of Minnesota Press, 2005.

Rahim, Jennifer. "Electronic Fictions and Tourist Currents: Constructing the Island-Body in Kempadoo's *Tide Running.*" *Anthurium: A Caribbean Studies Journal* 2.2 (Fall 2004). http://scholarlyrepository.miami.edu/anthurium/vol2/iss2/4.

Reiss, Timothy. "Descartes's Silences on Slavery and Race." *Race and Racism in Modern Philosophy.* Ed. Andrew Valls. Ithaca, NY: Cornell University Press, 2005. 16–42.

Réjouis, Rose. "Dark Horse Poetics: Lévi-Strauss, Benítez-Rojo, and Caribbean Epistemology." *Small Axe* 18.1 (2014): 103–13. doi:10.1215/07990537-2642791.

Rettberg, Jill Walker. *Blogging: Digital Media and Society Series.* Cambridge: Polity, 2008.

Reynolds, Dee. "Empathy, Contagion and Affect: The Role of Kinesthesia in Watching Dance." *Touching and Being Touched: Kinesthesia and Empathy in Dance and Movement.* Hawthorne: de Gruyter, 2013. 211–31.

Ricoeur, Paul. *Time and Narrative.* Trans. Kathleen McLaughlin and David Pellauer. Chicago: University of Chicago Press, 1990.

Rivera, Margarita. Lyrics. "Maquinolandera." Perf. Cortijo y su combo with Ismael Rivera. *Juntos otra vez (1974).* Musical Productions, 1997. CD.

Roach, Joseph. *Cities of the Dead: Circum-Atlantic Performance.* New York: Columbia University Press, 1996.

Rodríguez, Juana María. "Welcome to the Global Stage: Confessions of a Latina Cyber-Slut." *Queer Latinidad: Identity Practices, Discursive Spaces.* New York: NYU Press, 2003. 114–51.

Rodríguez Monegal, Emir. "Estructura y significaciones de tres tristes tigres." *Guillermo Cabrera Infante.* Ed. Julián Ríos. Madrid: Fundamentos, 1974: 81–127.

Rohter, Larry. "In Cuba, the Voice of a Blog Generation." *New York Times,* 6 July 2011. www.nytimes.com/2011/07/06/books/yoani-sanchez-cubas-voice-of-a-blogging-generation.html?_r=0.

Rosenthal, Judy. *Possession, Ecstasy, and Law in Ewe Voodoo.* Charlottesville: University of Virginia Press, 1998.

Rothberg, Michael. *Multidirectional Memory: Remembering the Holocaust in the Age of Decolonization.* Stanford: Stanford University Press, 2009.

Russell, Heather. *Legba's Crossing: Narratology in the African Atlantic.* Athens: University of Georgia Press, 2009.

Salwen, Michael Brian. *Radio and Televisión in Cuba: The Pre-Castro Era.* Ames: Iowa State University Press, 1994.

Santos-Febres, Mayra. *Sobre piel y papel.* San Juan: Ediciones Callejón, 2004.

Sartre, Jean-Paul. *Being and Nothingness: A Phenomenological Essay on Ontology.* Trans. Hazel Barnes. New York: Washington Square, 1956.

Saussy, Haun. "Communications and Constitutions: Transparency, Irony, and the Avatars of the Enlightenment Subject." Lecture. Greenberg Distinguished Scholar Program. 28 Jan. 2015, Reed College, Portland, OR.

Schechner, Richard. *Performance Studies: An Introduction.* 2nd ed. New York: Routledge, 2006.

Sedgwick, Eve Kosofsky. *Touching Feeling: Affect, Pedagogy, Performativity.* Durham: Duke University Press, 2003.

Sheller, Mimi. *Citizenship from Below: Erotic Agency and Caribbean Freedom.* Durham: Duke University Press, 2012.

———. *Consuming the Caribbean: From Arawaks to Zombies.* London: Routledge, 2003.

———. "Natural Hedonism: The Invention of the Caribbean as Tropical Playground." *Tourism in the Caribbean: Trends, Developments, Prospects.* Ed. David Duval. New York: Routledge, 2004. 23–38.

Silenieks, Juris. "Marronnage and the Canon: Theater to the Negritude Era." *Hispanic and Francophone Regions.* Ed. A. James Arnold, Julio Rodriguez-Luis, and J. Michael Dash. Vol. 1 of *A History of Literature in the Caribbean.* Amsterdam: John Benjamins, 1994. 507–16.

Sklar, Deidre. "Reprise: On Dance Ethnography." *Dance Research Journal* 32.1 (2000): 70–77.

Smith, Christian. *What Is a Person? Rethinking Humanity, Social Life, and the Moral Good from the Person Up.* Chicago: University of Chicago Press, 2010.

Smith, Matthew. *Red & Black in Haiti: Radicalism, Conflict, and Political Change, 1934–1957.* Chapel Hill: University of North Carolina Press, 2009.

Smith, Neil. "Contours of a Spatialized Politics: Homeless Vehicles and the Production of Geographical Scale." *Social Text* 33 (1992): 54–81.

Sommer, Doris. *Bilingual Aesthetics: A New Sentimental Education.* Durham: Duke University Press, 2004.

Stanley Niaah, Sonja. *Dancehall: From Slave Ship to Ghetto.* Ottawa: University of Ottawa Press, 2010.

Strachan, Ian. *Paradise and Plantation: Tourism and Culture in the Anglophone Caribbean.* Charlottesville: University of Virginia Press, 2002.

Strongman, Roberto. "Transcorporeality in Vodou." *Journal of Haitian Studies* 14.2 (2008): 4–29.

Sullivan, Andrew. "Why I Blog." *Atlantic.* Atlantic Monthly Group, 1 Nov. 2008.

Taylor, Diana. *The Archive and the Repertoire: Performing Cultural Memory in the Americas.* Durham: Duke University Press, 2003.

Taylor, Lucien. "Créolité Bites: A Conversation with Patrick Chamoiseau, Raphaël Confiant, and Jean Bernabé." *Transition* 74 (1998): 124–61.

Thompson, E. P. "Time, Work-Discipline, and Industrial Capitalism." *Past and Present* 38 (1967): 56–97. www.jstor.org/stable/649749.

Thompson, Krista. *An Eye for the Tropics: Tourism, Photography, and Framing the Caribbean Picturesque*. Durham: Duke University Press, 2006.

Tinsley, Omise'eke Natasha. *Thiefing Sugar: Eroticism between Women in Caribbean Literature*. Durham: Duke University Press, 2010.

Tom and Lorenzo (Tom Fitzgerald and Lorenzo Marquez). "T Lo Saw *Julie and Julia*." *Tomandlorenzo.com*, 10 Aug. 2009.

Torres-Saillant, Silvio. *An Intellectual History of the Caribbean*. New York: Palgrave, 2006.

"Tufo." *Real Academia Española diccionario de la lengua española*. 20th ed. 1992.

"Tufo." *The New Velázquez Spanish and English Dictionary*. 2005.

Turner, Victor. "Are There Universals of Performance in Myth, Ritual, and Drama?" *By Means of Performance: Intercultural Studies of Theatre and Ritual*. Ed. Richard Schechner and Willa Appel. Cambridge: University of Cambridge Press, 1990. 8–18.

Ulloa, Justo, and Leonor A. Ulloa. "Critical Readings from Exile." *Guillermo Cabrera Infante: Assays, Essays, and Other Arts*. Ed. Ardis Nelson. New York: Twayne, 1999. 140–58.

United States Department of State. *The American Republics*. Vol. 7 of *Foreign Relations of the United States Diplomatic Papers, 1944*. Washington: U.S. Government Printing Office, 1967. 1169–80. University of Wisconsin Digital Collections. PDF.

Valdés, Zoé. *Cuerdas para el lince*. Barcelona: Lumeneditorial, 1999.

———. "Historia de una foto 'pornopolítica.'" *Blog de Zoé Valdés*, 23 Oct. 2008.

———. "Información a los lectores. Information aux lecteurs." *Blog de Zoé Valdés*, 3 June 2009.

———. "Lía Villares en Habanemia." *Blog de Zoé Valdés*, 22 Oct. 2008.

———. "Memoria, libertad, supervivencia." *Blog de Zoé Valdés*, 18 Sept. 2008.

———. "Memoria del ciclón Flora." *Blog de Zoé Valdés*, 31 Aug. 2008.

———. "Partido Porno Poético." *Blog de Zoé Valdés*. Zoé Valdés, 22 Oct. 2008. 9 Jan. 2010.

———. "Partido Porno Poético." *Blog de Zoé Valdés*, 22 Oct. 2008.

———. "Recuerdos." *Blog de Zoé Valdés*, 13 Oct. 2008.

———. "Sergio Lastres y el Logo de PPP." *Blog de Zoé Valdés*, 26 Oct. 2008.

Vásquez, Sam. "Violent Liaisons: Historical Crossings and the Negotiation of Sex, Sexuality, and Race in *The Book of Night Women* and *The True History of Paradise*." *Small Axe* 16.2 (38) (2012): 43–59. doi:10.1215/07990537-1665668.

Villares, Lía. "y-llegó-la-policía-sí-señor." *Habanemia*, 20 Oct. 2008.

Watson, Hilbourne. "The 'Shiprider Solution' and Post-Cold War Imperialism:

Beyond Ontologies of State Sovereignty in the Caribbean." *Living at the Borderlines: Caribbean Sovereignty and Development.* Ed. Cynthia Barrow-Giles and Don Marshall. Kingston, Jamaica: Ian Randle, 2003. 226–74.

Webb, Ruth. *Ekphrasis, Imagination and Persuasion in Ancient Rhetorical Theory and Practice.* Burlington, VT: Ashgate, 2009.

Wenzel, Jennifer. "Remembering the Past's Future: Anti-Imperialist Nostalgia and Some Versions of the Third World." *Cultural Critique* 62 (2006): 1–32.

Whitfield, Esther. *Cuban Currency: The Dollar and "Special Period" Fiction.* Minneapolis: University of Minnesota Press, 2008.

Wilcken, Lois, and Frisner Augustin. *The Drums of Vodou.* Tempe, AZ: White Cliffs Media Company, 1992.

Winfree, Jason Kemp. "No More Beautiful Days: Situating Agamben's *Coming Community.*" *Epoché* 16.1 (2011): 79–92.

Winks, Christopher. *Symbolic Cities in Caribbean Literature.* New York: Palgrave Macmillan, 2009.

Wolska, Aleksandra. "Rabbits, Machines, and the Ontology of Performance." *Theatre Journal* 57 (2005): 83–95.

Wynter, Sylvia. "Unsettling the Coloniality of Being/Power/Truth/Freedom: Towards the Human, After Man, Its Overrepresentation—An Argument." *New Centennial Review* 3.3 (2003): 257–337.

Yancy, George, ed. *African-American Philosophers.* New York: Routledge, 1998.

———. "African-American Philosophy: Through the Lens of Socio-Existential Struggle." *Philosophy and Social Criticism* 37.5 (2011): 551–74. doi:10.1177/0191453711399252.

Zavala, Iris, and Rafael Rodríguez, eds. *The Intellectual Roots of Independence: An Anthology of Puerto Rican Political Essays.* New York: Monthly Review Press, 1980.

Index